高等学校交通运输与工程类专业规划教材
高 等 学 校 双 语 教 学 教 材
国 家 精 品 课 程 配 套 教 材
国 家 级 精 品 资 源 共 享 课 教 材

Introduction to Traffic Engineering

交通工程总论

(Second Edition)

(第2版)

杨孝宽　贺玉龙　著

人民交通出版社股份有限公司
China Communications Press Co.,Ltd.

内容提要

本教材为国家精品课程配套教材、国家级精品资源共享课教材、高等学校交通运输与各类专业规划教材、高等学校双语教学教材。本教材是在第一版的基础上修订而成，全书共分8章，包括：交通工程学的发展史概述；交通工程学的基本概念；流量、速度、密度的相互关系；地点速度、出行时间和延误的特性与调查；统计学在交通工程中的应用；道路通行能力；交叉口控制设计；交通控制设施。

本书可作为高等院校交通工程、交通运输、土木工程等专业的双语课程教学用书，也可供从事交通规划、道路规划与设计、交通工程规划与设计、交通管理研究的专业技术人员和研究人员参考。

图书在版编目(CIP)数据

交通工程总论 = Introduction to Traffic Engineering(the second edition) / 杨孝宽，贺玉龙著. — 2版. — 北京：人民交通出版社股份有限公司，2019.7

ISBN 978-7-114-15683-0

Ⅰ.①交… Ⅱ.①杨… ②贺… Ⅲ.①交通工程—双语教学—高等学校—教材 Ⅳ.①U491

中国版本图书馆CIP数据核字(2019)第139047号

国家精品课程配套教材
国家级精品资源共享课教材
高等学校交通运输与各类专业规划教材
高等学校双语教学教材

书　　名：	交通工程总论（第2版）
著 作 者：	杨孝宽　贺玉龙
责任编辑：	任雪莲
责任校对：	刘　芹
责任印制：	张　凯
出版发行：	人民交通出版社股份有限公司
地　　址：	(100011)北京市朝阳区安定门外外馆斜街3号
网　　址：	http://www.ccpress.com.cn
销售电话：	(010)59757973
总 经 销：	人民交通出版社股份有限公司发行部
经　　销：	各地新华书店
印　　刷：	北京印匠彩色印刷有限公司
开　　本：	787×1092　1/16
印　　张：	14.25
字　　数：	348千
版　　次：	2010年9月　第1版 2018年7月　第2版
印　　次：	2021年6月　第2版　第2次印刷
书　　号：	ISBN 978-7-114-15683-0
定　　价：	72.00元

(有印刷、装订质量问题的图书由本公司负责调换)

About Authors

Yang Xiaokuan, professor of Beijing University of Technology, got his Ph.D degree in Civil Engineering from the University of South Florida, USA in 2001. He has been working in transportation field for nearly 30 years and has taught bilingual course since 2004.

杨孝宽：现任北京工业大学教授，2001 年获得美国南佛罗里达大学博士学位，从事交通工程领域工作近 30 年，2004 年开始双语课程教学。

He Yulong, associate professor of Beijing University of Technology, got his Ph.D degree in Civil Engineering from the Beijing University of Technology in 2003. She has been teaching at the school since 1996 and worked on bilingual course since 2007. 贺玉龙：现任北京工业大学副教授，2003 年获得北京工业大学博士学位，1996 年留校任教并于 2007 年开始从事双语课程教学工作。

高等学校交通运输与工程(道路、桥梁、隧道与交通工程)教材建设委员会

主 任 委 员：沙爱民　（长安大学）
副主任委员：梁乃兴　（重庆交通大学）
　　　　　　陈艾荣　（同济大学）
　　　　　　徐　岳　（长安大学）
　　　　　　黄晓明　（东南大学）
　　　　　　韩　敏　（人民交通出版社股份有限公司）
委　　　员：(按姓氏笔画排序)

马松林　（哈尔滨工业大学）	王云鹏　（北京航空航天大学）
石　京　（清华大学）	申爱琴　（长安大学）
朱合华　（同济大学）	任伟新　（合肥工业大学）
向中富　（重庆交通大学）	刘　扬　（长沙理工大学）
刘朝晖　（长沙理工大学）	刘寒冰　（吉林大学）
关宏志　（北京工业大学）	李亚东　（西南交通大学）
杨晓光　（同济大学）	吴瑞麟　（华中科技大学）
何　民　（昆明理工大学）	何东坡　（东北林业大学）
张顶立　（北京交通大学）	张金喜　（北京工业大学）
陈　红　（长安大学）	陈　峻　（东南大学）
陈宝春　（福州大学）	陈静云　（大连理工大学）
邵旭东　（湖南大学）	项贻强　（浙江大学）
胡志坚　（武汉理工大学）	郭忠印　（同济大学）
黄　侨　（东南大学）	黄立葵　（湖南大学）
黄亚新　（解放军理工大学）	符锌砂　（华南理工大学）
葛耀君　（同济大学）	裴玉龙　（东北林业大学）
戴公连　（中南大学）	

秘 书 长：孙　玺　（人民交通出版社股份有限公司）

PREFACE

本教材是教育部国家精品课程和国家级精品资源共享课的配套双语教材,是在第一版教材的基础上修订而成。第二版保留了第一版的章节结构和学科的系统性,吸收了交通工程研究的新成果,并总结了作者十余载教学实践的经验和成果,融入了国内外研究成果与工程应用案例,浓缩了中文版《交通工程学》的内容,以适应双语教学的需要。为了方便读者理解和掌握,专业词汇采用了中英文对照和英文专业词附表。

本教材涵盖了交通工程的基础理论和工程应用。全书共分8章,第1章,概述交通工程学的发展史以及定义、研究范围和目标;第2章,交通工程中常用的基本概念包括:机动性和可达性,道路分类,连续流和间断流以及驾驶员和车辆的特性;第3章,流量、速度、密度以及三者之间的关系;第4章,地点速度、出行时间和延误的特性;第5章,统计学在交通工程中的应用;第6章,道路通行能力;第7章,交叉口控制设计;第8章,交通控制设施。

借此机会,谨向在该书修订过程中给予大力支持的陈艳艳、石建军、邵长桥、曹静、郑铮致谢,并感谢在修订工作中作出贡献的助教任振方、刘磊。还要特别感谢北京工业大学教务处和城市交通学院给予本书修订再版的支持,他们对双语教学强有力的支持和帮助促成了本书的修订再版。

本书作为双语教材,仍处于探索阶段,疏漏难免,敬请读者斧正。

作 者

2019 年夏于北京工业大学

CONTENTS

Chapter 1   Introduction ·· 1
  1.1   Definition, Scope and Objectives ··· 2
  1.2   Traffic System ··· 4
  1.3   Background of Development of Traffic Engineering ················· 6
  1.4   Responsibility and Liability (Professional Ethics) ····················· 8
  1.5   Transportation Legislation ··· 9
  1.6   Characteristics and Challenges of Traffic Engineering ············· 10
  1.7   Explanation of Some Technical Terms ···································· 12
  1.8   References ··· 13

Chapter 2   Basic Concepts and Components in Traffic Engineering ······ 15
  2.1   Right-of-way(通行权) ·· 16
  2.2   Mobility versus Accessibility(机动性和可达性) ······················ 16
  2.3   Classification of Roadways(道路分类) ···································· 17
  2.4   Uninterrupted(连续流) and Interrupted(间断流) Flows ············ 20
  2.5   Perception Reaction Time (PRT) ··· 21
  2.6   Visual Acuity——Static versus Dynamic ································· 22
  2.7   Walking Speed ·· 24
  2.8   Vehicle Characteristics ·· 26
  2.9   Geometric Characteristics of Roadways ·································· 30
  2.10 Traffic Control Devices ·· 31

Chapter 3   Volume, Density & Speed Studies ······································ 37
  3.1   Definition of Volumes ·· 38

1

3.2 Definition of Speed ·· 46
3.3 Density ··· 48
3.4 Relationship among Volume, Speed and Density ······················ 49
3.5 Derivation of Flow-Speed and Flow-Density Relationships ······ 51
3.6 Finding Capacity from Basic Speed-Flow-Density Curves ······ 51

Chapter 4 Spot Speed, Travel Time and Delay Studies ···················· 55
4.1 Spot Speed Studies ··· 56
4.2 Travel Time Studies ··· 62
4.3 Delay Studies ·· 66

Chapter 5 Statistics and Application in Traffic Engineering ············· 71
5.1 Some Basic Concepts ··· 72
5.2 Distribution of Traffic Flow ··· 75
5.3 M/M/1 System——Queuing Theory Application ······················ 83
5.4 Chi-square (χ^2) Goodness-of-fit Test ·· 85

Chapter 6 Highway Capacity Analysis ·· 93
6.1 Capacity, Level of Service and Other Related Concepts ········· 94
6.2 Two Types of Analysis ··· 106
6.3 Capacity Analysis for Two Lane Highway ······························· 112
6.4 Capacity & LOS Analysis for Weaving, Merging, and
    Diverging on Freeways and Multilane Highways ···················· 121
6.5 Exhibit for Chapter 6 ··· 135

Chapter 7 Fundamentals of Intersection Design ······························ 153
7.1 Introduction to Intersection Control ·· 154
7.2 Basic Principles and Steps of Intersection Signalization ········ 168
7.3 Fundamentals of Signal Timing and Design ··························· 174
7.4 Computer Software Related to Intersection Signal Timing ······ 179

Chapter 8 Traffic Control Devices ·· 181
8.1 Definition and categories of traffic control devices ················ 182
8.2 Introduction of the MUTCD ·· 183
8.3 Traffic markings ·· 187
8.4 Traffic signs ··· 191
8.5 Traffic signals ·· 198

GLOSSARY ··· 208
References ·· 218

Chapter 1   Introduction

In this chapter, the definition, scope and objectives of traffic engineering will be introduced, together with systems composing of traffic engineering field. In addition, the background of traffic engineering as a professional will also be elaborated. Technical terms related to traffic engineering that may confuse undergraduate students are illustrated to differentiate the meanings of the terms implied in this discipline. Challenges and issues of traffic engineers faced will be discussed at the final section of this chapter.

1.1 Definition, Scope and Objectives

In wake of growth of urbanization and development of automobile industry, traffic problems have become a big concern facing the urban planners and decision makers. As transportation facilities have been in place and used by road users so routinely that transportation system has become an important component in people's daily life. ***Traffic Engineering***(交通工程), one of the subsystems in ***transportation system***(运输系统), has gradually matured to become an independent discipline being taught at colleges and universities worldwide. The definition of traffic engineering is the phase of ***transportation engineering***(运输工程) that deals with the planning, geometric design and traffic operations of roads, streets and highways, networks, terminals, abutting lands, and the relationships with other ***modes of transportation***(运输方式). It should be noted here that if anyone flips over any textbook of traffic engineering, he/she will find there are many definitions for traffic engineering. In order not to make students being misled, we choose this definition as the best alternative in this book. This choice is based on authors' teaching and working experiences in China and the USA.

Transportation engineering is defined as a discipline applying technology and scientific principles to the planning, functional design, operation, and management of facilities for all modes of transportation. In general there are five modes of transportation including roadways, railways, waterways, air and pipe. Traffic engineering focuses on the roadway system, referring to land or surface transportation facilities. Likewise, ***traffic modes***(交通方式) refer to the conveyance means that are operated on highway system such as automobile, truck, bus, motorbike and bicycle (e-bike). Walking in some references is also considered a way of movement from one location to the others. However, since the majority of the walking behavior has nothing to do with the development of traffic facilities and it does not involve in the renovation and production of manufacturers like auto industry, walking is not included in traffic modes in this text.

The scope or coverage of traffic engineering deals with *surface* (*land*, *highway*, *roadway*) *transportation*(陆路运输或陆路交通) and relationships, and connection with other modes of transportation. Therefore, the main task of traffic engineering is intended to study how to move people and goods by highway or roadways and how to connect with other modes of transportation in an efficient way. As mentioned above the principal modes that traffic engineers have to deal with include automobile, bus, truck, motorbike, and bicycle. However, *terminals* (枢纽), *transfer center* (换乘中心) and *port* (*hub*, 港口) are also the facilities that traffic professionals have to work with. This kind of work should be accomplished through cooperation and coordination due to its comprehensiveness and interest-sharing feature. Though responsibility of traffic engineers has been broadened with development and expansion of transportation systems, they should keep in mind that their main duty is to plan, design, maintain, and manage highway systems.

The ultimate goal of traffic engineering is to explore how to provide for the safe, rapid, comfortable, convenient, economical, and environmentally compatible movement of people and goods. It should be pointed out that movement of a physical body does not necessarily formulate a trip unless this movement has a determined purpose. Any movement without specific purpose cannot constitute so-called traffic. Traffic denotes the movement with specific objective.

Safety is the priority that traffic engineers look after in their career. One of the responsibilities for traffic planners and engineers is to ensure the safety and security of traffic facilities. In addition to safety, high efficiency in terms of rapidness is also the objective traffic professionals try to seek. As is known that time has values. Thus, it is very important to move people and goods as quickly as possible. It should be mentioned that there is always a *tradeoff* (均衡) between safety and efficiency in the planning, design and management of highway facilities. Transportation industry plays a key role in economic development of any nations. As a result, the objective of traffic engineering is to promote economic growth and improve living standard of people. With improvement of quality of people's lives, road users expect to receive more comfortable, convenient, and environmentally friendly services of transportation. To achieve these objectives is not an easy thing. Some conflicts among the objectives may occur and the mission of traffic professionals is to make great efforts to compromise the conflicts, optimize the resources, in order to wake transportation systems best meet the requirements of road users.

1.2　Traffic System

To better understand function and characteristics of traffic facilities, it is necessary to know the elements that shape the traffic system. It is widely acknowledged that traffic system is composed of highway (or roadways), vehicles, road users, and general environment.

1.2.1　Highway Planning, Design, and Management

Highway is a general term describing any facilities providing services of vehicles running on it. Highway system can be as large as a national freeway network or as small as a town's street network. There are three things related to the highway system: planning, design and management.

Highway planning is defined as a process of comprehensive plan of highway system, involving land use plan, network plan of roadway with different categories, layout of traffic facilities, corridor plan, transit and parking planning. This process often needs more historical data and vision of decision makers who are responsible for the consequences of the planning. Highway planning is also considered as a part of transportation planning.

Highway design involves geometric characteristics of the roadway that mainly affect traffic flow and operation. ***Geometric designs***(几何设计) are the main tasks that traffic engineers have to accomplish to guarantee the safe and smooth movement of vehicles running on the roadways. As traffic engineers, they do not necessarily understand the structural design of highway facilities but should have some basic knowledge of structural features. Geometric design deals mainly with horizontal, vertical and cross section alignment of highway facilities. The principles and theories of geometric design in the past are generally based on the characteristics of vehicles, without putting human's element into consideration. However, it has been found from many studies that human related elements such as reaction time, vision deterioration, fear of height, comfort should also be incorporated in the design to make highway safer and more acceptable. As a result, the vehicle-based design has been gradually replaced by human-centered design over decades.

Highway management refers to the proper control and management of traffic facilities once upon they are in place. Lessons learned from the past indicate that highway facilities can't function efficiently without executing appropriate control and management strategies. ***Access management***(出入口管理) is a tool to deal with the control, design, and management of roadways in terms of layout of median, opening of driveway, as well as spacing of intersection signals.

1.2.2　Vehicle Characteristics

In traffic engineering, vehicles are an important element in the design and management of roadways. In light of the fact that design of vehicles is not what traffic engineering students need to master, some basic features of vehicles should be studied in the undergraduate course. What traffic engineers are concerned in terms of vehicles include physical size, turning characteristics, dynamic feature and *climbing capability*(爬坡能力). With regard to dynamic features of a vehicle, they indicate braking characteristics, acceleration rate and deceleration rate. In light of the fact that vehicles are so diverse, it is necessary to define a **standard vehicle** (标准车) or design vehicle as specification for the design of roadway facilities. Generally, a unit truck is designated as the standard vehicle in the highway design whereas a passenger car is designated as design vehicle only in parking area, either on street parking or off street parking.

Besides, electrical bike and bicycle should also be taken into consideration in the roadway design, particularly in the urban area. Bike lane should be incorporated in the profile of the urban roadways to separate bike traffic from vehicular traffic. Bicycle traffic draws more and more attention from traffic professionals with development of zero emission movement of transportation.

1.2.3　Road Users

Road users, in broad sense, include drivers, bikers and pedestrians. With regard to drivers, traffic engineers try to do everything possible to explore the *driving behavior* (驾驶行为) through various ways. *Visual acuity*(视力) and *reaction process* (反应过程) are considered as two utmost important factors related to drivers' characteristics. As is known, personality and psychology of the driver also greatly influence driving task but it is very difficult to search for.

As road users, bikers and pedestrians are also involved in the studies of traffic engineering for the sake of safety. This is particularly true for the populated cities. Walking speed and gap-acceptance behavior of pedestrians are the most important elements in traffic engineering studies. Observance of traffic law and regulations is also a key factor, which can be improved through education.

1.2.4　General Environment

General environment refers to the land use and landscaping along the highway, lighting along the roadway and weather, because these factors have greatly influence on the performance of traffic operation. Different land use will produce different type of trips, resulting in different traffic intensity. Likewise, varied landscaping provides drivers with different degree in comfort and ease during driving. In general, lighting is used on the urban roadways. The quality of lighting influences the safety of driving during night. Raining or snowing will deteriorate the driving quality and often trigger in *crashes*(事故). It is true that traffic engineers have no capacity to change general environment of highway. However, being aware of the consequences that these elements will bring about to the roadway operations will assist traffic planners and engineers in figuring out the preventing ways.

1.3 Background of Development of Traffic Engineering

In the next session, a brief introduction to history of development of traffic engineering abroad and in China will be traced. More detailed information on this topic will be found in other references. It is strongly recommended that students conduct wide *literature review*(文献阅读) for getting in-depth knowledge about how traffic engineering has been developed.

1.3.1 Brief History of Development of Traffic Engineering Abroad

It should be noted that two things have been considered as the pushing powers for the birth and development of traffic engineering. One is invention of automobile. In 1886 Douglip Damller produced the first experimental four-wheel vehicle. At the same year Carl Bentz in Germany produced a real three-wheel vehicle. In 1888 the Mercedes-Bentz was for the first time on sale in the market, signaling the development of contemporary vehicle.

The year 1904 marked the beginning of a new era in American transportation history with the advent of automobile in considerable numbers. Moreover, the American love affair with the automobile has grown greatly since the 1920s when Henry Ford made the car accessible to the general public.

The other factor that pushes development of traffic engineering is *urbanization* (城市化). After the Second World War more and more people have swarmed into the city to seek opportunities of making fortune. As a result, cities expanded and the distance between location of employment and living place was longer and longer. Residents living in the city had to construct roadways to connect their travel destinations. With the advancement of new technology of vehicles many types of public transit were seen on the streets to serve the public.

With economic reform and opening to the outside world since late 1980s China has seen mushroomed growth of urbanization. Statistics shows that there were only

11 metropolitans nationwide (metropolitan denotes the city with population over one million). However, this figure was 41 in 2002 and 225 in 2016. Comparisons of urbanization of China with other countries tell how quickly China's process of city's expansion is about. Percentage of urbanization is considered as a measure to assess expansion level of urbanization. Great Britain took 120 years to experience percentage change of urbanization from 20% to 40%. However, China just took 22 years to reach this target. Table 1.1 shows years taken in completing this process in different countries.

Table 1.1 Years Experienced by Different Countries from 20% to 40% of Urbanization

Country	Great Britain	France	German	America	Russia/Japan	China
Years	120	100	80	40	30	22

Besides, development of computer science and communication has improved traffic system. A good example is the introduction of **Intelligent Transportation System**(简称 ITS,智能交通系统), which brings transportation discipline into a new epoch.

Sustainable transportation development(可持续交通发展) is a more recent concept linking environmental, economic, and social values with the construction of traffic infrastructures. The ultimate goal is to identity the level of development that can be sustained without critical environmental damage, while meeting economic and social needs of present and future generations. Preservation of natural resources and exploration of new energy become vital steps toward sustainability. As a result environmental factors have been gradually involved in the development of transportation. It can be seen from current practice that hybrid and electric cars are the good examples of maintaining our transportation system in a sustainable fashion.

1.3.2 Development of Traffic Engineering in China

Traffic engineering was introduced into China rather late—compared to other countries. In 1980, traffic engineering course was first offered for undergraduate students at Beijing University of Technology in mainland China. In the following years many colleges and universities opened this course either affiliated to Civil Engineering Department or under Transportation College. Nowadays, there are 192 colleges and universities in China which can offer traffic engineering program with Bachelor, Master and Ph.D. degrees.

The Beijing Urban Planning Bureau started its comprehensive transportation planning work in 1982, conducing O-D survey for trucks, data collection for major and minor roadways, and delay investigation at signalized intersections. Since then transportation planning was considered an important element in the Urban Master Plan of Beijing. Traffic impact studies (TIS) have been required by transportation agencies to evaluate the potential transportation impacts of the proposed development on the surrounding neighborhood since the 1000s in Beijing, symbolizing that traffic issues invite considerable concerns from all levels of government.

In addition, all levels of government make high investments in highway and transportation infrastructure construction to better off the economy and to improve living standard of people. There is a very popular saying in China: "If you want to be rich, the first thing you need to do is to build a roadway." In 2004, the Ministry of Transportation of China worked out a plan to build up freeway systems nationwide in the next 30 years in the hope of shaping transportation network for national economic development.

1.4 Responsibility and Liability (Professional Ethics)

As a traffic engineer you have to be aware of your responsibilities when you plan, design or manage any traffic facilities, just as doctors who take **Hippocratic Oath** (希波克拉底誓言) before they practice medical work. (Hippocratic Oath, attributed to the ancient Greek physician Hippocrates, was adopted as a guide to conduct by the medical profession throughout the ages and still is used in graduation ceremonies of many medical schools. The text of the Oath itself is divided into two major sections. The first sets out the obligations of the physician to students of medicine and the duties of pupil to teachers. In the second section the physician pledges to prescribe only beneficial treatments, according to his/her abilities and judgment, to refrain from causing harm or hurt and to live an exemplary personal and professional life).

Like all engineers, traffic engineers must understand and comply with **professional ethics** (职业道德) codes. The fundamental ethical issue for traffic engineers is to provide for public safety through positive programs, good practice, knowledge, and proper procedure. In general good professional ethics requires that traffic engineers work only in their areas of expertise; do all work completely and thoroughly; be completely honest with the general public, employers, and clients; comply with all applicable codes and standards; and work to the best of their ability.

It can be observed that few engineers have so many people using their products so routinely and frequently and depending upon them so totally as traffic engineers. Therefore, traffic engineers should have special obligation to employ the available knowledge and state of art to enhance public safety and comfort.

Responsibilities for traffic engineers include:

(1) Public safety and security (after "9.11" event all levels of governments over the world pay much attention to the safety and security of transportation facilities in case of man-made disaster);

(2) Community protection (to better off the quality of living environment through *traffic calming*(交通静化) program such as installation of *speed hump*(减速丘), *roundabout*(环岛), narrowing of lane's width or reducing lanes);

(3) Legal obligation (control devices);

(4) Communication with people about what traffic engineers work for (e.g. public hearing).

1.5 Transportation Legislation

Transportation legislation plays key role in finance of construction, maintenance and management of transportation facilities. It is well known that transportation industry has been, and will be controlled and supervised under government. The government should guarantee the financial resources for the development of this industry by means of legislation. Some key legislative acts in the United States are shown as follows.

(1) *Federal-Aid Highway Act* (1916 to 1983)(联邦公路法)

The 1916 Act was the first allocation of federal-aid highway funds for highway construction by the states. It established the "A-B-C System" of primary, secondary, and tertiary federal-aid highways, and provided 50% of the funding for construction of highways in this system.

(2) **ISTEA** (Intermodal Surface Transportation Efficiency and Transportation Equity Act 1991 to 1997)(冰茶法案)

The key point of this act is to encourage *intermodality*(多模式) and integration of transportation systems. This act has allowed local agents to have more options to use federal-aid transportation funds.

(3) TEA-21 (*Transportation Equity Act for 21st Century*, 1998 to 2004) (21世纪交通衡平法)

The focus is to increase funding levels, further liberalize local options for allocation of funds.

(4) SAFETEA-LU (Safe, Accountable, Flexible, Efficient Transportation Equity Act: A Legacy for Users, 2005 to 2011)

(5) MAP-21 (Moving Ahead for Progress in the 21st Century, since 2005)

This act focuses on highway safety and public transportation.

It should be noted that China has so far not issued any legislative laws in transportation development.

1.6 Characteristics and Challenges of Traffic Engineering

The crystal clear fact in traffic engineering is that this field is so closely related to our daily lives. Traffic congestion has been a major headache for many years in major cities worldwide. Based on past experiences it is not always possible to solve congestion problems through capacity expansion. Traffic planners and engineers therefore are working out programs and strategies to manage demand in both time and space and to discourage growth wherever possible. However, some measures look good but are very hard to implement in practice. The characteristics of traffic engineering are so diverse that students who are studying for the first time will be more or less confused with or misled, to some extent. To make students better understand the traffic engineering theory and applications, it is necessary to have them to be aware of some facts as follows.

Traffic engineering is still not a rocket science in strict definition. It is known that traffic engineering is still quite young as compared to other disciplines. Thus, there leave rooms for improvement. Unlike mathematics, physics, chemistry, medicine or mechanics, traffic engineering have been developed not so matured as to be competitive. Theories and principles are in the debatable conditions due to different views from different schools. Most traffic models are still in the experimental stage and need to be tested and validated for application. Therefore, it is advisable that students are encouraged to carefully examine the preconditions, assumptions and boundaries of any traffic theory or model when applying them in their study.

The coverage is so broad that it is difficult to identify the boundary of the discipline. Although traffic engineering itself is engineering-oriented discipline with emphasis on technical importance, this field has close relationship with other fields such as computer science, communication technology, social science, psychology and urban planning. It is impossible for undergraduate students to get hand-on skills of these related fields during their four-year study. It would greatly benefit a student if he/she is, to some extent, knowledgeable about the information of these fields. It is recommended that students be aware of the diversity of traffic engineering.

The discipline is closely associated with the daily life of the public. Unlike professionals in other fields you can make decisions yourself without consulting with other people, it is very difficult for traffic engineers in determining what should be done and what should not be done without consulting with the public. It seems that communication skill is the key to success for traffic engineers to get projects approved from the public. As a traffic engineer or planner you should keep in mind that technologically sound solutions may not be socially acceptable.

Traffic planners and engineers worldwide are still experiencing never-ending traffic congestion in their cities. Some necessary measures have been implemented to control traffic demand and enhance the capacity of the facilities, but improvement is very limited. In addition to congestion safety and security of transportation infrastructures have been put into agenda since "9 · 11" terrorist attack in New York City, USA. All levels of government have paid much attention to security of transportation facilities since then. China has also worked out a plan for transportation emergency after suffering from snow storm at southern part of China and earthquake in Sichuan province in 2008, respectively. Besides, heavy rain caused traffic paralysis of Beijing in 2012. The following Figures (Figure 1.1 to Figure 1.4) provide some real situations of congestion and breakdown of transportation systems when unexpected hazardous events occurred.

Figure 1.1 Congestion on the Ring Road of Beijing

Figure 1.2 Twin Tower in Flame 2001, USA

Figure 1.3　Traffic Paralysis due to Snow Storm in Southern China,2008

Figure 1.4　Traffic Paralysis due to Heavy Rain in Beijing,2012

1.7　Explanation of Some Technical Terms

There are some technical terms that may misleading students when they encounter in their study. These technical terms include traffic, transport, transportation, and communication. Traffic tends to discuss issues being technical-oriented and engineering-oriented. Transportation refers to a comprehensive coverage of the discipline and emphases on political, social or legal activities rather than technical aspects. Transport is the British usage, interchangeable with transportation. Besides, transport can be used as a verb. Communication was used in China several years ago, representing transport when referring to *Ministry of Transport*(交通部) or *Beijing Municipal Commission of Transport*(北京市交通委员会). However, in the United States and other countries they use Department of Transportation (or DOT). It should be noted that "traffic" and "transportation" are interchangeable in use in China due to the different interpretation and explanation by different *schools*(学派).

1.8 References

In order to remain up to date and aware, traffic planners and engineers must keep up with new developments through regular review of key periodicals and awareness of the latest standard and criteria for professional practice. Like many other engineering fields, traffic engineering profession has many manuals and standard references as shown below.

(1)ITE:Institute of Transportation Engineers;
(2)TRB:Transportation Research Board;
(3)ASCE:American Society of Civil Engineers;
(4)MUTCD:Manual on Uniform Traffic Control Devices;
(5)HCM 2010: Highway Capacity Manual;
(6)"A Police on the Geometric Design of Highway and Street" by AASHTO (American Association of State Highway and Transportation Officials),6th Edition;
(7)The Traffic Engineering Handbook,ITE,Wiley,January-2016;
(8)Handbook of Transportation Engineering, Kutz,McGraw-Hill Education Mar 2011;
(9)Transportation Safety Manual;
(10)Trip Generation Handbook ITE,Sep. 2012;
(11)Access Management Manual,Mark A Marek, P.E. Design Division,June, 2011.

Since this textbook is made for bilingual teaching class, some Chinese references in traffic engineering are needed to be provided for undergraduate students as well as traffic professionals to access. More importantly these references are helpful and useful for Chinese students to obtain hand-on knowledge in traffic engineering. Major references in Chinese are listed below.

Key points of chapter

1. Discribe the definitions of traffic engineering and transportation engineering and the relationship between the two.
2. What is the goal of traffic engineering and what is the coverage of it?
3. What are the components that shape the traffic system?
4. What are the pushing powers that stimulate the development of traffic engineering?

5. What are the responsibilities and liabilities traffic engineers have to shoulder?
6. Describe the complexity and social characteristics of traffic problems.

本章要点

1. 简述交通工程学定义及它与运输工程学的关系。
2. 简述交通工程学的目标和研究对象。
3. 简述公路交通系统主要由什么构成?
4. 简述推动交通工程学发展的动力(主要因素)。
5. 简述交通工程师的责任与义务。
6. 简述交通问题的复杂性和社会性。

Chapter 2 Basic Concepts and Components in Traffic Engineering

In this chapter some fundamentals and main components in traffic engineering are introduced. The purpose of this introduction is to provide students with basic concepts often used in traffic engineering. The basic concepts include (not limited to) right of way, mobility/accessibility, roadway classification, interrupted/uninterrupted flows. Road users, vehicles, highway facilities, control devices and roadway environment are considered as the main elements that students majoring in traffic engineering have to master. Some of characteristics of road users will be discussed in this chapter and the detailed information about road users' behavior can be learned from Traffic Psychology course. In general, as traffic engineering students there is no need for them to study mechanical features of vehicles. However, it is necessary for them to know some basic characteristics of vehicles such as physical size and acceleration/deceleration rates.

Traffic engineering system deals with a broad aspect and has characteristics of multiple disciplines in strict sense. As indicated in the preface of this book the objective of writing this text is to provide students and traffic professionals with basic concepts and preliminary knowledge about what traffic engineering looks like. It is hoped that college students can lay a solid foundation through reading this book for their further study and research. For this reason some basic concepts in traffic engineering will be elaborated in this chapter.

2.1　Right-of-way(通行权)

This concept is the most important in the whole process of traffic engineering study, because almost all theories and models are built up on the observation of rules embedded in right-of-way. As a general term right-of-way is defined as a legal right of passage over another person's ground. In traffic engineering it refers to the right of traffic movement to take precedence over another movement. For example, the traffic on major roadway has priority to pass intersection over the traffic on minor roadway at an unsignalized intersection. At signalized intersection the left turn vehicles have to yield the opposing through traffic implying that through traffic has higher ranking of right-of-way than the opposing left turn traffic to pass the intersection. To quantify such right-of-way (priority) ranking of right-of-way has been proposed in traffic engineering. The ranking is numbered from high to low. The detailed ranking of right-of-way is illustrated in chapter 7. It should be noted that traffic movements may enjoy the same right-of-way if these movements have no conflict with each other.

2.2　Mobility versus Accessibility(机动性和可达性)

There are two primary categories of service provided by highway systems: mobility and accessibility. Mobility refers to the ability to travel to many different destinations, while accessibility refers to the ability to gain entry to a particular site or area. More specifically, mobility emphasizes the through movement of people, goods, and vehicles from point A to point B in the system. Accessibility denotes the direct connection to abutting lands or development such as home, stores, schools, office building, etc. (Michael D Meyer defined mobility as the ability and knowledge to travel from one location to another in a reasonable amount of time and for acceptable costs. Accessibility was defined as the means by which an individual can accomplish some economic or social activity through access to that activity.)

A good transportation system must provide for both mobility and accessibility in a balanced way and should be designed to separate the functions to the extent possible to ensure both safety and efficiency. Relationship between mobility and accessibility is as follows. With an increase of mobility, the ability to access any development decreases and vise versa. This relationship is shown in Figure 2.1.

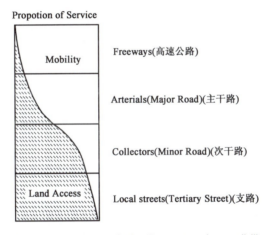

Figure 2.1　Relationship of Mobility versus Accessibility

Beijing-Tianjin-Tanggu highway is a freeway connecting Beijing and Tianjin. This roadway provides very good mobility for road users to move but less accessibility to the developments of abutting land. Chang'an avenue is a major road in the Beijing roadway network. It provides good accessibility to the buildings along the roadway. However, its mobility is not as good as Beijing-Tianjin-Tanggu highway due to many intersections on the route.

2.3　Classification of Roadways(道路分类)

In order to have roadway provide different services in terms of mobility and accessibility, it is necessary to stratify roadway system. In general hierarchy of highway classification is made based on traffic mobility and land access level. High-class highway has high-level of mobility whereas low-class highway has high-level of accessibility. Freeways provide high-level of mobility whereas local streets provide the best access to land development.

Different country has their own roadway classification based on their situations. All highway systems involve a hierarchal classification by the mix of mobility and accessibility functions provided. In the USA, they divide highway system into four major classes: freeways, arterials, collectors, and local streets. For different locations the classification can be different. In China, there are five classes for rural highway. They are freeway, first-class highway, second-class highway, third-class highway and fourth-class highway. For urban roadway there are also five categories. They are freeways, expressways, major streets, minor streets, and tertiary (or local) streets.

More details of roadway classification systems in the USA can be found in Table 2.1. Comparisons of typical categories of roadways between China and the USA are shown in Table 2.2. The purpose of conducting classification for highway is to clarify the functionality of each category of roadways in providing services from both mobility and accessibility.

Table 2.1 Typical Rural and Urban Roadway Classification Systems

Category	Subcategory	Rural	Urban
Freeways	Interstate Freeways	All freeways bearing interstate designation	All freeways bearing interstate designation
	Other Freeways	All other facilities with rull control of access	All other facilities with full control of access
	Expressways	Facilities with substantial control of access, but having some at-grade crossings or entrances	Facilities with substantial control of access, but having some at-grade crossings or entrances
Arterials	Major of Principal Arterials	Serving significant corridor movements, often between areas with populations over 25000 to 50000. High-type design and alignment prevail	Principal service for through movements, with very limited land-access functions that are incidental to the mobility function. High-type design prevails
	Minor Arterials	Provide linkage to significant traffic generators, including towns and cities with populations below the range for principal arterials; serve shorter trip lengths than principal arterials	Principal service for through movements, with moderate levels of access service also present

Continued table.

Subcategory		Rural	Urban
Collectors	Major Collectors	Serve generators of intra-county importance not served by arterials; provide connections to arterials and/or freeways	No subcategories usually used for urban collectors
	Minor Collectors	Link locally important generators with their rural hinterlands; provide connections to major collectors or arterials	Provide land access and circulation service within residential neighborhoods and/or commercial/industrial areas; collect trips from local generators and channel them to nearby arterials; distribute trips from arterials to their ultimate destination

Subcategory		Rural	Urban
Local streets	Residential	No subcategories generally used in rural classification schemes	Provide land access and circulation within residential neighborhoods
	Commercial	Provide access to adjacent lands of all types; serve travel over relatively short distances	Provide land access and circulation in areas of commercial development
	Industrial	—	Provide land access and circulation in areas of industrial development

Table 2.2 Comparison of Categories of Roadways between China and the USA

China		USA	
Urban	Rural	Urban	Rural
Freeway	Freeway	Freeway	Interstate
Expressway	1st Class Highway	—	—
Major Street	2nd Class Highway	Arterials	Primary
Minor Street	3rd Class Highway	Collector	Secondary
Tertiary Street	4th Class Highway	Local Street	Tertiary

In addition the classification of highways in South Africa, based on priority of traffic modes, is also given as indicated in Table 2.3.

Table 2.3 Priority-Based Highway Classification of South Africa

Primary Function	Class No.	Likely Features	Most Likely Authorities	Generic Description
Vehicle Priority (mobility)	1.	Long distance between cities, provinces or countries	National	Freeways, trunk roads
	2.	Relatively long distance between towns and cities	Provincial	Expressways, urban motorways, primary arteries

19

Continued table.

Primary Function	Class No.	Likely Features	Most Likely Authorities	Generic Description
Vehicle Priority (mobility)	3.	Medium distance between districts, municipalities	Metropolitan	Arterial roads, secondary arteries
Mixed Traffic (access)	4.	Short distance within districts/suburbs	Local/Municipal	Collector roads
	5.	Very short distance (500m max)	Local/Municipal	Local streets
Pedestrian Priority	6.	Suitable for walking, mobility impaired persons and cyclists	Local/Municipal	Footpaths/cycleways/sidewalks, parking lots

It should be noted that there are different ways to describe the classification of highways. For the purpose of simplicity it is suggested It should be noted that there are different ways to describe the classification of highways. For the purpose of simplicity it is suggested that students keep in mind that the ranking of highway is: freeway, expressway, major roadway, minor roadway, and local roadway, with highest to lowest in mobility. Motorway is British usage, synonymous word for freeway. Strictly speaking, there is a difference between freeway and expressway. However, their difference is disregarded in this text and we take them as a facility having same functionality.

2.4　Uninterrupted(连续流) and Interrupted (间断流) Flows

From characteristics of traffic movement traffic facilities are broadly divided into two principal categories: uninterrupted flow and interrupted flow.

Uninterrupted flow facilities(连续流道路设施) have no external interruptions to the traffic stream. Pure uninterrupted flow exists mainly on freeways and expressways, where there are no *at-grade intersections*(平面交叉口), traffic signals, STOP or YIELD signs, or any forms of direct access to such facilities. Therefore, the characteristics of the traffic stream are based solely on the interactions among vehicles and general roadway conditions.

Interrupted flow facilities(间断流道路设施) refer to those that incorporate fixed external interruptions into their design and operation. Such external interruptions include traffic signals, STOP or YIELD signs, *driveways*(接入道), *curb parking*(路侧停车区) and all forms of direct access connections. In fact all urban surface streets and highways are interrupted flow facilities.

The major difference between uninterrupted and interrupted flow facilities lies in continuously moving and discontinuously running of traffic flows on roadways. The traffic characteristics of both flows are quite different. It is true that interrupted flow is more difficult to study than uninterrupted flow.

A long segment of rural highway with no frequent accesses on both sides is also considered as an uninterrupted flow facility such as two-lane highway.

2.5 Perception Reaction Time (PRT)

As the major component of driver characteristics *perception reaction time* (PRT, 反应时间) is an important parameter in traffic engineering. It has many applications in the design of traffic facilities as well as in the traffic control management. Driver's perception reaction time is defined as the interval between seeing, feeling or hearing a traffic or highway situation and making an initial response to what has been perceived. Traditionally, the perception time includes the detection, identification, and decision elements involved in responding to a stimulus, whereas the reaction time is the time which takes to initiate the physical response such as foot touching the brake pedal. Some references refer it to the perception, identification, emotion, and volition time or PIEV, which is comparable in concept to the PRT. It varies with the complexity of the task, whether the event is expected or unexpected, and factors affecting human characteristics. MUTCD (Manual of Uniform Traffic Control Devices) recommend PIEV equals 3 to 10 seconds; AASHTO suggests a PRT of 2.5 seconds.

It is well known that elderly drivers have more difficulty than the young drivers in perceiving traffic situations and tend to pause longer between successive acts. Study conducted by Marsh indicates that on the average, simple reaction times for persons aged 65 are about 16 percent higher than for those aged 20. At the same time some studies show that the more information contents drivers come across, the higher the reaction times as depicted in Figure 2.2.

Driver *expectancy*(期望) is also a vial concept in traffic engineering study and particularly in the discussion of reaction times. Expectancy is defined in this text as readiness of a driver to respond to roadway conditions, traffic situations, or information systems. At locations where driver's expectancies are violated, drivers may require a longer response time as demonstrated in Figure 2.2. For example, drivers are all expected to enter or exit highway on the right-hand side. If the entrance or exit ramps of a highway are designed on the left-hand side, the traffic signs should be installed such that drivers have more time to respond this unexpected situation.

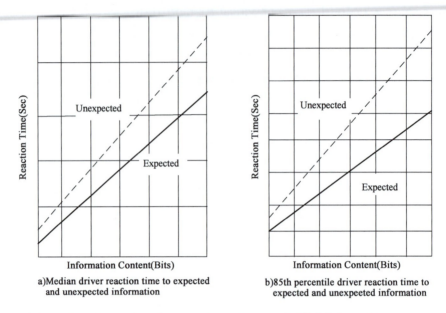

Figure 2.2　Perception Reaction Times from the AASHTO Green Book

2.6　Visual Acuity——Static versus Dynamic

Actions taken by drivers while driving on a roadway largely depend on their evaluation of information and reaction to information they receive from the *stimuli*(刺激物) that they see, feel or hear. Researchers report that about 90 percent of the information a driver obtains is visual. In the following session visual acuity is presented along with peripheral vision, color vision, and glare vision.

(1) *Visual Acuity*(视力) is defined as the ability to see fine details of an object. There are two types of visual acuity useful in traffic engineering: *static visual acuity* (静视力) is the ability to read letter at certain distance; *dynamic visual acuity*(动视力) is the ability to see objects in relative motion with the eyes. Generally, static visual acuity of a person is better than his/her dynamic visual acuity, which means that the ability of drivers to clearly see things diminishes with the increase of speed.

Mourant and Rockwell indicated in their study that experienced drivers scanned a wider range of horizontal fixation locations than novice drivers. The average horizontal fixation range for the experienced group varied from 30° to 48°.

Visual acuity declines and the *field of vision* (视野) narrows with advancing age, especially when lighting conditions are poor.

(2) **Peripheral Vision**(周边视力) is defined as the ability to see objects beyond the cone of clearest vision. The field may extend up to 90° to the right and left of the centerline of the pupil, and up to 60° above and 70° below the line of sight. This wide variation of the value results from the speed of the vehicle. The peripheral vision field narrows, as speed increases, to as little as 100° at 32km/h and to 40° at 96km/h.

(3) Color Vision is the ability to differentiate one color from another, but deficiency in this ability, usually referred to as **color blindness** (色盲), is not of great significance in highway driving because other ways of recognizing traffic information devices can compensate for it.

Glare Vision(眩光) and Recovery are also important characteristics of driver. Typically, direct and **specular glare visions**(反射眩光) are the two types of glare vision. Direct glare occurs when relatively bright light appears in the individual's field of vision. Specular glare occurs when the image reflected by the relatively bright light appears in the field of vision of a driver. Both types of glare result in the deterioration of visibility and cause discomfort to the eyes. Glare recovery is defined as the time required by driver to recover from the effects of glare after passing the light source. Studies show that the time is about 3 seconds when moving from dark to light and 6 seconds or more when moving from light to dark. Street lighting is designed for minimizing glare effects.

(4) **Depth Perception**(深度感觉) affects the ability of a person to estimate speed and distance. It is particularly important on the two-lane highway during passing maneuvers, when head-on crash may result from a lack of proper judgment of speed and distance.

For details about visual information please refer to Table 2.4.

Table 2.4 Visual Factors in the Driving Task

Visual Factor	Definition	Sample Related Driving Task
Accommodation	Change in the shape of the lens to bring images into focus	Changing focus from dashboard displays to roadway
Static Visual Acuity	Ability to see small details clearly	Reading distant traffic signs
Adaptation	Change in sensitivity to different levels of light	Adjust to changes in light upon entering a tunnel
Angular Movement	Seeing objects moving across the field of view	Judging the speed of cars crossing drivers' paths

Continued table.

Visual Factor	Definition	Sample Related Driving Task
Movement in Depth	Detecting changes in visual image size	Judging speed of an approaching vehicle
Color	Discrimination between different colors	Identifying the color of signals
Contrast Sensitivity	Seeing objects that are similar in brightness to their background	Detecting dark-clothed pedestrians at night
Depth Perception	Judgment of the distance of objects	Passing on two-lane roads with oncoming traffic
Dynamic Visual Acuity	Ability to see objects that are in motion relative to the eye	Reading traffic signs while moving
Eye Movement	Changing the direction of gaze	Scanning the road environment for hazards
Glare Sensitivity	Ability to resist and recover from the effects of glare	Reduction in visual performance due to headlight glare
Peripheral Vision	Detection of objects at the side of the visual field	Seeing a bicycle approaching from the left
Vergence(转角)	Angle between the eyes' line of sight	Change from looking at the dashboard to the road

Note: Dewar, R., "Road Users," Traffic Engineering Handbook, 5th Edition, Chapter 2, Table 2.2, pg. 8, 1999.

2.7 Walking Speed

This is a very important element reflecting pedestrian's characteristics and applied in traffic design for road users, particularly in *signal timing*(信号配时) at intersections. Empirical research has shown that under free-flow conditions pedestrian walking speeds tend to be approximately normally. It should be indicated that free-flow walking speeds will vary with the pedestrian's age and gender as well as trip purpose. The standard walking speed used in signal timing plan is 4.0ft/s with 3.5ft/s recommended where older pedestrians are predominant. Table 2.5 provides information relating to average walking speeds for different group of pedestrians.

Table 2.5 50th Percentile Walking Speeds for Pedestrians of Various Ages

Age(years)	50th Percentile Walking Speed(ft/s)	
	Males	Females
2	2.8	3.4
3	3.5	3.4
4	4.1	4.1
5	4.6	4.5
6	4.8	5.0
7	5.0	5.0
8	5.0	5.3
9	5.1	5.4
10	5.5	5.4
11	5.2	5.2
12	5.8	5.7
13	5.3	5.6
14	5.1	5.3
15	5.6	5.3
16	5.2	5.4
17	5.2	5.4
18	4.9	N/A
20~29	5.7	5.4
30~39	5.4	5.4
40~49	5.1	5.3
50~59	4.9	5.0
60+	4.1	4.1

Note: Compiled from Eubanks, J. and Hill, P., Pedestrian Accident Reconstruction and Litigation, 2nd Edition, Lawyers & Judges Publishing Co., Tucson, AZ, 1999.

With regard to road users characteristics only three components are introduced in this chapter. They are perception reaction time, visual acuity, and walking speeds. Since other characteristics of human factors can be studied in the course of traffic psychology, these components are not discussed in this text. However, some characteristics are listed below for students who are interested in.

(1) *Gap Acceptance*(可接受间隙). It is a very important element related to capacity analysis and safety and will be discussed in detail in chapter 6.

(2) Comprehension of Control Information. It is utmost important for pedestrians to understand and adherence to control devices while crossing streets and will be discussed in chapter 8.

(3) Impacts of Drugs and Alcohol. The past studies show that the effect of drugs and alcohol has impaired driver's ability to react, make correct judgment and execute necessary action. Enforcement and education are considered as major weapons in combating DWI (*Driving While Intoxicated* 醉酒驾车) and DUI (*Driving Under Influence* 酒后驾车), as there is not a great deal that can be done through design or control to address the issue.

(4) Impacts of Aging of Drivers. As life expectancy continues to rise, the number of older drivers has risen dramatically. It is keenly important for traffic engineers to understand how aging affects driver needs and limitations and how these should impact design and control decision.

It should be noted that the most important human factors that influence driving is the personality and psychology of the driver. However, this is beyond the scope of traffic engineering and not easily quantified. In reality it is difficult to consider these factors in planning, design, and management of traffic facilities.

2.8 Vehicle Characteristics

Traffic engineering students don't necessarily know much about mechanical features of motor vehicles. What they need to be familiar with is the physical size of a vehicle, acceleration and deceleration rates of a vehicle, braking performance, turning characteristics, and climbing capability. The information from these characteristics will assist traffic planners and engineers in determining the specifications and criteria of traffic facilities.

2.8.1 Design Vehicle (Standard Vehicle)

It is vital for traffic engineers to determine standard vehicle in order to guide the planning and design of highway facilities. The selection of design vehicles can have a profound effect on the use of roadway facilities such as turning radii, turning pocket length, U-turn from left-turn-bay, and design of parking lot. As rule of thumb, it must be remembered that all parts of the street and highway network should be accessible to emergency vehicles, including fire engines, ambulances, emergency evacuation vehicles. As a result, the single-unit truck is usually the minimum design vehicle selected for most local street applications. The passenger car is used as a design vehicle only in parking facilities. However, access to emergency vehicles must be considered in the design of the parking facilities.

For geometric design, AASHTO has defined 20 standard vehicles. In general design vehicles are mainly employed in the design of turning roadways and intersection curbs, and are used to determine the width of traffic lane. It is very important to determine design vehicle heights in the design of overpass whose overhead clearance should be sufficient to allow the largest anticipated vehicles to pass safely.

2.8.2 Acceleration and Deceleration Performance of Vehicles

Acceleration and deceleration properties of vehicles can help determine the length of acceleration/deceleration lane on highway when merging/diverging. Based on laws of motion, maximum acceleration rates vary with the size of the vehicles and its operating speed. Typically, vehicles are capable of obtaining the greatest acceleration at the lowest speeds. It should be indicated that there is a significant disparity in acceleration rate between passenger car and truck. In terms of acceleration distance, a truck is about 5 times longer than a passenger car.

A vehicle can decelerate when the driver releases the accelerator without braking, due to the drag of the engine, air resistance, grade resistance, and so forth. Under normal braking conditions the levels of deceleration developed usually do not reach the limit of a vehicle's braking capability nor that of the pavement-tireinterface. The magnitude of deceleration force developed under normal or nonskid braking depends on the force the driver applies to the brake pedal. That force is related to driver's comfort.

2.8.3 Braking Performance

What traffic engineers concern most about vehicle characteristics is braking property of vehicles, which is critical in the geometric design and safety management. The factors affecting braking performance include type and condition of the tires, roadway surface condition (wet or dry), and grade. The equation of braking distance is given as follows, based on the law of momentum.

$$d_b = \frac{S_i^2 - S_f^2}{254(F \pm G)} \tag{2-1}$$

Where: d_b——braking distance (meters);

S_i——initial vehicle speed (km/h);

S_f——final vehicle speed (km/h);

F——coefficient of forward friction between tires and roadway surface;

G——grade, expressed as a decimal.

For designation of grades, " + " is used for upgrade (uphill) and the " − " is used for downgrades (downhill). It should be noted that AASHTO Green Book observes that friction factors F should be based on wet pavements rather than dry. Readers should be careful in using this equation because metric system is applied. In some textbook the value of parameter in the braking distance equation is different from this equation. This is due to the use of different measurement system. In this textbook metric system is adopted unless specially noticed.

The braking distance formula is a useful tool of accident investigators. It can be used to estimate the initial speed of a vehicle using measured skid marks and an estimated final speed based on damage assessments.

2.8.4 Safe Stopping Sight Distance(SSD,停车视距)

The total distance to bring a vehicle to a full stop to avoid any unpleasant event is the sum of the reaction distance plus the braking distance, relating to perception-reaction time and braking performance of vehicle. This distance is called stopping sight distance and its mathematical equation is as follows.

$$d = 0.278 S_i t + \frac{S_i^2 - S_f^2}{254(F \pm G)} \quad (2\text{-}2)$$

Where d is in meters; S_i and S_f are in km/h; t stands for PRT in second.

One of the most fundamental principles of highway design is that the driver must be able to see far enough to avoid a potential hazard or collision. Thus, sight distance concept has been raised and this distance should at least be equivalent to the total stopping distance required at the design speed. The meaning of equation (2-2) is that for the entire length of highway section drivers must be able to see at least d ahead, otherwise collision may occur.

Example 2.1 Estimating Perception Reaction Time

A driver is driving at 65km/h when he/she observed that an accident has blocked the road ahead. The driver moves 45.15m before he/she could activate the brakes. Determine the perception reaction time.

Solution:

From the given condition we know the reaction distance is 45.15m. Thus, based on equation of reaction distance we have:

$$t = \frac{d_r}{0.278v} = \frac{45.15}{0.278 \times 65} = 2.5(s)$$

2.8.5 Decision Sight Distance(DSD,决策视距)

The SSD is provided when the stimulus is under driver's expectancy. However, when the stimulus is unexpected or when it is necessary for the driver to make unusual maneuvers, longer SSD is required. Decision Sight Distance is defined as the distance required for a driver to detect an unexpected or otherwise difficult-to-perceive information source or hazard in a roadway environment that may be visually cluttered. The DSD depends on the type of maneuver required to avoid the hazard on the roadway, and also on whether the roadway is located in a rural or in an urban area. The recommended DSD is shown in Table 2.6.

Table 2.6 Decision Sight Distance

Design Speed (mile/h)	Assumed Maneuver Time (s)	Decision Sight Distance for Avoidance Maneuver (ft)				
		A	B	C	D	E
Reaction Time (s)		3	9.1	11.2	12.9	14.5
30	4.5	219	488	692	767	838
40	4.5	330	688	923	1023	1117
50	4.0	460	908	1117	1242	1360
60	4.0	609	1147	1341	1491	1632
70	3.5	778	1406	1513	1688	1852
80	3.5	966	1683	1729	1929	2117

Note: A: Stop on a rural road;
B: Stop on an urban road;
C: Speed/path/direction change on a rural road;
D: Speed/path/direction change on a suburban road;
E: Speed/path/direction change on an urban road.

It should be mentioned that the English Unit System is used in Table 2.5.

Example 2.2   Calculating Stopping Sight Distance

A motorist traveling at 65km/h on a freeway intends to leave this freeway using an exit ramp with a maximum speed of 35km/h. At what point on the freeway should the motorist step on his/her brakes in order to reduce his/her speed to the maximum allowable on the ramp just before entering the ramp, if this section of the freeway has a downgrade of 3 percent and the coefficient of forward friction is 0.07.

Solution:
Use Equation(2-2):

$$d_b = \frac{S_i^2 - S_f^2}{254(F - G)}$$

Based on given conditions:
$F = 0.07$, $G = 0.03$, $S_i = 65 \text{km/h}$, $S_f = 35 \text{km/h}$

$$d_b = \frac{65^2 - 35^2}{254 \times (0.07 - 0.03)} = \frac{3000}{254 \times 0.04} = 295.3(\text{m})$$

The brakes should be applied at least 295.3m from the beginning of ramp.

Example 2.3 Finding the Distance Required

A motorist traveling at 55km/h down a grade of 5 percent on a highway observes an accident ahead of him/her, involving an overturned truck that is completely blocking the road. If the motorist was able to stop his vehicle 30m from the overturned truck, what was his/her distance from the truck when he/she first observed the accident? Assume perception-reaction time is 2.5s and the coefficient of forward friction is 0.08.

Solution:
Use Equation(2-2):

$$d = 0.278 S_i t + \frac{S_i^2 - S_f^2}{254(F-G)}$$

Based on given conditions:
$F = 0.08$, $G = 0.05$, $S_i = 55$km/h, $S_f = 0$, $t = 2.5$s

$$d = 0.278 \times 55 \times 2.5 + \frac{55^2}{254(0.08 - 0.05)} = 38.28 + 396.98 = 435.2(m)$$

Find the distance of the motorist when he/she first observed the accident:
$$d + 30 = 465.2(m)$$

2.9 Geometric Characteristics of Roadways

Geometric characteristics of roadways are the most components in traffic engineering practice, among other things. Since a comprehensive knowledge about geometric design will be learned in the course of highway design or from AASHTO Green Book, the detailed geometric characteristics will not be discussed in this text. The following is a brief description of geometric design.

2.9.1 *Horizontal Alignment*(平曲线)

The horizontal alignment refers to a plan view of the highway, including tangent sections, the horizontal curves and other transition elements that join them.

(1) Geometric characteristics of horizontal curves:
  a. Radius and degree of curvature;
  b. Review of trigonometric functions;
  c. Critical characteristics of circular horizontal curves;
  d. Length of tangent;
  e. Length of long chord;
  f. Superelevation of horizontal curves.

(2) Spiral transition curves:

a. Length of spiral;

b. Angle of deflection for the spiral;

c. Length of tangent distance.

(3) Sight distance on horizontal curves.

(4) Compound horizontal curves.

(5) Reverse horizontal curves.

2.9.2 *Vertical Alignment*(竖曲线)

Vertical alignment refers to the design of the facility in profile view. Straight grades are connected by vertical curves, which provide for transition between adjacent grades. The grade is defined as the longitudinal slope of the facility, expressed either as a decimal or as a percentage.

(1) Geometric characteristics of vertical curves—crest versus sag;

(2) Sight distance on vertical curves;

(3) Other minimum controls on length of vertical curves;

(4) Some design guidelines for vertical curves.

2.9.3 *Cross Section*(横断面)

The cross section refers to a cut across the plane of the highway and it includes the following elements to be discussed.

(1) Travel lanes and pavement.

(2) Shoulders-defined by AASHTO as portion of roadway contiguous with the traveled way that accommodates stopped vehicles, emergency use, and lateral support of sub-base, base, and surface courses of the roadway structure.

(3) Side-slopes for cuts and embankments.

(4) Guardrail-roadside guardrail is provided to prevent vehicles from entering a cross-slope than 4 : 1, or from colliding with roadside objects such as trees, culverts, lighting standards, sign posts. Median guardrail is primarily provided to prevent vehicles from encroaching into the opposing lane of traffic.

The current geometric design of roadways that is different from previous practice is the change from vehicle-oriented to human-centered concept.

2.10 Traffic Control Devices

The traffic control devices are defined as the media traffic engineers use to communicate with drivers. One of the objectives to install and manage traffic control devices is to communicate with road users in a manner that information delivered to users has a high level of expectancy and comfort. The other objective is to maintain consistent in providing standardization of sign, markings and signal for drivers to avoid confusing. MUTCD (Manual on Uniform Traffic Control Devices) can be considered a milestone in the development of traffic control devices. The following Table 2.7 shows the evolution of this manual.

Table 2.7 Evolution of the MUTCD

Year	Name	Month/Year Revised
1927	Manual and Specifications for the Manufacture, Display, and Erection of U.S. Standard Road Markers and Signs (for rural roads)	4/1929, 12/1931
1930	Manual on Street Traffic Signs, Signal, and Markings (for urban streets)	No revisions
1935	Manual on Uniform Traffic Control Devices for Streets and Highways (MUTCD)	2/1939
1942	Manual on Uniform Traffic Control Devices for Streets and Highways-War Emergency Edition	No revisions
1948	Manual on Uniform Traffic Control Devices for Streets and Highways	9/1954
1961	Manual on Uniform Traffic Control Devices for Streets and Highways	No revisions
1971	Manual on Uniform Traffic Control Devices for Streets and Highways	11/1971, 4/1972, 3/1973, 10/1973, 6/1974, 6/1975, 9/1976, 12/1977
1978	Manual on Uniform Traffic Control Devices for Streets and Highways	12/1979, 12/1983, 9/1984, 3/1986
1988	Manual on Uniform Traffic Control Devices for Streets and Highways	1/1990, 3/1992, 9/1993, 11/1994, 12/1996, 6/1998, 1/2000
2000	Manual on Uniform Traffic Control Devices for Streets and Highways-Millennium Edition	7/2002
2003	Manual on Uniform Traffic Control Devices for Streets and Highways	—
2009	Manual on Uniform Traffic Control Devices for Streets and Highways-2009 Edition	12/2009

In general traffic control devices cover three elements: traffic signs, traffic markings, and traffic signals. In this section brief introduction will be presented and the detailed characteristics of traffic control devices can be found in chapter 8.

2.10.1 Traffic Signs

Traffic signs are defined as specially-designed board with words, arrows, symbols, and legends, installed along roadways. They are designed for regulating, warning and guiding road users for completing their trips. Traffic signs include regulatory, warning, and guide signs.

(1) *Regulatory signs*(法令标志) are used to convey information related to specific traffic laws and regulations such as *right-of-way*(通行权), speed limit, lane usage, parking. Generally, regulatory signs have empowered road users to observe traffic laws and regulations, otherwise they must be fined.

(2) *Warning signs*(警告标志) are used to inform drivers about upcoming hazards that they might not see during driving. They are used to prevent unpleasant event from happening.

(3) *Guide signs* (指路标志) are used to provide information on routes, destinations and services that drivers may look for. They are used much more than regulatory and warning signs in practice.

2.10.2 Traffic Markings

Traffic markings are used to channelize traffic by painting or delineating on surface of road. In general there are three types of traffic markings: longitudinal markings, transverse markings, and object makers or delineators.

(1) *Longitudinal markings*(纵向标线) refer to those markings placed parallel to the direction of travel such as centerline, lane lines and pavement edge lines.

(2) *Transverse markings* (横向标线) refer to any markings with a component that cuts across a portion or all of the traveled way such as STOP lines, crosswalk markings, parking space markings, word and symbol markings.

(3) *Object markers and delineators*(物标和道钉). Object markers are used to denote obstructions; delineators are reflective devices mounted on the side of roadways to help denote its alignment.

2.10.3 Traffic Signals

Traffic signal is defined a power-operated traffic control device by which traffic is warned or directed to make movement at a particular location. It is mostly used at intersections and considered the ultimate form of intersection control approach. There are many types of traffic signal. Below are some of them.

(1) Traffic Control Signals

They are generally installed at intersections to control the vehicular movements.

(2) Pedestrian Signals

They are either installed at intersections to work with traffic control signals or installed at mid-block of roadway link to guide pedestrians crossing street.

(3) Signals at Freeway Entrance

As a measurement of traffic flow control on freeways signals are installed at the freeway entrance to control the entry of on-ramp traffic. This way of control is also called *ramp-metering*(匝道流量控制). This way of control is to guarantee the smooth movement of traffic on curb lane of freeway or expressway.

(4) Signal for *Draw Bridges*(开启桥)

When a draw bridge is located on the roadway it is necessary to install a signal to regulate the traffic on the roadway to stop before the elevated part of the bridge.

(5) Lane-use *Control Signal*(车道灯)

Lane-use control signal is often used to tell drivers if the lane is open or closed. This sort of signal is often installed overhead of the reversible lanes.

(6) *Flashing Beacon*(闪光标灯)

Flashing beacon is generally used during night at intersection when traffic is very low. It can also be used at school zone to regulate drivers to slow down.

Traffic control devices should be reasonable and appropriate for the traffic requirements at a specific location. The use of a traffic control device at a location where it is not warranted tends to invite drivers to disregard the device and to have less respect for traffic control devices in general. Therefore, traffic control devices should be properly designed and installed. The size of the device, its shape, colors, contrast with the background, and lighting or reflectorization should be designed such that they draw attention from road users.

The application of traffic control devices should be responsive to a driver's need for information. The information provided through traffic control devices must be correct and not confusing. Experiences indicate that wrong information will mislead road users, degrading level of service of travelers. The selection and design of traffic control devices should be an integral part of geometric design rather than a separate step.

Key points of the chapter

1. Describe the relationship between mobility and accessibility.
2. Why do we need to classify roadways?
3. What is difference between interrupted and uninterrupted flows?
4. What are the steps included in reaction time of drivers?
5. What are the static and dynamic visual acuities and relationship between the two?
6. Why do we have to determine the standard vehicle?
7. Remember the equations of braking distance and stopping sight distance and

applications of the equations.

8. What is major difference in geometric design between current and the past?

9. What is the objective of traffic control devices and what are composed of traffic control devices?

本章要点

1. 简述机动性与可达性关系。
2. 为什么要进行道路的分类？
3. 连续流与间断流的区别是什么？
4. 驾驶员反应时间包含哪几个过程？
5. 动视力与静视力的关系是什么？
6. 为什么要确定标准车？
7. 简述制动距离和安全停车视距的计算及其应用。
8. 现代几何设计与过去的主要区别是什么？
9. 交通控制设施设计的目标是什么？交通控制设施包含哪几方面？

Chapter 3 Volume, Density & Speed Studies

In traffic engineering volume, density and speed are the three most important parameters of interest. Percentile volumes, rate of flow, peak hour factor and percentile speeds have particular characteristics in the design and operation of traffic and highway facilities and will be introduced in this chapter. Besides, relationship among volume, density and speed will be briefly described since the detailed mathematical models of these three parameters are often discussed in the course of Traffic Flow Theory.

3.1 Definition of Volumes

Volume is defined as the number of vehicles (or persons) that pass a point on a transportation facility during a specified time period, which is usually one day or one hour, but need not be. In traffic engineering studies there are many volumes such as daily volume, hourly volume, peak hour volume, and rate of flow. In addition volumes of a day or an hour can vary greatly, depending on the different day of the week or different time period of a day.

In the following four daily volume parameters that are widely used in traffic engineering are introduced.

3.1.1 AADT (*Average Annual Daily Traffic*, 年平均日交通量)

This is the average of 24-hour traffic volume at a given location over a full 365-day year. AADT is estimated by dividing the total volume for the whole year by 365.

3.1.2 AAWT (*Average Annual Weekday Traffic*, 年平均工作日交通量)

This is the average 24-hour traffic volume occurring on weekdays over a full year, AAWT is computed by dividing the total weekday volume for the whole year by 260.

3.1.3 ADT (*Average Daily Traffic*, 平均日交通量)

This is the average 24-hour volume at a given location for some period of time less than a year.

3.1.4 AWT (*Average Weekday Traffic*, 平均工作日交通量)

This is the average 24-hour traffic volume occurring on weekdays for some period less than one year.

The relationship between AAWT and AWT is analogous to that between AADT and ADT. All of these four volumes are stated in terms of vehicles per day. Generally, daily volumes are not differentiated by direction or lane but are totals for an entire facility at particular location. It should be mentioned here that these four volumes are often used in transportation planning and shown in social or economic statistics. Most often they are called macroscopic parameters in traffic engineering and useful for planning purpose.

3.1.5 Daily Variation Factor (DF)

Daily variation factor is defined as ratio of AADT over yearly average volume for particular day of week (Monday, Tuesday, etc.). DF is often used to reflect fluctuation of daily volume over different weeks and Table 3.1 provides an example of how to estimate daily variation factor.

Table 3.1 Calibration of Daily Variation Factors

Day	Yearly Average Volume for Day (veh/day)	Daily Adjustment Factor DF
Monday	1820	1430/1820 = 0.79
Tuesday	1588	1430/1588 = 0.90
Wednesday	1406	1430/1406 = 1.02
Thursday	1300	1430/1300 = 1.10
Friday	1289	1430/1289 = 1.11
Saturday	1275	1430/1275 = 1.12
Sunday	1332	1430/1332 = 1.07
Total	10010	
Estimated AADT	1430	

3.1.6 Monthly Variation Factor (MF) is defined as ratio of AADT over

ADT is used for particular month of the year. Likewise, MF is often used to reflect fluctuation of daily volume over different month and Table 3.2 provides an example of how to estimate monthly variation factor.

Table 3.2 Calibration of Monthly Variation Factors

Month	Total Traffic (veh)	ADT for Month (veh/day)	Monthly Variation Factor MF
January	19840	290851/31 = 640	797/640 = 1.25
February	16660	290851/28 = 595	797/595 = 1.34
March	21235	290851/31 = 685	797/685 = 1.16
April	24300	290851/30 = 810	797/810 = 0.98
May	25885	290851/31 = 835	797/835 = 0.95
June	26280	290851/30 = 876	797/876 = 0.91
July	27652	290851/31 = 892	797/892 = 0.89
August	30008	290851/31 = 968	797/968 = 0.82
September	28620	290851/30 = 954	797/954 = 0.84

Continued table

Month	Total Traffic (veh)	ADT for Month (veh/day)	Monthly Variation Factor MF
October	26350	290851/31 =850	797/850 =0.94
November	22290	290851/30 =743	797/743 =1.07
December	21731	290851/31 =701	797/701 =1.14
Total	290851	AADT =290851/365 =797(veh/day)	

Daily variation factor and monthly variation factor are used to reflect the fluctuation of average daily traffic over a week or a month. If values of *DF* and *MF* are greater than 1.0, it indicates that average daily traffic for this week or month is lower than *AADT*. If values of *DF* and *MF* are less than 1.0, it indicates that average daily traffic for this week or month is higher than *AADT*.

From engineering design perspective hourly volumes are more often used to guide design and future operation practice.

3.1.7 Hourly Volumes and Peak Hour Volume

Hourly volumes are used to reflect variation (fluctuation) of traffic volume in a day, and peak hour volume is defined as the volume in the single hour that has the highest hourly volume. Sometimes, peak hour is also called rush hour. Unlike daily volumes hourly volumes are directional and lane based, which means any hourly volume should be both direction specific and lane specific.

Peak hour volume is of greatest interest to traffic engineers for design and operational analysis usage.

3.1.8 *Rate of Flow* (流率)

For in-depth operational analysis of hourly volume the concept of rate of flow has been raised. It is defined as an equivalent hourly volume for a given *interval* (时段) (interval can be 5,10,15 minutes). The following is an example of estimation of rate of flow, given interval of 5,10 and 15 minutes in Table 3.3.

Table 3.3 Estimation of Rate of Flow

Interval	Volume(veh)	Interval	Volume(veh)
7:00~7:05	15	7:30~7:35	17
7:05~7:10	25	7:35~7:40	35
7:10~7:15	18	7:40~7:45	28
7:15~7:20	42	7:45~7:50	32
7:20~7:25	31	7:50~7:55	26
7:25~7:30	18	7:55~8:00	20

Assuming V_5, V_{10}, and V_{15} representing rate of flow for 5, 10 and 15 minutes intervals, so we have twelve rates of flow for 5-minute interval, six rates of flow for 10-minute interval, and four rates of flow for 15-minute interval as demonstrated below.

V_5 = (180,300,216,504,372,216,204,420,336,384,312,240)

V_{10} = (240,360,294,312,360,276)

V_{15} = (232,364,320,312)

Thus:

Max V_5 = 504, Max V_{10} = 360, Max V_{15} = 364

It is widely accepted that 15-minute interval is considered the standard time period used, primarily based on the belief that this is the shortest period of time over which flow rates are "statistically stable". The difference between volume and rate of flow for the above example is illustrated in Table 3.4. The very reason to make use of rate of flow instead of hourly volume in operational analysis lies in the fact that short-term peaks of flow within an hour may exceed handling capacity of the facility and create a breakdown.

Table 3.4 Illustration of Volumes and Rates of Flow

Time Interval	Volume for 15-minute Interval (veh)	Rate of Flow (veh/h)
7:00 ~7:15	58	58 ×4 =232
7:15 ~7:30	91	91 ×4 =364
7:30 ~7:45	80	80 ×4 =320
7:45 ~8:00	78	78 ×4 =312
7:00 ~8:00	Σ =307	

3.1.9 *Peak Hour Factor*(高峰小时系数)

Peak Hour Factor (*PHF*) is defined the ratio of peak hour volume over maximum rate of flow. It is used to reflect the stability of volume distribution within peak hour.

For the above case we have:

PHF_5 = 307/504 = 0.61

PHF_{10} = 307/360 = 0.85

PHF_{15} = 307/364 = 0.84

Two features of *PHF* should be remembered: (1) 0 < *PHF* < 1; (2) the less the value of PHF, the more the *fluctuation*(波动) of the traffic flow within an hour.

In general *PHF* is used to reflect the *evenness*(均匀程度) of peak-hourly flow. If the value of *PHF* is very small it shows that the coming traffic flow during peak hour is not evenly distributed. If the value of *PHF* is close to 1.0 it indicates that the coming traffic flow is evenly distributed. The *PHF* is descriptive of trip generation patterns and may apply to an area or portion of street and highway system. Once the value of

PHF is known it can be used to estimate a maximum flow rate within an hour for analysis purpose.

3.1.10 The 30th Hourly Volume (第30位小时交通量)

It is defined as an hourly volume at which its ranking on yearly-counting curve counts 30th among 8760 hourly volumes in a year. The value of this point is considered in the planning and design of roadway facilities because the volume-ranking curve begins to "flatten out" after this point.

3.1.11 The 30th Highest Hourly Volume

This volume is defined as an hourly volume at which its ranking on yearly-counting curve counts 30th among 365 peak hour volumes in a year. This volume is not often used in practice.

3.1.12 DDHV (Directional Design Hour Volume, 设计小时流量)

$DDHV = AADT = AA$, where: K is proportion of daily traffic occurring during the peak hour, expressed as a decimal; D is proportion of peak-hour traffic traveling in the peak direction, expressed as a decimal. For design purpose, the K factor often represents the proportion of $AADT$ occurring during the 30th peak hour of the year.

Factors K and D are based on local or regional characteristics at existing locations. The data bank of K and D has been maintained in some states of the USA for many years. Therefore, some locations similar to characteristics of the area having such data bank can borrow the values of K and D in estimation of $DDHV$.

Typically, K decreases with increasing development density in the areas served by the facility. In high-density areas, substantial demand during off-peak periods exists, resulting in low proportion of traffic occurring during the peak hour of the day. The volume generated by high-density development is generally larger than that generated by lower-density areas. Thus, it is important to remember that a high proportion of traffic occurring in the peak hour does not imply that the peak-hour volume is large.

As development density increases, the D factor tends to decrease. As density increases, it is more likely to have substantial bi-directional demands. The value of D is between 0.45 and 0.55. If this value is 0.65 or over for a particular segment of highway this demonstrates that directional disparity is significant. The *reversible lanes* (潮汐车道) are sometimes installed, accordingly.

Example 3.1 Determine DDHV

Consider an urban roadway on which it was projected that $AADT$ in 10 years would reach 50000 vehicles per day. For the same type of roadway and region in question, it is known that peak-hour traffic remains approximately 15% of the *AADT*, and that the peak direction generally carries 60% of the peak-hour traffic. Determine the *DDHV* of this roadway.

Solution:

Given the condition it is known that the proportion of daily traffic $K=0.15$ and directional factor $D=0.6$.

Thus, an approximate *DDHV* could be estimated as:
$DDHV = AADT \cdot K \cdot D = 50,000 \times 0.15 \times 0.60 = 4500 (\text{veh/h})$

3.1.13 VMT (Vehicle Miles Traveled) or VKT (Vehicle Kilometers Traveled)

Vehicle Miles Traveled (VMT, 车公里) is another parameter to estimate product of volume and average travel length for a trip. This element is often used as an important statistics to measure intensity of vehicles using roadway network as well as to evaluate strength of local economy from transportation perspective. Table 3.5 illustrates an example of estimation of *VMT*.

Table 3.5 Estimation of Vehicle Miles Traveled on a Limited Network: An Example

Station	8-Hour Count (veh)	Link Length (mile)	Link VMT (veh-miles)
A	6967	0.25	1741.75
1	5159	0.25	1289.75
2	5254	0.25	1313.50
3	5820	0.25	1455.00
4	4058	0.25	1014.50
5	8710	0.25	2177.50
6	7274	0.25	1818.50
Network Total			10810.50

3.1.14 *PCU* (*or PCE*)——*Passenger Car Unit* (*Passenger Car Equivalent*) (标准小汽车当量)

In traffic engineering design vehicle dictates the geometric design. In traffic volume estimation passenger car plays key role to integrate mix traffic counts into a uniform or standard counting unit. The concept of passenger car unit has then been introduced. It is defined as the number of passenger cars displaced by one truck, bus or *RV* (*Recreational Vehicle*, 房车) in a given traffic stream. In order to reflect the different impact or intensity on the roadway due to the different vehicles in terms of size, operating characteristics, passenger car unit (passenger car equivalent) is applied in the estimation of traffic volume. Passenger car equivalents for trucks, buses and RVs are given in Table 3.6, 3.7 and 3.8, respectively. It should be noted that the values in these Tables are based on the American experiences and should be used with care.

Table 3.6 Passenger-Car Equivalents for Trucks and Buses on Upgrades

Upgrade (%)	Length (km)	E_T Percentage of Trucks and Buses								
		2	4	5	6	8	10	15	20	25
<2	All	1.5	1.5	1.5	1.5	1.5	1.5	1.5	1.5	1.5
≥2~3	0.0~0.4	1.5	1.5	1.5	1.5	1.5	1.5	1.5	1.5	1.5
	>0.4~0.8	1.5	1.5	1.5	1.5	1.5	1.5	1.5	1.5	1.5
	>0.8~1.2	1.5	1.5	1.5	1.5	1.5	1.5	1.5	1.5	1.5
	>1.2~1.6	2.0	2.0	2.0	2.0	1.5	1.5	1.5	1.5	1.5
	>1.6~2.4	2.5	2.5	2.5	2.5	2.0	2.0	2.0	2.0	2.0
	>2.4	3.0	3.0	2.5	2.5	2.0	2.0	2.0	2.0	2.0
>3~4	0.0~0.4	1.5	1.5	1.5	1.5	1.5	1.5	1.5	1.5	1.5
	>0.4~0.8	2.0	2.0	2.0	2.0	2.0	2.0	1.5	1.5	1.5
	>0.8~1.2	2.5	2.5	2.0	2.0	2.0	2.0	2.0	2.0	2.0
	>1.2~1.6	3.0	3.0	2.5	2.5	2.5	2.5	2.0	2.0	2.0
	>1.6~2.4	3.5	3.5	3.0	3.0	3.0	3.0	2.5	2.5	2.5
	>2.4	4.0	3.5	3.0	3.0	3.0	3.0	2.5	2.5	2.5
>4~5	0.0~0.4	1.5	1.5	1.5	1.5	1.5	1.5	1.5	1.5	1.5
	>0.4~0.8	3.0	2.5	2.5	2.5	2.0	2.0	2.0	2.0	2.0
	>0.8~1.2	3.5	3.0	3.0	3.0	2.5	2.5	2.5	2.5	2.5
	>1.2~1.6	4.0	3.5	3.5	3.5	3.0	3.0	3.0	3.0	3.0
	>1.6	5.0	4.0	4.0	4.0	3.5	3.5	3.0	3.0	3.0
>5~6	0.0~0.4	2.0	2.0	1.5	1.5	1.5	1.5	1.5	1.5	1.5
	>0.4~0.5	4.0	3.0	2.5	2.5	2.0	2.0	2.0	2.0	2.0
	>0.5~0.8	4.5	4.0	3.5	3.0	2.5	2.5	2.5	2.5	2.5
	>0.8~1.2	5.0	4.5	4.0	3.5	3.0	3.0	3.0	3.0	3.0
	>1.2~1.6	5.5	5.0	4.5	4.0	3.0	3.0	3.0	3.0	3.0
	>1.6	6.0	5.0	5.0	4.5	3.5	3.5	3.5	3.5	3.5
>6	0.0~0.4	4.0	3.0	2.5	2.5	2.5	2.5	2.0	2.0	2.0
	>0.4~0.5	4.5	4.0	3.5	3.5	3.5	3.0	2.5	2.5	2.5
	>0.5~0.8	5.0	4.5	4.0	4.0	3.5	3.0	2.5	2.5	2.5
	>0.8~1.2	5.5	5.0	4.5	4.5	4.0	3.5	3.0	3.0	3.0
	>1.2~1.6	6.0	5.5	5.0	5.0	4.5	4.0	3.5	3.5	3.5
	>1.6	7.0	6.0	5.5	5.5	5.0	4.5	4.0	4.0	4.0

Note:HCM 2000,Exhibit 23-9,p. 23-9.

Table 3.7 Passenger-Car Equivalents for RVs on Upgrades

Upgrade (%)	Length (km)	E_R Percentage of RVs								
		2	4	5	6	8	10	15	20	25
<2	All	1.2	1.2	1.2	1.2	1.2	1.2	1.2	1.2	1.2
>2~3	0.0~0.8	1.2	1.2	1.2	1.2	1.2	1.2	1.2	1.2	1.2
	>0.8	3.0	1.5	1.5	1.5	1.5	1.5	1.2	1.2	1.2
>3~4	0.0~0.4	1.2	1.2	1.2	1.2	1.2	1.2	1.2	1.2	1.2
	>0.4~0.8	2.5	2.5	2.0	2.0	2.0	2.0	1.5	1.5	1.5
	>0.8	3.0	2.5	2.5	2.5	2.0	2.0	2.0	1.5	1.5
>4~5	0.0~0.4	2.5	2.0	2.0	2.0	1.5	1.5	1.5	1.5	1.5
	>0.4~0.8	4.0	3.0	3.0	3.0	2.5	2.5	2.0	2.0	2.0
	>0.8	4.5	3.5	3.0	3.0	3.0	2.5	2.5	2.0	2.0
>5	0.0~0.4	4.0	3.0	2.5	2.5	2.5	2.0	2.0	2.0	1.5
	>0.4~0.8	6.0	4.0	4.0	3.5	3.0	3.0	2.5	2.5	2.0
	>0.8	6.0	4.5	4.0	4.5	3.5	3.0	3.0	2.5	2.0

Note: HCM 2000, Exhibit 23-10, p. 23-10.

Table 3.8 Passenger-Car Equivalents for Trucks and Buses on Downgrades

Downgrade (%)	Length (km)	E_T Percentage of Trucks			
		5	10	15	20
<4	All	1.5	1.5	1.5	1.5
4~5	≤6.4	1.5	1.5	1.5	1.5
4~5	>6.4	2.0	2.0	2.0	1.5
>5~6	≤6.4	1.5	1.5	1.5	1.5
>5~6	>6.4	5.5	4.0	4.0	3.0
>6	≤6.4	1.5	1.5	1.5	1.5
>6	>6.4	7.5	6.0	5.5	4.5

Note: HCM 2000, Exhibit 23-11, p. 23-11.

The above tables reflect research results from the USA. The results are based on HCM 2000. It should be noted that passenger car equivalent values for truck have greatly changed. The maximum value of this value for HCM 1985 version was 17. However, the maximum value for HCM 2000 is 7 as indicated in Table 3.5, which demonstrates that the discrepancy in operation between truck and passenger car shrinks. There are numerous studies on passenger car equivalent in China. However, there is no widely accepted criterion for the use of this parameter.

The introduction of PCE is because heavy vehicles take more roadway space for than passenger car. It is difficult for traffic engineers to compare traffic counts without converting mix traffic into standard unit. In traffic engineering field heavy vehicles include trucks, buses and recreational vehicles. It is also observed that when heavy vehicles travel on uphill section of highway their running speed decreases sharply. Thus, the more the grade of roadway is, the higher the PCE values of heavy vehicles are. It is interesting to find that with the increase of the percent of heavy vehicles, the PCE values decrease.

3.2　Definition of Speed

Speed is the second macroscopic parameter describing the state of a traffic stream. It is defined as a rate of motion, in distance per unit of time. For engineering students, speed is not a difficult factor in their studies. However, in traffic engineering there are some concepts in terms of speed that students need to be familiar with.

3.2.1　*Time Mean Speed*(*TMS*, 时间平均速度)

Time mean speed is defined as the average speed of all vehicles passing a point on a highway over some specified time period. Its mathematical equation is as follows.

$$TMS = \frac{1}{n}\Sigma V_i \tag{3-1}$$

$$TMS = \frac{\Sigma \frac{d}{t_i}}{n} \tag{3-2}$$

Where: V_i——spot speed;
　　　　n——sample size;
　　　TMS——time mean speed;
　　　　d——distance traversed;
　　　　t_i——travel time for the ith vehicle.

3.2.2　*Space Mean Speed* (*SMS*, 空间平均速度)

Space mean speed is defined as the average speed of all vehicles occupying a given section of a highway over some specified time period. Its mathematical equation is as follows.

$$SMS = \frac{1}{\frac{1}{n}\Sigma \frac{1}{V_i}} \quad (harmonic\ mean, 调和中项) \tag{3-3}$$

$$SMS = \frac{d}{\Sigma \frac{t_i}{n}} = \frac{nd}{\Sigma t_i} \tag{3-4}$$

Where: *SMS*——space mean speed.

TMS is a point measure, while *SMS* is a measure relating to a length of highway or lane. *TMS* is calculated by finding each individual vehicle speed and taking a simple average of the results. *SMS* is estimated by finding the average travel time for a vehicle to traverse the section and using the average travel time to compute a speed. The *TMS* is no less than *SMS* at any conditions. The two speeds may be equal if all vehicles in the section are traveling at exactly the same speed.

Example 3.2 Calculating Time Mean Speed and Space Mean

An observer located at point X observes the four vehicles passing point X during a period of T sec. The velocities of the vehicles are measured as 45, 45, 40 and 30 km/h, respectively. Calculate the time mean speed, and the space mean speed.

Solution:

The time mean speed is found by

$$TMS = \frac{1}{n}\sum V_i = \frac{30+40+45+45}{4} = 40 \text{ (km/h)}$$

The space mean speed is found by

$$SMS = \frac{1}{\frac{1}{n}\sum \frac{1}{V_i}} = \frac{1}{\frac{1}{4}\left(\frac{1}{45}+\frac{1}{45}+\frac{1}{40}+\frac{1}{30}\right)} = 38.9 \text{ (km/h)}$$

Spot speed(地点速度), occurring in the equations of both speeds, is an important element in traffic engineering study and will be discussed in detailed in chapter 4.

3.2.3 Percentile Speeds

Percentile speed(百分位速度) is a speed below which the stated percent of vehicles in the traffic stream travel. Percentile speed values can be obtained from the cumulative curve of spot speed. In traffic engineering, 85th percentile speed is often used as a measure of the maximum reasonable speed for the traffic stream (upper limit), while the 15th percentile speed may be used as a measure of the minimum reasonable speed for the traffic stream. The 50th percentile or median speed is used to describe the midpoint of the speed distribution.

(1) Critical speed is defined as the speed at which maximum flow rate can be achieved. This definition has been used since traffic engineering course was officially

offered at colleges and universities. Before that the critical speed was defined as the speed at which gas consumption of vehicles is at the lowest. Sometimes critical speed is also called optimal speed.

(2) Average travel speed and average running speed are often used to evaluate operation performance of roadways or transit lines. The former is equal to the total travel distance divided by travel time; the latter is equal to the total travel distance divided by running time that is equal to the travel time minus stopped time.

3.3 Density

Density, the third primary measure of traffic stream characteristics, is defined as the number of vehicles occupying a given length of highway or lane and is generally expressed as vehicles per kilometer per lane. In reality, density is difficult to measure from field as compared to volume and speed. However, it is considered the most important parameter of the three traffic-stream elements, because it is the measure most directly related to traffic demand.

Density is also a vital measure of the quality of traffic movement, as it is a measure of the proximity of other vehicles, a factor which influences freedom to maneuver and the psychological comfort of drivers. As an indirect measure of density *occupancy* (占有率) is used. Occupancy is defined as the proportion of time that a detector is occupied or covered by a vehicle in a defined time period.

Relationship of density and occupancy:

$$D = \frac{1000 \cdot O}{L_v + L_d} \tag{3-5}$$

Where: L_v——average length of vehicle(m);

L_d——length of detector(m);

O——time occupancy defined as $O = \frac{\Sigma t_i}{T}$;

T——length of survey period, 15, 30, or 60 minutes;

t_i——time occupied or covered by vehicle i.

Two elements in traffic engineering are closely related to traffic density. They are *spacing*(车头间距) and *headway*(车头时距). Spacing is defined as the distance between successive vehicles in a traffic lane, measured from some common reference point on the vehicle such as the front bumper. The relationship between density and average spacing can be shown below.

$$D = \frac{1000}{d_a}$$

Headway is defined as the time interval between successive vehicles as they pass a point along the lane. The relationship between volume and average headway can be expressed in the following format.

$$v = \frac{3600}{h_a}$$

It should be noted that both spacing and headway are the microscopic parameters in traffic analysis. Practically, headway has been used more often than spacing.

3.4 Relationship among Volume, Speed and Density

The following equations are based on the observation on freeways, namely the models described below are applicable for uninterrupted flow only.

$$v = S \cdot D$$
$$D = \frac{v}{S} \tag{3-6}$$

Where: v——rate of flow or volume (veh/h);

S——space mean speed (km/h);

D——density (veh/km).

This is a macroscopic equation among these three parameters. This equation applies to the traffic stream as a whole. It should be pointed out that the exact shape and calibration of these relationships depends upon prevailing conditions, which vary from location to location and even over time at the same location.

Over the years, many researchers have studied speed-flow-density relationships and have attempted to develop many mathematical descriptions for these curves. In the 1930s Bruce Greenshields conducted the first formal studies of traffic flow, with assuming that the speed-density relationship was linear.

Greenberg assumed a logarithmic curve for speed-density, while Underwood used an exponential model for this relationship. All of these historic studies focused on calibration of the speed-density relationship because once this relationship has been established, the speed-flow and flow-density relationships are derived thereafter. Models set by Greenshields, Greenberg and Underwood are considered classical models. These models are discussed in the following section. Readers should keep in mind that most recent studies on speed-flow-density relationship do not start from exploration of speed-density curve, but speed-flow curve. For further information about calibration of base speed-flow-density models, please read chapter 12 of textbook of "Traffic Engineering" by Roger P. Roess.

3.4.1 The Greenshields Linear Model (Figure 3.1)

Figure 3.1 The Greenshields Linear Model

$$S = S_f\left(1 - \frac{D}{D_j}\right) \quad (3\text{-}7)$$

$$S = S_f - \frac{S_f}{D_j}D$$

Where: $a = S_f$ (free speed), $b = -\dfrac{S_f}{D_j\text{(jam density)}}$

3.4.2 Greenberg's Logarithmic Model (Figure 3.2)

$$S = S_c \ln \frac{D_j}{D} \quad (3\text{-}8)$$

$$S = S_c \ln D_j - S_c \ln D$$

$$= a + bD_1$$

Where: $a = S_c \ln D_j$;

$b = -S_c$;

$D_1 = \ln D$.

S_c——critical speed;

It is assumed in the model that D is a nonzero parameter.

3.4.3 Underwood's Exponential Model (Figure 3.3)

$$S = S_f\, e^{-\frac{1}{D_c}D}$$

$$\ln S = \ln S_f - \frac{1}{D_c}D;$$

$$S_1 = a + bD. \quad (3\text{-}9)$$

Where: D_c——critical density;

$S_1 = \ln S$; $a = \ln S_f$; $b = -\dfrac{1}{D_c}$.

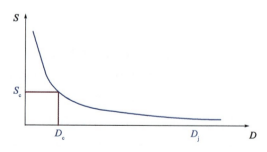

Figure 3.2 Greenberg's logarithmic Model

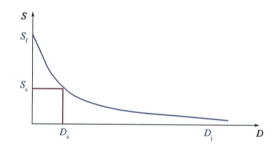

Figure 3.3 Underwood's Exponential Model

This model is reasonable at low densities, as it collapses to $S = S_f$ when D is zero.

3.5 Derivation of Flow-Speed and Flow-Density Relationships

Given a Greenshields speed-density model, we can have:
$$S = S_f\left(1 - \frac{D}{D_j}\right) = S_f - \frac{S_f}{D_j}D$$

When plug in $D = v/S$, we get:
$$S = S_f - \frac{S_f}{D_j}\frac{v}{S}$$
$$v = D_j S - \frac{D_j}{S_f}S^2 \tag{3-10}$$

By the same token, we can have v-D equation
$$\frac{v}{D} = S_f - \frac{S_f}{D_j}D$$
$$v = S_f D - \frac{S_f}{D_j}D^2 \tag{3-11}$$

Notes:

(1) Equations (3-10) and Equations (3-11) represent the macroscopic relationship among volume, speed and density.

(2) Equations (3-10) and Equations (3-11) need to do parameter calibration before applying to the real world.

(3) By the same procedures, we can get Greenberg-based flow-speed and flow-density equations, Underwood-based low-speed and flow-density equations.

(4) These equations are useful for the theoretical analysis, but not necessarily applicable for the real situation.

3.6 Finding Capacity from Basic Speed-Flow-Density Curves

From Greenshields-based equation (3-11) (which is parabolic flow-density curve); We can derive this equation and find the maximum point of volume.
$$\frac{dv}{dD} = 0 = S_f - 2\frac{S_f}{D_j}D$$
$$\text{so}: D = D_j/2$$
$$S = S_f - \frac{S_f}{D_j}D = S_f - \frac{S_f}{D_j}\frac{D_j}{2} = \frac{S_f}{2}$$

$$V_m = c = \frac{S_f}{2} \frac{D_j}{2} = \frac{S_f D_j}{4} \qquad (3\text{-}12)$$

It is evident that critical density and critical speed are the ones at which capacity occurs.

Similarly, we can obtain:

$$c(Greenberg) = S_c \frac{D_j}{e} \qquad (3\text{-}13)$$

$$c(Underwood) = D_c \frac{S_f}{e} \qquad (3\text{-}14)$$

(1) Capacity is defined as the maximum rate of flow that can be achieved on roadway facilities under prevailing roadway, traffic and control conditions.

(2) Capacity is a characteristic of the roadway. Volume can never be observed at levels higher than the true capacity of the section. Demand, defined as the number of vehicles (or persons) that desire to travel past a point of roadway facility during a specified period, can be higher than capacity.

(3) Capacity is not a constant value for the reason that there is no clear consensus among traffic engineers as to whether a discontinuous or continuous approach is more universally applicable. For details about capacity please read chapter 6.

Example 3.3 Relationship among Volume, Density and Speed

Given the relationship between speed and density:
$$S = 70(1 - 0.008 \cdot D)$$

(1) Find the free-flow speed and jam density;

(2) Derive equations describing flow versus speed and flow versus density;

(3) Determine the capacity mathematically;

(4) Sketch the speed-density, flow-speed and flow-density curves and indicate the congested and uncongested area.

Solution:

(1) Based on equation $S = 70(1 - 0.008 \cdot D)$, we can get free flow speed:
$S_f = 70$ km/h, and jam density $D_j = 1/0.008 = 125$ veh/km

(2) Plug equation $S = 70(1 - 0.008 \cdot D)$ into $v = S \cdot D$

We can get: $v = 70D(1 - 0.008 \cdot D)$, and $V = \frac{1}{0.56} S(70 - S)$

(3) Do derivation of volume over density and let it be zero we can have:

$$\frac{dV}{dD} = 70 - 0.56 \cdot 2 \cdot D = 0$$

Thus density at capacity can be derived $D_m = 62.5 \text{veh/km}$.

Therefore, we can get capacity:

$c = v_m = 70 D_m (1 - 0.008 \cdot D_m) = 70 \cdot 62.5 \cdot (1 - 0.008 \times 6.25) = 2188$ (veh/h) Similarly we can use equation $V_m = \dfrac{S_f \cdot D_j}{4}$ to get the same result:

$$V_m = \frac{70 \times 125}{4} = 2188 (\text{veh/h})$$

(4) The curves are shown in Figure 3.4.

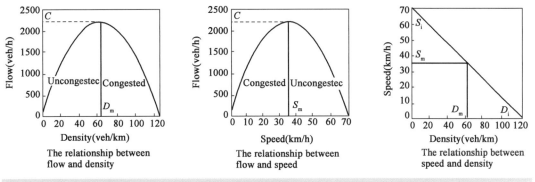

Figure 3.4 The Relationship Between Flow, Density and speed

Key points of the chapter

1. What is the difference between hourly volume and rate of flow?
2. What are peak hour volume and peak hour factor?
3. What is passenger car unit?
4. What is 30th hourly volume and why is it selected in the design?
5. Describe relationship among volume, density and speed.
6. What is percentile speed and how is it applicable in practice?

本章要点

1. 流量与流率的定义是什么？二者有何不同？
2. 什么是高峰小时流量与高峰小时系数？
3. 什么是标准小汽车当量？
4. 什么是第30位小时交通量？
5. 流量、速度和密度三者的关系如何？
6. 什么是百分位速度及在交通工程中的应用？

Chapter 4 Spot Speed, Travel Time and Delay Studies

In this chapter spot speed, travel time and delay are described. Spot speed is an important parameter in traffic engineering studies. In many textbooks it is discussed as an individual section because this speed has many applications in traffic engineering practice. Travel times are often applied to evaluate level of service that roadway network has provided. The concept of delays and some survey approaches are illustrated at the end of this chapter.

In traffic engineering studies there are three categories: (1) inventories; (2) administrative;(3) dynamic studies. Inventories provide a list or graphic display of existing information, such as roadway widths, parking spaces, transit routes, traffic regulations, and so forth. Administrative studies use existing engineering records, available in government agencies and departments. This kind of information is used to prepare an inventory of the relevant data. Administrative studies include the results of surveys, which may involve field measurements or aerial photography. Dynamic traffic studies deal with the collection of data under operational conditions and include studies of speed, traffic volume, travel time and delays, parking and crashes. Spot speed, travel time and delay are considered basic elements in dynamic traffic studies. Therefore, these three things are discussed in this chapter.

4.1 Spot Speed Studies

4.1.1 *Spot Speed*(地点车速)

Spot speed is defined as the average speed of vehicles passing a point. It is the mostly used indicator that traffic engineers use to measure the speed that drivers freely select, meaning that spot speed studies are under free flow conditions. Free flow conditions denote that volumes are below 1000 veh/h/ln on freeways or 500 veh/h/ln on other types of uninterrupted flow facilities.

Generally, spot speed studies are conducted to estimate the distribution of speeds of vehicles in a stream of traffic at a particular location on a highway. This is time mean speed as introduced in chapter 2. What traffic engineers are interested in is its distribution rather than absolute values.

4.1.2 Some Useful Speed Definitions

4.1.2.1 *Mean Speed* (平均速度)

Mean speed in traffic engineering is defined as average speed. It usually is estimated as the sum of the observed values divided by the number of observations. However, in a spot speed study, individual values of speed are not recorded; rather, the frequency of observations within defined speed groups is known.

4.1.2.2 *Mode Speed*(众速度)

Mode speed is defined as the most frequent single value among observation.

4.1.2.3 *Median Speed*(中位速度)

Median speed is defined as the speed that equally divides the distribution of spot speeds meaning there are as many vehicles traveling at higher speeds as at lower speeds.

These three parameters are considered as the measure of **central tendency**(集中趋势) of the speed at which vehicles travel.

(1) Applications of spot speeds

①Speed limit build-up;

②Trends establishment;

③Specific design applications;

④Specific control applications;

⑤High-crash investigation.

(2) Spot speed collection methods

①Radar meters (hand-held or mounted on a vehicle) (Figure 4.1a));

②Stop-watch method (manual);

③*Loop detector*(线圈探测器) method;

④*Microwaved-detector*(微波探测器);

⑤*Video-frequency detector*(视频探测器) (Figure 4.1b)).

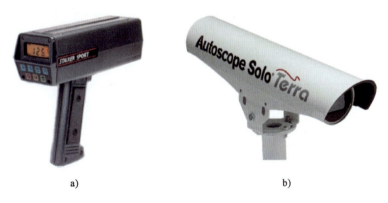

Figure 4.1 Radar Meter (left) and Video frequency Detector (right)

These methods of conducting spot speed studies will be introduced in the traffic experiment course and they are not discussed in this text. With regard to radar meters they are either hand-held or vehicle-mounted and are used often by police to monitor running speed of vehicles on the roadway segment with posted speed limit. These devices measure speed directly by reflecting an emitted radar wave off an oncoming vehicle and measuring the difference in the frequency between the emitted and reflected radar wave. This difference in frequency is referred to as the "*Dopplor Effcct*" (多普勒效应), and is proportional to the speed of the oncoming vehicle.

The accuracy of various radar meters vary, generally limited to plus or minus 1 ~ 2 mph range. Radar meters are difficult to conceal in practice. Motorists may slow down when they observe radar meters, which affects the results of measurements.

4.1.3 Presentation of Spot Speed Data

4.1.3.1 Frequency Distribution Table

Frequency distribution table is the result of reduction of spot speed data observed from the field. The raw data typically are indicated in tabular sheet prepared for data collection. The first thing of data reduction is to group data. The number of groups for spot speed study varies depending on data characteristics and analytical objective, but not less than 10 at least. Apart from that it is widely accepted that speed groups of more than 5 mph are not used. For principle or guidance of data grouping, students can read statistical references. Table 4.1 is a typical frequency distribution table used for processing collected spot speed data.

Table 4.1 Frequency Distribution Table for Illustrative Spot Speed Study

Speed Group		Middle Speed S(mile/h)	Observed Freq-in Group n	Freq-in Group (%)	Cum·Freq(%)
Lower Limit (mile/h)	Upper Limit (mile/h)				
32	34	33	0	0.0	0.0
34	36	35	5	1.8	1.8
36	38	37	5	1.8	3.5
38	40	39	7	2.5	6.0
40	42	41	13	4.6	10.6
42	44	43	21	7.4	18.0
44	46	45	33	11.7	29.7
46	48	47	46	16.3	45.9
48	50	49	62	21.9	67.8
50	52	51	37	13.1	80.9
52	54	53	24	8.5	89.4
54	56	55	14	4.9	94.3
56	58	57	9	3.2	97.5
58	60	59	5	1.8	99.3
60	62	61	2	0.7	100.0
62	64	63	0	0.0	100.0
			283	**100.0**	

4.1.3.2 Frequency and Cumulative Frequency Distribution Curves

These two curves are plotted based on frequency distribution table. The more groups of the data, the smoother the curves are. The purpose to plot frequency curves is to find interesting points such as percentile values. It is also recommended to plot the frequency distribution curve directly above the cumulative frequency distribution curve, using the same horizontal scale. This makes it easier to use the curves to graphically pick up statistical values as indicated in Figure 4.2. From this figure we can get values of percentile spot speed, mode speed and pace. To estimate range of true mean of spot speed at given *level of confidence* (置信水平) is the procedure of calculation of some statistics. These statistics is described in next section.

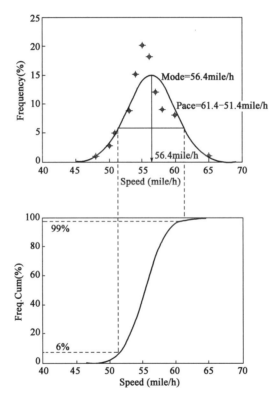

Figure 4.2 Frequency & Cumulative Frequency Curves for Spot Speed Study

4.1.4 Common Descriptive Statistics

4.1.4.1 *Pace*(速度差幅度)

Pace in traffic engineering is defined as the 10 mile/h increment in speed in which the highest percentage of drivers is observed. The pace itself is a measure of the center of the distribution. The percentage of vehicles traveling within the pace speeds is a measure of both central tendency and dispersion. The smaller the percentage of vehicles traveling within the pace, the greater the degree of dispersion in the distribution.

To find a pace of spot speed, the following procedure should be taken. A 10km/h (or 16km/h) template is scaled from the horizontal axis. Keeping this template horizontal, place an end on the lower left side of the frequency curve and move slowly along the curve. When the right side of the template intersects the right side of the curve, the pace has been located. If the percentage of vehicles traveling within the pace is smaller, it shows that the dispersion of spot speed distribution is greater. From safety point of view, this situation is not safe because higher percentage of vehicles traveling whose difference in speed is beyond 10 mph. That is the reason 10-mile value is taken as a *threshold*(域值), beyond which it is thought to have high potential of *traffic crash*(交通事故).

4.1.4.2 *Standard Deviation*(标准差)

Standard deviation is a measure of dispersion in the distribution of collected data. It can tell how far data spreads around the mean value, indicating the degree of dispersion of the data. Its mathematical equation is expressed as below.

$$S = \sqrt{\frac{\sum_{i=1}^{n} f_i (X_i - \bar{X})^2}{n-1}} = \sqrt{\frac{\sum f_i X_i^2}{n-1} - \frac{n\bar{X}^2}{n-1}} \qquad (4\text{-}1)$$

Where: S——the standard deviation;

X_i——observation i;

$\bar{X}$——average of all observations;

f_i——frequency of observation i;

n——number of observations.

4.1.4.3 Standard Error of the Mean

Standard error of the mean is defined as the standard deviation of a distribution of sample means and its mathematical equation is shown below.

$$E = \frac{S}{\sqrt{n}} \qquad (4\text{-}2)$$

Where: E——standard error of the mean;

S——standard deviation of the original distribution of individual values;

n——number of samples in each group of observations.

4.1.4.4 Range of True Mean of Spot Speed

$$\mu = \bar{X} \pm 1.96E, \text{when confidence level is } 95\%$$
$$\mu = \bar{X} \pm 3.0E, \text{when confidence level is } 99.7\% \qquad (4\text{-}3)$$

Where: μ——range of true mean spot speed under given confidence level.

The values of 1.96 and 3.0 are the *t*-values, assuming that the estimation of mean is in accord with the *t* distribution. As the confidence level increases, the precision of the estimate decreases. As rule of thumb, 95% confidence level is very common in spot speed studies.

4.1.5 Required Sample Size

The minimum number of observations from field in order to satisfy the predetermined precision and confidence level.

$$n \geq \frac{S^2 K^2}{e^2} \qquad (4\text{-}4)$$

Where: n——minimum number of sample required;

S——standard deviation of sample;

e——*tolerance in error* (*given*) (允许误差);

K——t-value for given confidence level;

$K = 1.96$ when confidence level $= 95\%$;

$K = 3.0$ when confidence level $= 99.7\%$.

It should be noted that in order to reduce sample size for reasons of finance it is necessary to either reduce the confidence or increase the tolerance. In traffic engineering 95% confidence level is considered the minimum that is acceptable. Therefore, increase of tolerance seems unavoidable. It has been proved that the increase of just 0.3 mile per hour in tolerance results in a decrease of 2017 samples required as indicated in textbook of "Traffic Engineering" (Fourth Edition) by Roge P. Roess et.. Sample size N should be rechecked after the speed study is completed.

Example 4.1 Determine Sample Size for Spot Speed

As part of a class project a group of students collected a total of 120 spot speed samples at a location and determined from this data that the standard variation of the speeds was ±6km/h. If the project required that the confidence level be 95.0 percent and the limit of acceptable error was ±1.5km/h, determine whether these students satisfied the project requirement.

Solution:

Use equation (4-4) to determine the minimum sample size to satisfy the project requirement.

$$n \geq \frac{S^2 K^2}{e^2}$$

Where: $K = 1.96; S = \pm 6; e = 1.5$.

$$n \geq \frac{S^2 K^2}{e^2} = \frac{6^2 \times 1.96^2}{1.5^2} = 61.45$$

Therefore, the minimum number of spot speeds collected to satisfy the project requirement is 62. Since the students collected 120 samples they satisfied the project requirements.

It should also be pointed out that the guiding philosophy behind spot speed studies is that measurement should include drivers freely selecting their speeds, unaffected by traffic congestion. Thus, spot speed studies are rarely made under conditions of heavy, or even moderate, traffic.

4.2　Travel Time Studies

In general, travel time studies involve significant lengths of a facility or group of facilities forming a route. It is often conducted on the arterial or major roadway, along which there are several intersections (signalized or stop/yield signs). Travel time plays key role in city's life and it indicates the level of service of roadway network performance. From mobility point of view travel time reflects degree of convenience from one point to the other point.

4.2.1　Purpose of Travel Time Studies

(1) to identify problem locations on facilities;

(2) to determine level of service of the facility;

(3) to provide some inputs for traffic assignment process;

(4) to provide travel time for economic evaluation of transportation improvement;

(5) to develop time contour maps and other depictions of traffic congestion in a area or region;

(6) to provide information for travelers.

4.2.2　Techniques for Travel Time Studies

Techniques for travel time studies include:

(1) *floating-car approach*(浮动车法);

(2) *license-plate approach*(牌照法);

(3) *car-following approach*(跟车法);

(4) GPS based approach.

The following equations show how to estimated travel time through floating car approach. This approach is generally applicable only on two-lane highways, where passing is rare and length of roadway link is not long (Figure 4.3). The number of test-car runs ranges from 6 to 12, depending on the type of facility and the amount of traffic.

$$V_w = \frac{(N_e + O_w - P_w) \cdot 60}{T_e + T_w}$$

$$\overline{T}_w = T_w - \frac{60 \cdot (O_w - P_w)}{V_w}$$

Where: V_w——traffic flow westbound in vehicles per hour;
N_e——opposing volume in vehicle per survey period;
O_w——traffic overtaking the testing car in vehicle per survey period;
P_w——traffic overtaken by the testing car in vehicle per survey period;
T_e——travel time eastbound in minutes;
T_w——travel time westbound in minutes;
$\overline{T}_w$——average travel time westbound in minutes.

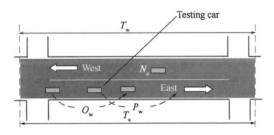

Figure 4.3 Diagram Display of Floating Car Method

Example 4.2 Estimation of Volume and Travel Time Using Moving-Vehicle Technique

The data in Table 4.2 were obtained in a travel time study on a section of highway using the moving-vehicle technique. Determine the travel and volume in each direction at this section of the highway.

Based on information given in Table 4.2, we have:
(1) Mean time it takes to travel eastward T_e =2.85 min;
(2) Mean time it takes to travel westbound T_w =3.07 min.

Table 4.2 Data from Travel Time Study Using the Moving-Vehicle Technique

Run Direction/ Number	Travel Time (min)	No. of Vehicles Traveling in Opposite Direction	No. of Vehicles That Overtook Test Vehicle	No. of Vehicles Overtaken by Test Vehicle
Eastward				
1	2.75	80	1	1
2	2.55	75	2	1
3	2.85	83	0	3
4	3.00	78	0	1
5	3.05	81	1	1
6	2.70	79	3	2
7	2.82	82	1	1
8	3.08	78	0	2
Average	2.85	79.50	1.00	1.50
Westward				
1	2.95	78	2	0
2	3.15	83	1	1
3	3.20	89	1	1
4	2.83	86	1	0
5	3.30	80	2	1
6	3.00	79	1	2
7	3.22	82	2	1
8	2.91	81	0	1
Average	3.07	82.25	1.25	0.875

(3) Average number of vehicles traveling westward when test vehicle is traveling eastward N_e =79.50.

(4) Average number of vehicles traveling eastward when test vehicle is traveling westward N_w =82.25.

(5) Average number of vehicles that overtake test vehicle while it is traveling westward O_w =1.25.

(6) Average number of vehicles that overtake test vehicle while it is traveling eastward O_e =1.00.

(7) Average number of vehicles the test vehicle passes while traveling westward P_w =0.875.

(8) Average number of vehicles the test vehicle passes while traveling eastward $P_e = 1.5$.

Solution:

From the equation, find the volume in westbound direction:

$$V_w = \frac{(N_e + O_w - P_w) \times 60}{T_e + T_w} = \frac{(79.50 + 1.25 - 0.875) \times 60}{2.85 + 3.07} = 810(\text{veh/h})$$

Similarly, calculate the volume in the eastbound direction:

$$V_e = \frac{(82.25 + 1.00 - 1.5) \times 60}{2.85 + 3.07} = 829(\text{veh/h})$$

Find the average travel time in the westbound direction:

$$\bar{T}_w = 3.07 - \frac{1.25 - 0.875}{810} \times 60 = 3.0(\text{min})$$

Find the average travel time in the eastbound direction:

$$\bar{T}_e = 2.85 - \frac{1.00 - 1.5}{829} \times 60 = 2.0(\text{min})$$

The license plate approach is also used for conducting travel time studies. However, since a lot of in-house work involved and low match-up rate in practice, this method is only used for a small network with few nodes.

The car-following approach is used to conduct travel time studies for a rather long arterial or traffic corridor. The objective of conducting such study attempts to estimate the operating performance of traffic movement in a region such as Key West, Florida.

GPS based approach is the update method to get developed in recent years. The GPS device is installed at each testing vehicle (taxi in Beijing) and movement information of each vehicle on the roadways will be received by the control center. The travel time will be then calculated based on predetermined algorithm. This approach is still at the testing stage.

4.2.3 Travel Time Displays

Travel time data can be displayed in many interesting and informative ways. One method that is often used for overall traffic planning in a region is the development of a travel time contour map as shown in Figure 4.4. It should be noted that the closer together *contour lines* (等时线) plot, the longer the travel time to progress any set distance. The contour line methodology is generally used for planning purpose. It can also be applied to help identify network problem from roadways layout and efficiency of roadway network.

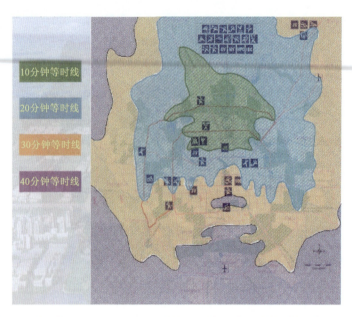

Figure 4.4   Contour Line Graph of Travel Time for 2008 Olympic Games

4.3   Delay Studies

Delay is defined as an extra time spent by drivers against their expectation. Delay can have many forms depending on different locations. Therefore, in many cases delay study is often accompanied with travel time study. The motivation of conducting delay study resides in the fact that time has values. The study of delays has two major applications in practice. The first one is to estimate economic costs such as: fuel consumption and time value. The second one is to determine the operating performance of a facility in terms of level of service.

The focus of delay study is put on the intersection delays. For this reason the following listed delays are all related to the conditions at intersections.

(1) *Stopped-time delay*(停车延误)

It is defined as the time a vehicle is stopped in queue waiting to proceed through a signalized or STOP-controlled intersection.

(2) *Approach delay*(引道延误)

Approach delay includes stopped-time delay but adds adds the time loss due to deceleration from the approach speed to a stop and the time loss due to reacceleration back to the desired speed.

(3) *Time-in-queue delay*(排队延误)

It is the total time from a vehicle joining an intersection queue to its discharge across the STOP line one departure.

(4) *Control delay*(控制延误)

Control delay denotes the total delay at an intersection caused by a control device, including both time-in-queue delay plus delays due to acceleration and deceleration.

Figure 4.5 provides delays occurring at a signalized intersection.

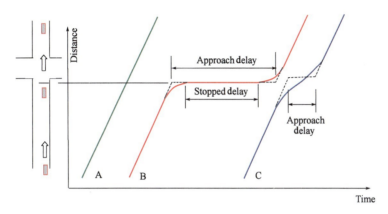

Figure 4.5   Display Diagram of Delays Occurring at Intersection

From Figure 4.5 it can be seen that line A has no any delay; whereas line B demonstrates that vehicles experience stopped and approach delays. Line C shows that vehicles do not stop at intersection but experience deceleration process when approaching intersection.

Due to the fact that delay at signalized intersections is of particular interest, many efforts are put on the intersection delay study. Accurate estimation of delays has many implications in traffic engineering studies. Transportation planners will use delay to evaluate economic loses, whereas traffic engineers will use delays to determine level of service at signalized intersections. In general the methodology used in analyzing intersection delay comes from the HCM (Highway Capacity Manual).

The 1985 HCM and its 1994 update define intersection level of service on the basis of average individual stopped-time delay per vehicles. In its 1997 and 2000 update versions, stopped delay is replaced by control delay.

Methods of conducting intersection delays include:

a. License-plate method;

b. Sample-counting method;

c. HCM 2000 method (or called cycle-based method).

At one approach of an intersection two observers are needed to conduct HCM based delay study. One person counts the arriving vehicles and number of stopping vehicles during survey period, while the other person keeps track of the queue for each cycle (counting number of vehicles being queued).

$$T_Q = 0.9 \left(I_s \times \frac{\sum V_{iq}}{V_T} \right) \quad (4-5)$$

Where: T_Q——average time-in-queue(s/veh);
　　　I_s——time interval between time-in-queue counts(s);
　　　$\sum V_{iq}$——sum of all vehicle-in-queue counts during survey period(vehs);
　　　V_T——total number of vehicles arriving during survey period(vehs).

To make adjustment for acceleration/deceleration delays it is necessary to estimate fraction of vehicles stopping as follows.

$$V_{SLC} = \frac{V_{STOP}}{N_c \cdot N_L} \quad (4-6)$$

$$FVS = \frac{V_{STOP}}{V_T} \quad (4-7)$$

Where: V_{SLC}——number of vehicles stopping(veh/ln/cycle);
　　　V_{STOP}——total count of stopping vehicles(vehs);
　　　N_c——number of cycles in the survey;
　　　N_L——number of lanes in the survey lane group;
　　　FVS——fraction of stopping vehicles.

The final estimate of control delay can be calculated as follows.

$$d = T_Q + FVS \cdot CF \quad (4-8)$$

The value of CF is a correction factor that is given at the Table 4.3.

Table 4.3　Adjustment Factor for Acceleration/Deceleration Delays

Free Flow Speed (mile/h)	Vehicles Stopping per lane, per Cycle V_{SLC}		
	<7 vehs	8~19 vehs	20~30 vehs
<37	+5	+2	−1
>37~45	+7	+4	+2
>45	+9	+7	+5

Example of survey data on a signalized intersection approach is given as indicated in Table 4.4. The approach has two lanes, and the signal cycle length is 60 seconds. Ten cycles were survey with vehicle-in-queue count interval being 20 seconds.

$$T_Q = 0.9 \left(I_s \cdot \frac{\sum V_{iq}}{V_T} \right) = 0.9 \times \left(20 \times \frac{132}{120} \right) = 19.8 (s/veh)$$

$$V_{SLC} = \frac{V_{STOP}}{N_c \cdot N_L} = \frac{75}{10 \times 2} = 3.75 (veh)$$

$$FVS = \frac{V_{STOP}}{V_T} = \frac{75}{120} = 0.625$$

$$d = T_Q + FVS \cdot CF = 19.8 + 0.625 \times 5 = 22.9 \,(\text{mile/veh})$$

Table 4.4 Sample Data for HCM Based Delay Study

Clock Time	Cycle Number	Number of Vehicles in Queue		
		+0 s	+20 s	+40 s
5:00 pm	1	4	7	5
5:01 pm	2	6	6	5
5:02 pm	3	3	5	5
5:03 pm	4	2	6	4
5:04 pm	5	5	3	3
5:05 pm	6	5	4	5
5:06 pm	7	6	8	4
5:07 pm	8	3	4	3
5:08 pm	9	2	4	3
5:09 pm	10	4	3	5
	Total	40	50	42

$\sum V_{iq} = 132\,\text{vehs}$ $V_T = 120\,\text{vehs}$ $V_{STOP} = 75\,\text{vehs}$ $FFS = 35\,\text{mile/h}$

The cycle based method is an approximate way to estimate control delays at intersections. The license-plate method can estimate delays at intersections in relatively accurate manner. However, this method needs more investment in time and human power.

Key points of the chapter

1. How to count and process spot speed data?

2. What is the estimation range of mean spot speed?

3. The concept of pace and its implication.

4. What is the purpose of travel time (trip time) study?

5. What are the three approaches in conducting travel time and what is floating car method?

6. Be aware of the definitions of four delays at intersections and usual method of investigation.

本章要点

1. 如何进行地点车速数据调查和数据的处理？

2. 地点车速区间估计是如何确定的？
3. 简述速度差幅度的概念及其应用。
4. 研究旅行时间（出行时间）的目的是什么？
5. 旅行时间调查常用的三种方法是什么？采用浮动车法如何进行旅行时间调查？
6. 交叉口延误的四类延误的定义是什么？交叉口延误常用的调查方法是什么？

Chapter 5 Statistics and Application in Traffic Engineering

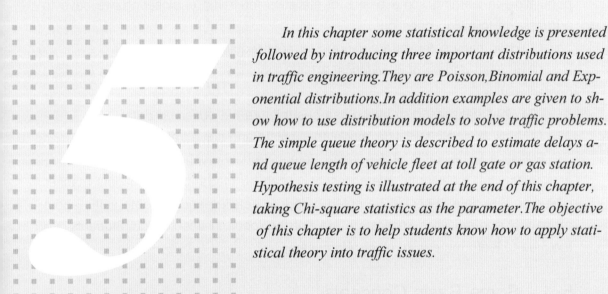

In this chapter some statistical knowledge is presented ,followed by introducing three important distributions used in traffic engineering.They are Poisson,Binomial and Exponential distributions.In addition examples are given to show how to use distribution models to solve traffic problems. The simple queue theory is described to estimate delays and queue length of vehicle fleet at toll gate or gas station. Hypothesis testing is illustrated at the end of this chapter, taking Chi-square statistics as the parameter.The objective of this chapter is to help students know how to apply statistical theory into traffic issues.

Traffic engineering needs a lot of data for analysis and statistics is the best tool to process the data. Due to the limited resources in terms of time and money, traffic engineers can't observe and measure the characteristics of ***population***(全体). Instead, they have to collect ***sample*** (样本) to represent the features of the population. In learning some basics of statistics for traffic engineering, we have to address the following questions.

(1) How many samples are needed to meet requirement for analysis?

(2) In what ***degree of confidence***(置信度) should we have in estimation of traffic characteristics?

(3) What statistical distribution can best picture the observed data?

(4) How to apply statistical model to simulate and solve traffic problems?

Statistics helps traffic professionals determine how much data will be required, as well as what meaningful ***inferences***(推论) can be made in the confident manner based on that data. It should be noted here that detailed and in-depth stuffs about probability and statistics knowledge are not the focus in this section. Students are required to learn more from other references.

5.1　Some Basic Concepts

5.1.1　Population versus Sample

There are at least two reasons for traffic engineers to use sample instead of using population to figure out the characteristics of traffic flow. First, it is out of the question to collect population data in real world or it is absolutely unnecessary to do so with regard to issues in traffic studies. Second, due to uncertainty of traffic phenomenon what can be reasonably concluded from traffic data is still unpredictable. Therefore, using sample will meet the requirement to draw conclusion in sensible way.

5.1.2　***Discrete versus Continuous***(离散与连续)

Discrete functions are made up of discrete variables——that is, they can assure only specific whole values and not any value in between. Examples of discrete probability functions are the *Bernoulli*(伯努利), *binomial*(二项), and *Poisson*(泊松) distributions.

Continuous functions, made up of continuous variable, can assume any value between two given values. Examples of this kind of function are the *normal*(正态), *exponential*(负指数), and *Chi-square* (卡方) distributions. Any process that is the sum of many parts tends to be normally distributed. In traffic engineering, speed, travel time, and delay are all described using the normal distribution.

5.1.3 *Data Grouping*(数据分组)

It can be observed that most traffic data set will fit into a common distribution, which means that there are some data whose value is same or so close to put them into one class. Before conducting statistical analysis for traffic data set it is necessary to summarize the raw data into classes and create so-called frequency distribution table. Assuming the height of each student in class is known and the frequency distribution table is established as shown in Table 5.1.

Table 5.1 Frequency Distribution of Student's Height

Number of Group	Height Group (m)	Number of Observation
1	1.56~1.60	1
2	1.61~1.65	3
3	1.66~1.70	5
4	1.71~1.75	12
5	1.76~1.80	7
6	1.81~1.85	4
7	1.86~1.90	2
		Total = 34

Even though the details of the individual data points on student's height are lost, the grouping of the data set adds much clarity to the character of the height distribution.

5.1.4 *Statistical Estimators*(统计量)

From statistical point of view statistical estimators are those parameters that are used to demonstrate the tendency of data development. There are four main estimators: measure of *central tendency*(集中趋势); *measure of dispersion*(离散); *coefficient of variation*(变异系数) and *skewness* (非对称性).

(1) Measure of central tendency

In general there are three main parameters to represent central tendency of any data set. They are *mean*(均值), *median*(中位值) and *mode*(众值).

Mean is defined the weighted average of all observations.

$$\bar{x} = \frac{\sum_i f_i m_i}{N} \tag{5-1}$$

Where: $\bar{x}$——mean of a data set;

f_i——number of observations for group i (or frequency of group i);

m_i——middle value of variable in group i;

N——total sample size or number of observations.

As for the student's height case the mean of this data set can be calculated as follows.

$$\bar{x} = \frac{1.58 \times 1 + 1.63 \times 3 + 1.68 \times 5 + 1.73 \times 12 + 1.78 \times 7 + 1.83 \times 4 + 1.88 \times 2}{34}$$

$$= 1.74 \tag{5-2}$$

Median is defined the middle value of all data when arranged in an array (ascending or descending order). The median divides a distribution in half: half of all observed values are higher than the median, half are lower. For grouped data set, median is at the 50% percentile point off a cumulative frequency distribution curve. Thus, the median of student's height is in the neighborhood of 1.73 meters.

Mode is defined the value that occurs most frequently. For the above case the mode of student's height is estimated as the peak of the frequency distribution curve, close to 1.73 meters.

(2) Measure of dispersion

There are two parameters to describe the dispersion of a data set. They are **variance**(方差) and **standard deviation**(标准差).

$$s^2 = \frac{\sum (x_i - \bar{x})^2}{N-1} \tag{5-3}$$

Where: s^2——variance of the data set;

N——sample size, number of observations.

All other variables are previously defined. It can be seen that variance and standard deviation are used to describe the magnitude of variation around the mean.

(3) Coefficient of variation

It is a ratio of the standard deviation to the mean, indicating the spread of outcomes relative to the mean.

(4) Skewness

It defined as the $\frac{\text{mean} - \text{mode}}{\text{standard deviation}}$, If a distribution is negatively skewed, it means that the data are concentrated to the left of the most frequent value in Figure 5.1; whereas if a distribution is positively skewed, then data are concentrated to the right in Figure 5.2.

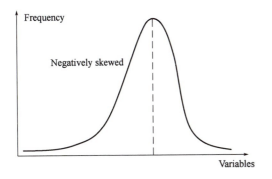

Figure 5.1 Diagram of Negatively Skewed Distribution

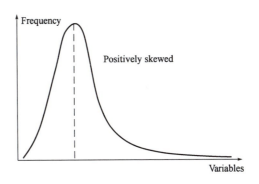

Figure 5.2 Diagram of Positively Skewed Distribution

5.2 Distribution of Traffic Flow

Some useful statistical distribution equations and their implications in traffic engineering are introduced in the next section.

5.2.1 Poisson Distribution(泊松分布)

The Poisson distribution is known in traffic engineering as the "counting" distribution because this distribution is often used to estimate the probability of a number of events X occurring in a specified counting interval of duration T. The mathematical descriptive format of Poisson distribution is as follows:

$$P(X=x) = \frac{(\lambda T)^x e^{-\lambda T}}{x!} \tag{5-4}$$

Where: $P(X=x)$——probability of event occurring (vehicles arriving) when $X=x$ at given T period;

T——given period of time;

λ——the average rate of event occurring (vehicles arriving) within T period;

x——variable of event occurring (number of vehicles).

Below are some statistical features of Poisson distribution.

(1) Poisson distribution belongs to discrete function with only one parameter.

(2) In traffic engineering Poisson distribution equation is used to describe the arrivals of vehicles at intersections or toll booth, as well as number of accident (crash).

(3) Poisson distribution is appropriate to describe vehicle's arrival when traffic volume is not high.

(4) The recurrence formula for Poisson distribution:

$$P(x) = \frac{\lambda T}{x} P(x-1) \tag{5-5}$$

This recurrence formula can be used to simplify the calculation procedure when x is relatively large in question. To help students better understand and know how to use Poisson distribution to solve traffic problems, we take some examples from different patterns to explain how to correctly translate traffic problems into each parameter in Poisson distribution.

Example 5.1

Based on field observation it is found that the volume of traffic flow passing a point of highway segment is 720 veh/h. Calculate the probability that there is no vehicle passing this point in 5 seconds, assuming the arrival of vehicles is in accord with Poisson distribution.

Solution:

$T=5, x=0, \lambda=720/3600=0.2$ veh/s (vehicle per second)

We have:

$$P(X=0) = \frac{(0.2 \times 5)^0 e^{-0.2 \times 5}}{0!} = e^{-0.2 \times 5} = 0.37$$

So, the probability of no vehicles coming in 5 second is 0.37.

Suppose we want to calculate the probability of exact 5 vehicles passing this point in 5 seconds. Thus, in this case we have:

$T=5, x=5, \lambda=720/3600=0.2$ veh/s (vehicle per second)

$$P(X=5) = \frac{(0.2 \times 5)^5 e^{-0.2 \times 5}}{5!} = \frac{e^{-0.2 \times 5}}{5!} = 0.0031$$

So, the probability of exact 5 vehicles coming in 5 second is 0.0031. Furthermore, if we want to estimate the probability of less than 5 vehicles passing this point in 5 seconds under the same conditions above, we have the information.

$T=5, x=5, \lambda=720/3600=0.2$ veh/s (vehicle per second)

The Poisson equation at this moment has changed to the form:

$$P(X<x) = \sum_{i=0}^{x-1} \frac{(\lambda T)^i e^{-\lambda T}}{i!} \quad (i=0,1,2,3,4) \tag{5-6}$$

We have to sum up the probability of when x = 0, 1, 2, 3, and 4.

$$P(X<5) = \sum_{i=0}^{x-1} \frac{(0.2 \times 5)^i e^{-0.2 \times 5}}{i!} = \frac{1}{e} + \frac{1}{e} + \frac{1}{e \times 2} + \frac{1}{e \times 6} + \frac{1}{e \times 24} = 0.995$$

So, conclusion can be drawn that the probability of less than 5 vehicles passing this point in 5 seconds is 0.995.

Based on that, we can obtain the probability of greater than 5 vehicles passing this point in 5 seconds. Based on the property of probability $P(X>x) = 1 - P(X \leq x)$, we have:

$$P(X>5) = 1 - P(X \leq 5)$$

Therefore,

$$P(X>5) = 1 - P(X<5) - P(X=5) = 1 - 0.995 - 0.0031 = 0.002$$

Example 5.2

The cycle length of a signalized intersection is 90 seconds. Based on the field study we have learned that the arrival rate of vehicles is 400 veh/h, assuming the arrival agrees with the Poisson distribution. Estimate the probability that no more than 10 vehicles will arrive at this intersection within a cycle.

Solution:

$T = 90, x = 10, \lambda = 400/3600 = 1/9$ veh/s (vehicle per second)

We have:

$$P(X \leq 10) = \sum_{i=0}^{10} \frac{\left(\frac{1}{9} \times 90\right)^i e^{-\frac{1}{9} \times 90}}{i!} = 0.583$$

Example 5.3

The cycle length of a signalized intersection is 60 seconds and the arrival rate is 360 veh/h (Poisson distribution). Estimate the least number of vehicles arriving in a cycle with its probability being no less than 95%.

Solution:

In this problem it is not to calculate the probability. Instead, this probability is given, namely 0.95. The question is to find out the least number of vehicles arriving in 60 seconds. In this case recurrence equation can be applied to conduct calculation.

$$T=60, \quad \lambda = 360/3600 = 1/10, x = ?$$

Based on question, we have:

$$P(X \leqslant x) \geqslant 0.95$$

Therefore,

$$\sum_{i=0}^{x} \frac{6^x e^{-6}}{x!} \geqslant 0.95 \quad x = 0,1,2,3,\cdots,i$$

The number of arrived vehicle in a cycle is 10, which satisfies the confidence of 95%. The calculation process is shown in Table 5.2.

Table 5.2 Calculation Procedure for Example 5.3

x	P(X=x)	P(X≤x)
0	0.002478762	0.002478762
1	0.014872573	0.017351335
2	0.044617719	0.061969055
3	0.089235439	0.151204493
4	0.133853158	0.285057651
5	0.160623789	0.44568144
6	0.160623789	0.606305229
7	0.137677534	0.743982763
8	0.10325815	0.847240913
9	0.068838767	0.91607968
10	0.04130326	0.95738294

5.2.2 *Binomial Distribution*(二项分布)

As is known the third step in the so-called four-step procedure of forecasting traffic demand is *mode split*(方式分担) in which the choice between transit and auto will be determined. This procedure is similar to the toss of a coin because this event has only two outcomes. Therefore, Binomial distribution can be applied to model the mode split procedure. The mathematical descriptive format of Binomial distribution is as follows:

$$P(X=x) = \frac{N!}{(N-x)! \, x!} p^x (1-p)^{N-x} \qquad (5-7)$$

where: $P(X=x)$——probability of event occurring (choose transit or auto) when $X=x$;

p——probability of event (choose transit or auto);
N——sample size (taken as variable);
x——variable for the event.

Below are some statistical features of Binomial distribution.

(1) Binomial distribution is used to describe mode split, namely, choice between transit and auto.

(2) Binomial distribution can also simulate the arrival of turning vehicles.

(3) Binomial distribution is also a discrete equation and can only be used when an event has two outcomes.

Similarly, we have:

$$P(X \leq x) = \sum_{i=0}^{x} \frac{N!}{(N-x)! \, x!} p^x (1-p)^{N-x} \tag{5-8}$$

Example 5.4

Based on the OD survey, 25% commuters choose transit for their daily trip. There are 5 commuters being randomly selected from an organization. Estimate the probability that 1 person among 5 will choose transit for travel.

Solution:

$$p = 0.25, N = 5, x = 1$$

$$P(X=1) = \frac{5!}{(5-1)! \, 1!} 0.25^1 (1-0.25)^{5-1} = 0.39$$

Example 5.5

It is found that the percentage of left turn vehicles from eastbound approach is 20% and average hourly volume of eastbound is 2000 veh/h. The cycle length for this intersection is 90 seconds. Estimate the probability that no more than 4 left turn vehicles will come in a cycle.

Solution:

$$p = 0.20, N = \frac{2000 \times 90}{3600} = 50 \text{ (vehicles per cycle)}, x = 4$$

We have:

$$P(X \leq 4) = \sum_{i=0}^{4} \frac{N!}{(N-i)! \, i!} p^i (1-p)^{N-i} = 0.2^0 \times 0.8^{50} + \frac{50!}{49! \, 1!} 0.2^1 \times 0.8^{49} +$$

$$\frac{50!}{48!\ 2!} \times 0.2^2 \times 0.8^{48} + \frac{50!}{47!\ 3!} \times 0.2^3 \times 0.8^{47} + \frac{50!}{46!\ 4!} \times 0.2^4 \times 0.8^{46} = 0.02$$

Relationship between Poisson and Binomial distributions is as follows.

When N is very large and p is very small, Binomial distribution equation can approximate to Poisson distribution as follows.

$$P(X=x)\frac{N!}{(N-x)!\ x!}p^x(1-p)^{N-x} \approx \frac{\lambda^x e^{-\lambda}}{x!} \quad (\lambda = N \cdot p) \tag{5-9}$$

As a rule of thumb, N should be at least 50, and p is less than 0.01.

Example 5.6

Based on the survey conducted at a busy bus stop in the past 10 years, it is found that the probability of each bus having a crash from 8:00am to 8:00pm is 0.0005. The average volume of buses arriving at this stop from 8:00am to 8:00pm is 2000. Estimate the probability of having no less than 2 crashes from 8:00am to 8:00pm at this stop.

Solution:

$$p = 0.0005, x = 2, N = 2000$$

By applying equation (5-9), we have

$$\lambda = N \cdot p = 2000 \times 0.0005 = 1$$

Thus,

$$P(X \geqslant 2) = 1 - P(X < 2) = 1 - P(X=0) - P(X=1) = 0.26$$

5.2.3 *Exponential Distribution*(负指数分布)

When we plug $x=0$ in the Poisson distribution equation we can get:

$$P(X=0) = \frac{(\lambda T)^0 e^{-\lambda T}}{0!} = e^{-\lambda T}$$

At this moment the probability of headway between two consecutive vehicles no less than T second equals to $e^{-\lambda T}$. This transformation can be described as below.

$$P(h \geqslant T) = e^{-\lambda T} \tag{5-10}$$

Where: $P(h \geqslant T)$——probability of a headway no less than T in traffic stream;

T——headway (s);

λ——the average rate of flow within T period of time.

This is a good case that discrete distribution changes to continued distribution. Its traffic engineering meaning is evident that the probability of headway can be expressed as shown in equation (5-10). As traffic engineers what they concern is

not the probability of headway but the number of headway. The number of headways whose value is no less than T second is defined as:
$$M(h \geq T) = V \times P(h \geq T) = V \cdot e^{-\lambda T} \quad (5\text{-}11)$$
Where: V——traffic volume.

Example 5.7

Given that the volume of a segment of roadway is 720 veh/h, and traffic movement is in accord with Poisson distribution. Calculate: (i) the probability of headway no less than 5 seconds, (ii) number of headways whose value is less than 5 seconds in an hour.

Solution:
$$T = 5, \lambda = 720/3600 = 0.2 \text{ (veh/s)}$$
$$P(h \geq 5) = e^{-0.2 \times 5} = e^{-1} = 0.37$$
$$M(h < 5) = V \cdot P(h < 5) = 720 \times (1 - P(h \geq 5)) = 454$$

Therefore, we know that number of headways whose value is less than 5 seconds in an hour is 454 among 720.

Below are some statistical features for exponential distribution.
(1) Exponential distribution is the special case of Poisson distribution.
(2) Exponential distribution equation is a continuous one with the headway being as its variable.
(3) Exponential distribution is applicable when traffic flow is light or moderate.
(4) Traffic engineers are concerned with headways greater than or equal to a specific period of time
(5) It is easily substantiated that the number of headway whose value is between T_1 and T_2 can be expressed as:
$$M(T_1 < h < T_2) = V \cdot (e^{-\lambda T_1} - e^{-\lambda T_2}) \quad (5\text{-}12)$$

Example 5.8

The traffic volume of roadway is 720 veh/h and its headway is distributed in the form of exponential equation. Estimate the number of the headways between 15 seconds and 20 seconds within two hours.

Solution:
$$T_1 = 15 \text{ sec}, T_2 = 20 \text{ sec}, \lambda = 720/3600 = 0.2, V = 2 \times 720 = 1440$$
$$M(15 \leqslant h \leqslant 20) = V \times P(15 \leqslant h \leqslant 20) = V \times [P(h \geqslant 15) - P(h \geqslant 20)]$$
$$= 1440 \times (e^{-0.2 \times 15} - e^{-0.2 \times 20}) = 1440 \times (0.0498 - 0.0183)$$
$$= 46$$

Therefore, the number of the headways between 15 seconds and 20 seconds within two hours is 46.

Example 5.9

The peak hour volume on the right-most lane of an expressway is 1800veh/h. It is assumed that the arrival of expressway vehicles can be described by a Poisson distribution. The critical gap (headway) for merging vehicles is 3.5 seconds. Determine the expected number of acceptable gaps for ramp vehicles that will occur on the expressway during the peak hour.

Solution:
$$T = 3600, \quad \lambda = 1800/3600 = 0.5 (\text{veh/s})$$
$$V = 1800 (\text{veh/h})$$
$$M(h \geqslant 3.5) = V \cdot P(h \geqslant 3.5) = 1800 \times e^{-0.5 \times 3.5} = 312 (\text{veh/h})$$

Therefore, the maximum merging rate of flow (or on-ramp capacity) is 312veh/h. The number of different lengths of gaps corresponding to volume of 1800 is given in Table 5.3.

Table 5.3 Number of Different Lengths of Gaps for Volume is 1800

Gap t(secs)	Probability		No. of Gaps	
	$P(h \geqslant t)$	$P(h < t)$	$h \geqslant t$	$h < t$
0	1.0000	0.0000	1799	0
0.5	0.7788	0.2212	1401	398
1.0	0.6065	0.3935	1091	708
1.5	0.4724	0.5276	849	950
2.0	0.3679	0.6321	661	1138
2.5	0.2865	0.7135	515	1284
3.0	0.2231	0.7769	401	1398
3.5	0.1738	0.8262	312	1487
4.0	0.1353	0.8647	243	1556
4.5	0.1054	0.8946	189	1610
5.0	0.0821	0.9179	147	1652

From Table 5.3 it can be seen that the main discrepancies occur at gaps of short lengths (less than 1 second). The reason for this is that although theoretically there are definite probabilities for the occurrence of gaps between 0 and 1 second, in reality these gaps very rarely occur, since a driver will tend to keep a safe distance between his or her vehicle and the vehicle immediately in front. One alternative used to deal with this situation is to restrict the range of headways by introducing a minimum gap as shown in the following equation.

$$P(h \geq T) = e^{-\lambda(T-\tau)} \tag{5-13}$$

Where: τ——the minimum headway.

It should be noted that in addition to these three distributions there are other distributions such as negative Binomial, M3 and Erlang distributions. For more details about these distributions please refer to some references.

5.3 M/M/1 System——Queuing Theory Application

This system has only one service station to receive vehicle. The other vehicles have to be in the queue waiting for service. The first come first service policy is adopted in the system. Assuming the average arrival rate is λ and average service rate is μ, so the $\rho = \lambda/\mu$ is defined as traffic intensity, which represents the status of the queuing.

Based on queuing theory:

$\rho < 1.0$ status of queuing is stable; $\rho > 1.0$ status of queuing is unstable.

The following equations are used only when status of queuing is stable.

Probability of no units in system: $P_0 = 1 - \rho$

Probability of having N units in system: $P_n = \rho^n (1 - \rho)$

Average unit in system: $\bar{n} = \dfrac{\rho}{1-\rho}$

Average (mean) queue length: $\bar{q} = \dfrac{\rho^2}{1-\rho}$

Average queue length in the system: $\bar{q}_w = \dfrac{1}{1-\rho}$

Average waiting time in system: $d = \dfrac{1}{\mu - \lambda}$

Average waiting time in queue: $\bar{w} = \dfrac{\lambda}{\mu(\mu - \lambda)} = d - \dfrac{1}{\mu}$

The probability that number of customer in the system is greater than k:

$$P(n > k) = \rho^{k+1}$$

The probability that number of customer in the queue is greater than k:

$$P(Q>k) = \rho^{k+2}$$

Examples of M/M/1 system application are as follows.

Example 5.10

The toll booth has opened only one window to collect toll. The traffic arriving at this toll plaza is in accord with Poisson distribution and an hourly volume is 800 vehicles. The fee collection process needs 4 seconds for each vehicle. Estimate the parameters of interest.

Solution:

First, we have to determine average arrival rate λ and average rate of service μ:

$$\lambda = 800/3600 = 2/9 \text{ (veh/s)}$$
$$\mu = 1/4 \text{ (vehicle/s)}$$

Due to $\rho = \lambda/\mu = 8/9 < 1$

So that the system is in stable status.

Average vehicles in system:

$$\bar{n} = \frac{\rho}{1-\rho} = \frac{\frac{8}{9}}{1-\frac{8}{9}} = 8 \text{ (veh)}$$

Average queue length:

$$\bar{q} = \frac{\rho^2}{1-\rho} = \frac{\frac{8^2}{9^2}}{1-\frac{8}{9}} = \frac{64}{9} = 7 \text{ (veh)}$$

Average queue length in the system:

$$\bar{q}_w = \frac{1}{1-\rho} = \frac{1}{1-\frac{8}{9}} = 9 \text{ (veh)}$$

Average time-in-queue delay in system:

$$d = \frac{1}{\mu-\lambda} = \frac{1}{\frac{1}{4}-\frac{2}{9}} = 36 \text{ (s/veh)}$$

Average time-in-queue delay in the queuing line:

$$\bar{w} = \frac{\lambda}{\mu(\mu-\lambda)} = d - \frac{1}{\mu} = 36 - 4 = 32 \text{ (s/veh)}$$

It should be mentioned here that the unit for average queue length is in terms of number of vehicles not meters.

5.4 Chi-square (χ^2) Goodness-of-fit Test

In traffic engineering it has always been assumed that the frequency distribution of the observed data is in accord with the known statistical distribution. The objective of statistical test is to confirm that the hypothesis (assumption) is valid. A statistical hypothesis is defined as an assertion or *conjecture* (推断) about the distribution of one or more random variables. If a statistical hypothesis completely specifies the distribution, it is referred to as a simple hypothesis; if not, it is referred to as a composite hypothesis. Specifically, Chi-square *goodness-of-fit* (拟合优度) test is used to determine whether the difference between an observed distribution and its assumed mathematical form is significant. Generally, a goodness-of-fit test applies to situations in which we want to determine whether a set of data may be looked upon as a random sample from a population having a given distribution.

The basic steps of conducting Chi-square test:

(1) Set hypothesis H_0: the underlying distribution agrees to the known mathematical form.

(2) Grouping the raw data and compute both observed frequencies and theoretical frequencies for each group.

(3) Compute quantity:

$$\chi^2 = \sum_{i=1}^{g} \frac{(f_i - F_i)^2}{F_i} \quad (5\text{-}14)$$

Where: χ^2——Chi-squared statistic;

f_i——observed frequency for each group;

F_i——theoretical frequency for each group (greater than 5 in practice);

g——number of groups (after final grouping to meet $F_i > 5$).

(4) Determine the value of α which is called level of significance. The α is defined as the probability of making first-type error or "truth-forsaking" error, which means that the true hypothesis is declined. Even it is true that the smaller the α, the lower the probability of making first-type error. However, reducing value of α triggers in increasing the probability of producing second-kind error, which is often expressed by β. This error is also called "false-acceptance" error, which means that the false hypothesis is accepted. As α decreases β will go up. Therefore, there is a balance in the selection of confidence level $1 - \alpha$.

(5) Determine the decision value of χ^2_α (Table 5.4) based on the given confidence level ($1 - \alpha$) and degree of freedom (Table 5.5) defined as:

$$DF = g - a - 1$$

where: g——number of group;

a——number of variable in distribution.

Table 5.4 Number of Degree of Freedom versus Distribution

DF	0.995	0.990	0.975	0.950	0.900	0.750	0.500	0.250	0.100	0.050	0.025	0.010	0.005
1	3927×10^{-2}	1571×10^{-7}	9821×10^{-7}	3932×10^{-8}	0.01579	0.1015	0.4549	1.323	2.706	3.841	5.024	6.635	7.879
2	0.01003	0.02010	0.05064	0.1026	0.2107	0.5754	1.386	2.773	4.605	5.991	7.378	9.210	10.60
3	0.07172	0.1148	0.2158	0.3578	0.5844	1.213	2.366	4.108	6.251	7.815	9.348	11.34	12.34
4	0.2070	0.2971	0.4844	0.7107	1.064	1.923	3.357	5.585	7.779	9.488	11.14	13.28	14.86
5	0.4117	0.5543	0.8312	1.145	1.610	2.675	4.351	6.626	9.236	11.07	12.83	15.09	16.75
6	0.6757	0.8721	1.237	1.635	2.204	3.455	5.348	7.841	10.64	12.59	14.45	16.81	18.55
7	0.9893	1.259	1.690	2.167	2.833	4.255	6.346	9.037	12.02	14.07	16.01	18.48	20.28
8	1.344	1.646	2.180	2.733	3.199	5.071	7.344	10.22	13.36	15.51	17.63	20.09	21.98
9	1.735	2.088	2.700	3.325	4.168	5.899	8.343	11.39	14.68	16.92	19.02	21.67	23.59
10	2.150	2.558	3.247	3.940	4.865	6.737	9.342	12.55	15.99	18.31	20.48	23.21	25.19
11	2.603	3.053	3.816	4.575	5.578	7.584	10.34	13.70	17.28	19.68	21.92	24.72	26.76
12	3.074	3.571	4.404	5.226	6.304	8.458	11.34	14.85	18.55	21.03	23.34	26.22	28.30
13	3.565	4.107	5.009	5.892	7.042	9.299	12.34	15.98	19.81	22.36	24.74	27.69	29.82
14	4.075	4.660	5.629	6.571	7.790	10.17	13.34	17.12	21.06	23.68	26.12	29.14	31.32
15	4.601	5.229	6.262	7.261	8.547	11.04	14.34	18.25	22.31	25.00	27.49	30.58	32.80
16	5.142	5.812	6.908	7.962	9.312	11.91	15.34	19.37	23.54	26.30	28.85	32.00	34.27
17	5.697	5.408	7.564	8.672	10.09	12.79	16.34	20.49	24.77	27.59	30.19	33.41	35.72
18	6.265	7.015	8.231	9.390	10.86	13.68	17.34	21.60	25.99	28.87	31.53	34.81	37.16
19	6.844	7.644	8.907	10.12	11.65	14.56	18.34	22.72	27.20	30.14	32.85	36.19	38.58
20	7.434	8.260	9.591	10.85	12.44	15.45	19.34	23.83	28.41	31.41	34.17	37.57	40.00
21	8.034	8.897	10.28	11.59	13.24	16.34	20.34	24.93	29.62	32.67	35.48	38.93	41.40
22	8.643	9.542	10.98	12.34	14.04	17.24	21.34	26.04	30.81	33.92	36.78	40.29	42.60
23	9.260	10.20	11.69	13.09	14.85	18.14	22.34	27.14	32.01	35.17	38.08	41.64	44.18
24	9.886	10.86	12.40	13.85	15.66	19.04	23.34	28.24	33.20	36.42	39.36	42.98	45.58
25	10.52	11.52	13.12	14.61	16.47	19.94	24.34	29.34	34.38	37.65	40.65	44.31	46.93
26	11.16	12.20	13.84	15.38	17.29	20.84	25.34	30.43	35.56	38.89	41.92	45.64	48.29
27	11.81	12.88	14.57	16.15	18.11	21.75	26.34	31.53	36.74	40.11	43.19	46.96	49.64
28	12.46	13.56	15.31	16.93	18.94	22.66	27.34	32.62	37.92	41.34	44.46	48.28	50.99
29	13.12	14.26	16.05	17.71	19.77	23.57	28.34	33.71	39.09	42.58	45.72	49.59	52.34
30	13.79	14.95	16.79	18.49	20.60	24.48	29.34	34.80	43.26	43.77	46.98	50.89	53.67
40	20.71	22.16	24.43	26.51	29.05	33.66	39.34	45.62	51.80	55.76	59.34	63.69	66.77
50	27.99	29.71	32.36	34.76	37.69	42.94	49.33	56.33	63.17	67.50	71.42	76.15	79.49

Continued table

DF	0.995	0.990	0.975	0.950	0.900	0.750	0.500	0.250	0.100	0.050	0.025	0.010	0.005
60	35.53	37.48	40.48	43.19	46.46	52.29	59.33	66.98	79.08	79.08	83.30	88.38	91.95
70	43.28	45.44	48.76	51.74	55.33	61.70	69.33	77.58	85.53	90.53	95.02	100.42	104.22
80	51.17	53.54	57.15	60.39	64.28	71.14	79.33	88.13	96.58	101.88	106.63	112.33	116.32
90	59.20	61.75	65.65	69.13	73.29	80.62	89.33	98.65	107.56	113.14	118.14	124.12	128.30
100	67.33	70.00	74.22	77.93	82.36	90.13	99.33	109.14	118.50	124.34	129.56	135.81	140.17
	−2.576	−2.326	1.960	−1.645	−1.28	−0.6745	0.0000	0.6745	+1.282	+1.645	+1.960	+2.326	576

Source: E. L. Crow, F. A. Davis, and M. W. Maxwell, Statistics Manual, Dover Publications, Mineola, NY, 1960.

The number of degree of freedom versus distribution is given in Table 5.5.

(6) Draw conclusion of testing the hypothesis: accept or reject. When $\chi_\alpha^2 \geq \chi^2$, the hypothesis is accepted, otherwise hypothesis is rejected.

Attention should be paid to the number of group. This number is the final grouping after computing theoretical frequency to meet $F_i > 5$. The Relationship between Number of Degree of Freedom and Distribution are listed in Table 5.5. The above procedure is best illustrated by an example. For this reason three examples are described in next section.

Table 5.5 Number of Degree of Freedom versus Distribution

Distribution	a	DF
Normal	2	$g-3$
Poisson	1	$g-2$
Binomial	2	$g-3$
Exponential	1	$g-2$

Example 5.11 Chi-squared test(I)

The spot speed data were collected and shown in Table 5.6. The null hypothesis for this example is: spot speed data is in accord with normal distribution under confidence levels of 90% and 75%, respectively.

Table 5.6 Chi-Square Test for Normalcy on Illustrative Spot Speed Data

Average Speed =48.10mile/h Standard Deviation =4.96mile/h Sample Size =283									
Speed Group		Observed Frequency n	Upper Limit (Std. Normal) z_d	Prob. $z \leq z_d$ Table 7.3	Prob. of Occurrence in Group	Theoretical Frequency f	Combined Groups n	Combined Groups f	χ^2 Group
Upper Limit (mile/h)	Lower Limit (mile/h)								
∞	60	2	∞	1.0000	0.0082	2.3206			
60	58	5	2.40	0.9918	0.0146	4.1318	7	6.4524	0.0465
58	56	9	2.00	0.9772	0.0331	9.3673	9	9.3673	0.0144

87

Continued table

Speed Group		Observed Frequency n	Upper Limit (Std. Normal) z_d	Prob. $z \leq z_d$ Table 7.3	Prob. of Occurrence in Group	Theoretical Frequency f	Combined Groups n	Combined Groups f	χ^2 Group
Upper Limit (mile/h)	Lower Limit (mile/h)								
56	54	14	1.59	0.9441	0.0611	17.2913	14	17.2913	0.6265
54	52	24	1.19	0.8830	0.0978	27.6774	24	27.6774	0.4886
52	50	37	0.79	0.7852	0.1372	38.8276	37	38.8276	0.0860
50	48	62	0.38	0.6480	0.1560	44.1480	62	44.1480	7.2188
48	46	46	−0.02	0.4920	0.1548	43.8084	46	43.8084	0.1096
46	44	33	−0.42	0.3372	0.1339	37.8937	33	37.8937	0.6320
44	42	21	−0.83	0.2033	0.0940	26.6020	21	26.6020	1.1797
42	40	13	−1.23	0.1093	0.0577	16.3291	13	16.3291	0.6787
40	38	7	−1.63	0.0516	0.0309	8.7447	7	8.7447	0.3481
38	36	5	−2.04	0.0207	0.0134	3.7922	10	5.8581	2.9285
36	34	5	−2.44	0.0073	0.0073	2.0659			
Total					1.0000	283	283	283	14.3574

$$\chi^2 = 14.3574$$
$$\text{Degrees of Freedom} = 12 - 3 = 9$$

When confidence level is 90%, namely $\alpha = 0.10$ then $\chi^2_{0.10}(DF=9) = 14.68$, the hypothesis is accepted. When confidence level is 75%, namely $\alpha = 0.25$ then $\chi^2_{0.25}(DF=9) = 11.39$, the hypothesis is rejected. The explanations of the results are as follows.

When we believe that there is 90% chance that the spot speed data is in accord with normal distribution. This belief is then accepted through Chi-square testing. However, when we believe that there is 75% chance that the spot speed data is in accord with normal distribution. This time our belief is rejected. Therefore, conclusion can be drawn that the higher the confidence level is, the more likely the hypothesis is accepted.

Example 5.12 Chi-squared test(II)

The data in Table 5.7 illustrate vehicles approaching at intersection in a minute. The null hypothesis for this group of data is: the arrival of vehicles is in accord with Poisson distribution under 95% confidence level.

Table 5.7 Chi-Square Test for Poisson Distribution on Illustrative Number of Arrival

No. of coming vehicles x_i	Observed Frequency f_i	$P(X=x_i)$	Theoretical Frequency F_i		$f_i - F_i$	$(f_i - F_i)^2$	$(f_i - F_i)^2 / F_i$
0	3	0.0086	2.83	16.28	0.72	0.5231	0.0321
1	14	0.0410	13.45				
2	30	0.0974	31.96		-1.96	3.8336	0.1200
3	41	0.1544	50.63		-9.63	92.7769	1.8324
4	61	0.1834	60.16		0.84	0.6996	0.0116
5	69	0.1744	57.19		11.81	139.4410	2.4381
6	46	0.1381	45.31		0.69	0.4828	0.0107
7	31	0.0938	30.76		0.24	0.0565	0.0018
8	22	0.0557	18.28		3.72	13.8637	0.7585
9	8	0.0294	9.65		-1.65	2.7294	0.2828
10	2	0.0140	4.59				
11	0	0.0060	1.98	7.78	-4.78	22.87	2.94
≥12	1	0.0037	1.21				
Total	328	1.00	328		—	—	8.3945
		$\chi^2 = 8.3945$					
		Degrees of Freedom = 10 - 1 - 1 = 8					

Due to $\chi^2_{0.05}(DF=8) = 15.51 > 8.3945$, so the hypothesis is accepted. Thus, conclusion can be drawn that the arrivals of vehicles are in accord with Poisson distribution and its form is as follows.

$$P(X=x) = \frac{(4.753)^x e^{-4.753}}{x!}$$

Example 5.13 Chi-squared test(Ⅲ)

In this example a group of headway data has been collected as illustrated in Table 5.8. Likewise, the null hypothesis for this group of data is: the headway is in accord with exponential distribution under 95% confidence level.

Table 5.8 Chi-Square Test for Exponential Distribution on Illustrative Headway Data

Raw Data Group		Middle Value	Observed Frequency f_i	Prob. of $t_i \in (a,b]$	Theoretical Frequency F_i	$f_i - F_i$	$(f_i - F_i)^2$	$(f_i - F_i)^2 / F_i$
Lower Limit	Upper Limit							
0	1.5	0.75	16	0.2819	58.08	−42.0778	1770.5387	30.4857
1.5	2.5	2.00	43	0.1423	29.31	13.6940	187.5267	6.3989
2.5	3.5	3.00	43	0.1141	23.50	19.5001	380.2523	16.1810
3.5	4.5	4.00	29	0.0915	18.84	10.1558	103.1404	5.4733
4.5	5.5	5.00	18	0.0734	15.11	2.8892	8.3473	0.5524
5.5	6.5	6.00	13	0.0588	12.12	0.8829	0.7795	0.0643
6.5	7.5	7.00	7	0.0472	9.72	−2.7165	7.3794	0.7595
7.5	8.5	8.00	9	0.0378	7.79	1.2085	1.4605	0.1874
8.5	9.5	9.00	18	0.0303	6.25	11.7521	138.1127	22.1056
10.5	12.5	11.50	4	0.0351	7.24	−3.2390	10.4913	1.4493
12.5	16.5	14.50	3	0.0371	7.65	−4.6479	21.6031	2.8247
>16.5		16.5	3	0.0505	10.40	−7.4014	54.7805	5.2667
Total			206	1.00	206	—	—	91.7487

$$\chi^2 = 91.7487$$
Degrees of Freedom = 12 − 1 − 1 = 10

Because $\chi^2_{0.05}(DF = 10) = 18.307 < 91.7484$, thus the hypothesis that group of data agrees with exponential distribution is rejected.

It is important to point out that rejection of the null hypothesis when it is true is called a type I error. The probability of committing this type of error is denoted by α that is also called level of significance. However, acceptance of null hypothesis when it is false is called a type II error. The probability of committing this type of error is denoted by β. A good test procedure is one in which both are small, thereby giving us a good chance of making the correct decision. The only way to keep values of both as smaller as possible is to increase sample size.

Key points of the chapter

1. What is skewness and what does it imply?
2. Be aware of the preconditions to use any statistical models and know how to use models to do calculations.

3. Be familiar with M/M/1 model and related calculations.
4. Hand on the Chi-square testing procedure and points worthy noticing.
5. How has freedom been determined for different distribution assumed?

本章要点

1. 简述非对称 Skewness 的定义及其应用？
2. 简述泊松分布、二项分布和负指数分布的使用条件和计算。
3. 简述 M/M/1 分布计算公式的使用条件和公式。
4. 简述卡方检验的过程和注意事项。
5. 对于不同的分布，自由度是如何确定的？

Chapter 6 Highway Capacity Analysis

In this chapter highway capacity and level of services are introduced. Capacity and level of services are the most important elements in traffic engineering studies. First, the definitions of capacity in general and level of services are presented. Then, the procedures to estimate capacity and level of services for freeway basic segment and multilane highway are described. Two lane highways are considered vital traffic facilities and capacity analysis for this type of facility is illustrated. Finally, capacity analysis for the merging, diverging and weaving areas of freeway is summarized. It should be pointed out that capacity analysis covers a wide range of topics. The objective of this chapter attempts to provide fundamentals of the analytical methodology and logic procedure for the estimation of capacity of freeways and two-lane highways. With regard to the capacity analysis of signalized intersections or other traffic facilities readers can read Highway Capacity Manual.

Capacity analysis is considered the most important procedure in traffic engineering. It takes about 70 years to study, involving huge amount of investment in time and man's power. It has many useful applications in traffic operation analysis as well as roadway design.

US Highway Capacity Manual (HCM) is said the milestone of capacity analysis. The first edition of HCM was published by Bureau of Public Roads (BPR) in 1950. The second edition was published in 1965. The third edition was born in 1985 and it experienced two-time update in 1994 and 1997, respectively. The fourth edition of the HCM was published in December 2000 and is generally refered to as HCM 2000. The fifth edition was published in December of 2010, and more often called HCM 2010.

In general, capacity analysis is conducted with regard to different type of roadway facilities. Most capacity analysis results are based on vehicular traffic only without considering mixed traffic in which non-motorized vehicles (such as bicycles) involve in traffic stream.

6.1 Capacity, Level of Service and Other Related Concepts

6.1.1 *Definition of Capacity*(通行能力)

Based on HCM 2010 capacity of a facility is the maximum sustainable hourly flow rate at which persons or vehicles reasonably can be expected to traverse a point or a uniform section of a lane or roadway during a given time period under prevailing roadway, traffic, and control conditions.

(1) Time period for analysis: as rule of thumb, the peak 15 minutes rate is taken in most cases, even leaving some discretions.

(2) Capacity: can be expressed in terms of persons or vehicles depending on element in question.

(3) Prevailing conditions: are generally categorized as roadway condition,

traffic composition, and control approach.

Roadway conditions refer to the geometric characteristics of the street or highway, including types of facility, number of lanes, lane and shoulder widths, *lateral clearances* (侧向净空), horizontal and vertical alignments.

Traffic conditions refer to the composition of the traffic stream, particularly the presence of trucks and other heavy vehicles.

Control conditions refer to interrupted flow facilities. Control devices such as "STOP" or "YIELD" signs, lane use restrictions, turn restrictions, type and timing of traffic signals have significant impacts on capacity.

(4) Point or uniform section: meaning a uniform section must have consistent prevailing conditions. Based on definition it can be seen that capacity itself refers to a particular point of section of interest. However, in practice it implies the capability to handle traffic flow of the facilities such as a segment of roadway.

(5) Capacity is subject to variation in both time and space.

Capacity is rather clear in concept than in estimation. It should be noted that there has so far been no analytical solution to estimate capacity for any kind of the facilities. Field observation has been often used to find possibly stated capacities as a substitute in practice. In addition the methodology used in data processing has no established criterion resulting in the discrepancy of the results in the estimation of capacity.

The capacities for basic segment of freeways and multilane highway according to free-flow speed are summarized in Table 6.1.

Table 6.1 Basic Values of Uninterrupted Flow Capacity (HCM 2010)

Type of Facility	Free-flow Speed (mile/h)	Capacity (passenger cars/h/lane)	Approx Speed at Capacity (mile/h)
Basic Segment of Freeway	70	2,400	53
	65	2.350	52
	60	2,300	51
	55	2.250	50
Multilane Highway	60	2,200	55
	55	2,100	51
	50	2,000	48
	45	1,900	42

The values in the column of capacity are derived from field observations and the unit of each value is expressed in passenger car Unit(PCU) per hour per lane. The values of capacity in different edition of HCM are varied due to variation of the results from field observation over time.

6.1.2 *Concept of Level of Service*(服务水平) *and Measure of Effectiveness* (效率指标)

Level of Service (LOS), introduced in 1965 edition of HCM, is a quality measure describing operational conditions within a traffic stream. Generally the quality measures include speed and travel time, freedom to maneuver, traffic interruption, comfort and convenience.

The level of service is also described as the quality that road users receive from roadway facilities in terms of speed, freedom to drive and comfort he/she feels to obtain. To quantify this kind of quality measure it is necessary to use indicators that are tangible in practice. In traffic engineering Measure Of Effectiveness (MOE) is used as an indicator to quantify traffic performance. Density, travel speed and delay are often used as measure of effectiveness as indicated in Table 6.2.

Table 6.2 The MOEs of Level of Service Used in Capacity Analysis

Facilities	Measure of Effectiveness	Unit
Freeway Basic Sections	Density	pc/mile(or km)/ln
Freeway Weaving Section	Density	pc/mile(or km)/ln
Freeway Ramp Influence Area	Density	pc/mile(or km)/ln
Multilane Highways	Density (based on Q/S)	pc/mile(or km)/ln
Two-Way Highway Links	Travel Speed	mile (or km)/h
Signalized Intersections	Control Delay	s/veh
Unsignalized Intersections	Control Delay	s/veh
Arterial	Travel Speed	mile (or km)/h

The determination of level of service is as follows.

HCM 2010(USA) defines six grades in terms of LOS for each type of basic freeway segment. Letters designate each level, from A to F(Figure 6.1), with LOS A representing the best operating conditions and LOS F the worst. Each level of service represents a range of operating conditions and the driver's perception of those conditions.

LOS A describes free-flow operations. Vehicles are almost completely unimpeded in their ability to maneuver within the traffic stream.

LOS B represents reasonably free flow, and free-flow speeds are maintained. The ability to maneuver within the traffic stream is only slightly restricted, and the general level of physical and psychological comfort provided to drivers is still high.

LOS C provides for flow with speeds at or near the FFS of the freeway. Freedom to maneuver within the traffic stream is noticeably restricted, and lane changes require more care and vigilance on the part of the driver.

LOS D is the level at which speeds begin to decline slightly with increase of flows and density begins to increase somewhat more quickly. Freedom to maneuver within the traffic stream is more noticeably limited, and the driver experiences reduced physical and psychological comfort levels. Even minor incidents can be expected to create queuing.

LOS E describes operation at capacity. Operations at this level are in an unstable condition, because there are virtually no usable gaps in the traffic stream. Vehicles are closely spaced leaving little room to maneuver within the traffic stream

Figure 6.1 Diagram of Level of Service on Freeways in USA

at speeds that still exceed 80 km/h. Any disruption of the traffic stream, such as vehicles entering from a ramp or a vehicle changing lanes, can establish a disruption wave that propagates throughout the upstream traffic flow.

LOS F describes breakdowns in vehicular flow. Such conditions generally exist within queues forming behind breakdown points. This situation can be described as parking scenario.

However, traffic engineers in China have graded four LOS up to 2014 for basic segment of freeway as showed in Figure 6.2. Based on *Technical Standard of Highway Engineering*(JTG B01—2014) current LOS has divided into 6 grades.

a)LOS I b)LOS II c)LOS III d)LOS IV

Figure 6.2　Diagram of Level of Service on Freeways in China

This is the level-of-service criterion for basic segment of freeways as shown in Table 6.3 and density is expressed in passenger cars per mile per lane. It should be noted that level of service is for a specified roadway facility, not for systems or networks.

The basic segment of freeways is defined a section of freeways on which movement of traffic flows is not influenced by the merge or diverge maneuver as indicated in Figure 6.3, 6.4, 6.5, 6.6 and 6.7, respectively.

Table 6.3 The Level of Service Used in Capacity (USA and China)

Level of Service	Density (USA) (pc/mile/ln)	Level of Service	Density (China) (pc/mile/ln)
A	≤11	1	≤12
B	≤18	2	≤19
C	≤26	3	≤26
D	≤35	4	>26
E	≤45		
F	>45		

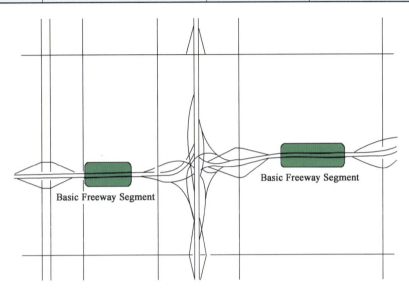

Figure 6.3 Diagram of Basic Segment of Freeway

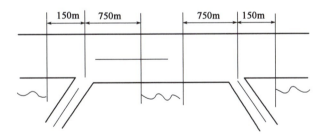

Figure 6.4 Basic Segment (M-D)

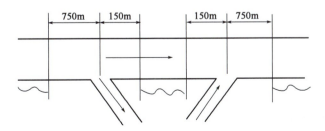

Figure 6.5 Basic Segment (D-M) of Freeway

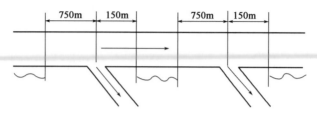

Figure 6.6 Basic Segment (D-D)

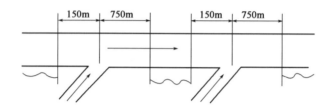

Figure 6.7 Basic Segment (M-M) of Freeway

6.1.3 Other Related Concepts

In order to conduct capacity analysis for basic segment of freeway in a more meaningful sense there are some concepts that should be presented in the next section.

6.1.3.1 *Service Flow Rate*(服务流率)

This is flow rate that can be accommodated by various facility types at each level of service(A to E), in which vehicles can be reasonably expected to traverse a point or roadway, during a given time period (15 min), under prevailing roadway, traffic and control conditions, while maintaining a designated level of service. This parameter provides a range of flow rate within which traffic operation maintains at a given level of service. Thus, service flow rate can be called LOS-related flow rate.

6.1.3.2 *Maximum Service Flow Rate*(MSF,最大服务流率)

Defined as the capacity of single lane for given level of service usually from A to E, without F, which represents unstable flow or unacceptably poor service quality. Similarly, maximum service flow rate can be called LOS-related capacity.

The values of MSF can be found in Exhibit 6.1 for basic freeway section and Exhibit 6.12 for multilane highways. Maximum service flow rates are stated in terms of pc/h/ln and reflect the ideal conditions.

The ideal conditions refer to:

(1) The standard width of a traffic lane (12 feet for USA and 3.75 meter for China);

(2) Enough lateral clearance;

(3) No heavy vehicles in traffic stream;

(4) No unfamiliar driver populations.

It is true that MSF is a good indicator to connect capacity with level of service.

6.1.3.3 Relationship of *SF*(服务流率) and *MSF*(最大服务流率)

$$SF_i = MSF_i \cdot N \cdot f_{HV} \cdot f_p \tag{6-1}$$

Where: SF_i——service flow rate for level of service " i " (pc/h);

MSF_i——maximum service flow rate for level of service " i " (pc/h/ln);

N——number of lanes (in one direction) on the facility;

f_p——adjustment factor for presence of occasional or non-familiar user of facility;

f_{HV}——adjustment factor for presence of heavy vehicles.

$$f_{HV} = \frac{1}{1 + P_T \cdot (E_T - 1) + P_R \cdot (E_R - 1)} \tag{6-2}$$

Over time, the operation of heavy vehicles has improved relative to passenger cars. Trucks in particular, now have considerably more power than in the past, primarily due to turbo-charged engines. Thus, the maximum passenger-car equivalent shown in Exhibit 6.4 and Exhibit 6.5 is 7.0. In the 1965 HCM, the value was as high as 17.0.

6.1.3.4 Equivalents for Extended Freeway Segments

Extended segment analysis can be used where no one grade of 3 percent or greater is longer than 0.5 km or where no one grade of less than 3 percent is longer than 1.0 km. the terrain of the freeway must be classified as level, rolling, or mountainous.

(1) *Level terrain*(平原地形)

Level terrain is any combination of grades and horizontal or vertical alignment that permits heavy vehicles to maintain the same speed as passenger cars. This type of terrain includes short grades of no more than 2 percent.

(2) *Rolling terrain*(丘陵地形)

Rolling terrain is any combination of grades and horizontal or vertical alignment that causes heavy vehicles to reduce their speeds substantially below those of passenger cars but that does not cause heavy vehicles to operate at crawl speeds for any significant length of time or at frequent intervals.

If any grade is long enough, trucks will be forced to decelerate to the crawl speed, which they will then be able to maintain for extended distances.

(3) *Mountainous terrain*(山岭地形)

Mountainous terrain is any combination of grades and horizontal or vertical alignment that causes heavy vehicles to operate at *crawl speeds*(爬行速度) for significant distances or at frequent intervals.

Exhibit 6.3 gives passenger-car equivalents for extended freeway segments.

6.1.3.5　Equivalents for Specific Grades

Any freeway grade of more than 1.0 km for grades less than 3 percent or 0.5 km for grades of 3 percent or more should be considered as a separate segment. Analysis of such segments must consider the upgrade and downgrade conditions and whether the grade is a single and isolated grade of constant percentage or part of a series forming a composite grade.

Exhibits 6.4 and 6.5 give values of E_T and E_R for upgrade segments. These factors vary with the percent of grade, length of grade, and the proportion of heavy vehicles in the traffic stream. Exhibit 6.6 gives values of E_T for RVs, downgrades may be treated as level terrain.

6.1.3.6　*Volume/Capacity Ratio* (负荷度)

The *v/c* ratio, known as volume/capacity ratio, is defined as the ratio of current or projected demand flow to the capacity of the facility, ranges from 0 to 1.0. Volume/capacity ratio (*v/c* ratio) is often used to measure the operation performance of roadway facilities. It is also measure of effectiveness for level of service.

It is impossible for a measured departure flow to exceed the actual capacity of a facility, which means the *v/c* ratio can't be over 1.0. However, when we deal with future projections, the forecasted demand flow is then used and compared with the capacity. At that time *v/c* ratio can be over 1.0, implying that the estimated capacity is not sufficient to handle the forecast demand flows.

6.1.3.7　*Free-flow Speed* (自由流速度)

Free flow speed is a descriptive parameter to indicate degree of freedom of driver operating on the segment of roadways. It is defined as the average speed measured in field when flow is less than or equal to 1300 vehicles per hour per lane. Exhibits 6.7 and 6.13 show the relationship of capacity varies by free-flow speed for basic segment of freeway and multilane highway separately.

6.1.4　Factors Affecting Capacity & LOS (Base Conditions)

6.1.4.1　Base Conditions

Base conditions assume good weather, good pavement conditions, user's familiarity with the facility, and no impediments to traffic flow. Examples of base conditions for uninterrupted-flow facilities and for intersection approaches are given below. Base conditions for basic freeway segments include the following:

(1) Minimum lane widths of 3.6 m;

(2) Minimum right-shoulder lateral clearance between the edge of the travel lane

and the nearest obstacle or object that influences traffic behavior of 1.8 m;

(3) Minimum median lateral clearance of 0.6 m;

(4) Traffic stream composed entirely of passenger cars;

(5) Five or more lanes for one direction (in urban areas only);

(6) Interchange spacing at 3 km or greater;

(7) Level terrain, with grades no greater than 2 percent; and

(8) A driver population composed principally of regular users of the facility.

6.1.4.2 Base conditions for multilane highways.

Base conditions for multilane highways are as follows:

(1) 3.6-m minimum lane widths;

(2) 3.6-m minimum total lateral clearance in the direction of travel-this represents the total lateral clearances from the edge of the traveled lanes to obstructions along the edge of the road and in the median (in computations, lateral clearances greater than 1.8 m are considered in computations to be equal to 1.8 m);

(3) Only passenger cars in the traffic stream;

(4) No direct access points along the roadway;

(5) A divided highway; and

(6) Free-flow Speed (FFS) higher than 100 km/h.

In most capacity analyses, prevailing conditions differ from the base conditions, and computations of capacity, service flow rate, and level of service must include adjustments.

6.1.5 Factors Affecting the Free-flow Speed

A lot of factors will affect the free-flow speed on freeways and multilane highways. However, the main factors are discussed only.

6.1.5.1 Factors Affecting the Free-flow Speed on Freeways

(1) Lane width (f_{LW}): the standard width of a lane is 12 feet or 3.66 meters.

(2) Lateral clearance (f_{LC}): base lateral clearance is 6 feet on the right side and 2 feet on the median or left.

(3) Number of lanes (f_N): base condition for number of lanes in one direction on a freeway is five and it should be noted that this modification is very debatable and for rural area there is no adjustment.

(4) *Interchange density* (f_{ID}立交密度): this is defined as the average number of interchanges per mile over a six-mile section of the facility and the base condition for interchange density is 0.50 which implies an average interchange spacing of two miles.

$$FFS = BFFS - f_{LW} - f_{LC} - f_N - f_{ID} \quad \text{(for freeways)} \quad (6\text{-}3)$$

Equation (6-3) provides the procedure of adjustments for the base free flow speed for freeways. The corresponding adjustments to free flow speed for freeways can be found in Exhibits 6.8, 6.9, 6.10, and 6.11, respectively.

In general BFFS is 70mile/h for urban and suburban freeways, 75mile/h for rural freeways.

6.1.5.2　Factors Affecting the free-flow Speed on Multilane Highways

(1) Lane width (f_{LW}): the standard width of a lane is 12 feet or 3.66 meters.

(2) Lateral clearance (f_{LC}): this adjustment is based on the total lateral clearance, the left or median lateral clearance on an undivided highway is assumed to be 6 feet;

(3) Median-type (f_M): Median is an important part of roadway and in general there are four types of **median** (中央分隔带) including: undivided, divided (or raised), TWLTL❶(Two Way Left Turn Lane), and fence median as indicated in Figure 6.8. TWLTL can only be found in the USA; whereas fence median is used very often on the roadways in China's cities.

Figure 6.8　Types of Roadway Median

---

❶　TWLTL：Two-Way Left Turn Lane (median treatment on roadways that allows left turns from both directions).

(4) Access-point density (f_A): The access-point density on a divided roadway is determined by dividing the total number of access points (i. e. intersections and driveways) on the right side of the roadway in the direction of travel by the segment's total length in kilometers.

$$FFS = BFFS - f_{LW} - f_{LC} - f_M - f_A \quad \text{(for multilane highways)} \quad (6\text{-}4)$$

A base free-flow speed of 60mile/h may be used for rural and suburban multilane highways, if field data is unavailable.

The base free-flow speed may also be estimated by referencing the ***posted speed*** (限速值). For speed limits of 40 and 45 mile/h in USA, the base free-flow speed is approximately 100 mile/h higher than the posted speed limit. The base free-flow speed is approximately 5 mile/h higher than the limit when speed limits are 50 and 55 mile/h.

Adjustments to free flow speed for multilane highways can be found in Exhibit 6.14, 6.15, 6.16, and 6.17, respectively.

6.1.6 Samples for Free-Flow Speed Estimation

Example 6.1 An Urban Freeway

An old 6-lane urban freeway has the following characteristics: 11-ft lanes; frequent roadside obstructions located 2 ft from the right pavement edge; and an interchange density of 2.00 interchanges per mile (i. e., average interchange spacing of 0.50 mile). What is the free-flow speed of this freeway?

Solution:

The free-flow speed of a freeway may be estimated using Equation (6-3):

$$FFS = BFFS - f_{LW} - f_{LC} - f_N - f_{ID}$$

The following values are used in this computation:

BFFS = 70 mile/h (based condition for urban freeways)
f_{LW} = 1.9 mile/h (Exhibit 6.8, 11-ft lanes)
f_{LC} = 1.6 mile/h (Exhibit 6.9, 2-ft lateral clearance, 3 lanes)
f_N = 3.0 mile/h (Exhibit 6.10, 3 lanes in one direction)
f_{ID} = 7.5 mile/h (Exhibit 6.11, 2.00 interchanges per mile)
Then,
FFS = 70.0 − 1.9 − 1.6 − 3.0 − 7.5 = 56.0 (mile/h)

Example 6.2 A Four-Lane Suburban Multilane Highway

A 4-lane undivided multilane highway in a suburban area has the following characteristics: posted speed limit =50 mile/h; 11-ft lanes; frequent obstructions located 4 ft from the right pavement edge; 30 access points/mile on the right side of the facility. What is the free-flow speed for the direction described?

Solution:

The free-flow speed for a multilane highway is computed using Equation (6-4).

$$FFS = BFFS - f_{LW} - f_{LC} - f_M - f_A$$

The base free-flow speed for a multilane highway may be taken as 60 mile/h as a default or may be related to the posted speed limit. In the latter case, for a posted speed limit of 50 mile/h, the base free-flow speed may be taken to be 5 mile/h more than the limit, or $50 + 5 = 55$ mile/h. This is the value that will be used.

Adjustments to the base free-flow speed are as followings:

f_{LW} = 1.9 mile/h (Exhibit 6.14, 11-ft lanes)

f_{LC} = 0.4 mile/h (Exhibit 6.15, total lateral clearance = 10 ft, 4-lanes highway)

f_M = 1.6 mile/h (Exhibit 6.16, undivided highway)

f_A = 7.5 mile/h (Exhibit 6.17, 30 access points/mile)

Then,

$$FFS = 55.0 - 1.9 - 0.4 - 1.6 - 7.5 = 43.6 (mile/h)$$

Note that in selecting the adjustment for lateral clearance, the total lateral clearance is 4 ft (for the right side) plus an assumed value of 6.0 ft (for the left or median side) of an undivided highway.

6.2 Two Types of Analysis

The following section introduces procedures for determining level of service (LOS), lane requirements, and effects of traffic on basic freeway segments, and multilane highway.

6.2.1 Steps for Operational Analysis (运行状态分析)

Operational analysis is to determine level of service based on demand flow rate under equivalent ideal conditions. The procedure of determining LOS is as follows:

Step 1 Determine the measured or estimated *FFS*, construct an appropriate speed-flow curve of the same shape as the typical curves shown in Exhibit 6.7/ Exhibit 6.13. The curve should intercept the *y*-axis at the *FFS*.

Step 2 Determine the demand flow rate v_p according to Equation (6-5).

$$v_p = \frac{V}{PHF \cdot N \cdot f_{HV} \cdot f_p} \qquad (6\text{-}5)$$

Where: v_p——demand flow rate under equivalent ideal conditions(pc/h/ln);

V——actual volume(veh/h);

PHF——peak hour factor;

N——number of lanes (in one direction) on the facility;

f_p——adjustment factor for presence of occasional or non-familiar user of facility, this value is not well defined and 0.85 is considered the worst-case scenario;

f_{HV}——adjustment factor for presence of heavy vehicles (Equation (6-2));

$$f_{HV} = \frac{1}{1 + P_T(E_T - 1) + P_R(E_R - 1)}$$

E_T、E_R——passenger-car equivalents for trucks/buses and recreational vehicles (RVs) in the traffic stream, respectively; referring to Exhibit 6.3/6.4/ 6.5/ 6.6;

P_T、P_R——proportion of trucks/buses and RVs in the traffic stream, respectively.

Step 3 Determine Level of Service.

Method A: Based on reading up to the *FFS* curve identified in Step 1 and the demand flow rate V_p in Step 2, Determine LOS corresponding to that point in Exhibit 6.7.

Method B: Determine the density of flow according to Equation (6-6).

$$D = \frac{v_p}{S} \qquad (6\text{-}6)$$

Where: D——density (pc/km/ln);

v_p——flow rate (pc/h/ln);

S——average passenger-car travel speed (km/h).

6.2.2 Example for Operational Analysis

Example 6.3

Figure 6.9 shows a section of an old freeway in New York City. It is a four-lane freeway (additional service roads are shown in the picture) with the following characteristics: Ten-foot travel lane, Lateral obstructions at 0 ft at the roadside, Interchange density is 2.0 interchanges per mile, with rolling terrain.

Figure 6.9 An Old Freeway in New York City

The roadway has a current peak demand volume of 3500veh/h. The peak-hour factor is 0.95, and there are no trucks, buses, or RVs in the traffic stream, as the roadway is classified as a parkway and such vehicles are prohibited.

At what level of service will the freeway operate during its peak period of demand?

Solution:

Step 1 Determine *FFS*

The free-flow speed of a freeway may be estimated using Equation(6-3):

$$FFS = BFFS - f_{LW} - f_{LC} - f_N - f_{ID}$$

The following values are used in this computation:

$BFFS$ = 70 mile/h (based condition for urban freeways)

f_{LW} = 6.6 mile/h (Exhibit 6.8, 10-ft lanes)

f_{LC} = 3.6 mile/h (Exhibit 6.9, 0-ft lateral clearance, 2 lanes)

f_N = 4.5 mile/h (Exhibit 6.10, 2 lanes in one direction)

f_{ID} = 7.5 mile/h (Exhibit 6.11, 2.0 interchanges/mile)

Then,

$$FFS = 70.0 - 6.6 - 3.6 - 4.5 - 7.5 = 47.8 (\text{mile/h})$$

Step 2 Determine demand flow rate

The demand flow rate may be estimated using Equation(6-5):

$$v_p = \frac{V}{PHF \cdot N \cdot f_{HV} \cdot f_p}$$

The following values are used in this computation:

V = 3500 veh/h

PHF = 0.95

N = 2 lanes

f_p = 1.0 (assumed commuter driver population)

$f_{HV} = 1$ (no trucks, buses, or RVs in the traffic stream)

Then,

$$v_p = \frac{V}{PHF \cdot N \cdot f_{HV} \cdot f_p}$$

$$= \frac{3500}{0.95 \times 2 \times 1 \times 1} = 1842 \quad (\text{pc/h/ln})$$

Step 3 Determine Level of Service

Method A:

Use Figure.10, LOS = E.

Method B: Computer Density:

The Density may be estimated using Equation(6-6):

$$D = \frac{V_p}{S} = \frac{1842}{48} = 38.4 \quad (\text{pc/h/ln})$$

Use Table 6.3/ Figure 6.10, LOS = E.

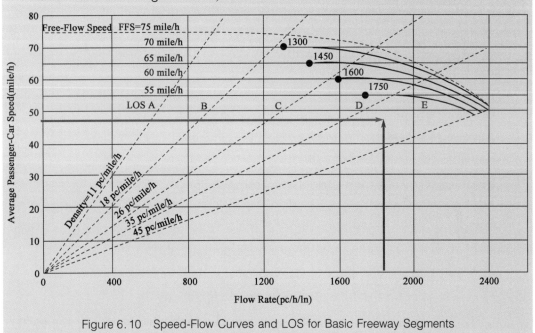

Figure 6.10 Speed-Flow Curves and LOS for Basic Freeway Segments

6.2.3 *Steps for Design Analysis* (道路设计分析)

The objective of design analysis is to determine number of lanes for a specified level of service.

$$N = \frac{DDHV}{PHF \cdot MSF_i \cdot f_{HV} \cdot f_p} \tag{6-7}$$

Most often, this is an iterative process, by entering assumed number of lanes and testing if it meets the requirement of level of service.

The procedure of determining number of lanes is as follows:

Step 1　Determine the measured or estimated *FFS*;

Step 2　Determine Maximum Service Flow Rate;

Step 3　Find number of lanes *N*.

6.2.4　Example for Design Analysis

Example 6.4

A new freeway is being designed through a rural area. The directional design hour volume (DDHV) has been forecast to be 2700veh/h during the peak hour, with a PHF of 0.85 and 15% trucks in the traffic stream.

A long section of the facility will have level terrain characteristics, but one 2-mile section involves a sustained grade of 4%. If the objective is to provide level of service C, with a minimum acceptable level of D, how many lanes must be provided?

Solution:

Step 1　Determine the measured or estimated *FFS*.

The free-flow speed of a freeway may be estimated using Equation(6-3):

$$FFS = BFFS - f_{LW} - f_{LC} - f_{N} - f_{ID}$$

The following values are used in this computation:

BFFS = 75 mile/h (based condition for rural freeways)

No lane widths, lateral clearance, number of lanes and interchange density are noted, it would assumed that all are base conditions.

f_{LW} = 0.0 mile/h (Exhibit 6.8, 12-ft lanes)

f_{LC} = 0.0 mile/h (Exhibit 6.9, ⩾6ft lateral clearance)

f_{N} = 0.0 mile/h (Exhibit 6.10 footnote, For all rural highways, f_{N} = 0.0 mile/h)

f_{ID} = 0.0 mile/h (Exhibit 6.11, assumed ⩽0.5 interchanges/mile)

Then,

$$FFS = BFFS - 0 = 120 km/h = 75 mile/h$$
$$FFS = BFFS - f_{LW} - f_{LC} - f_{N} - f_{ID}$$
$$= 120 - 0 - 0 - 0 - 0 = 120(km/h) = 75(mile/h)$$

Step 2　Determine Maximum Service Flow Rate

The Maximum Service Flow Rate may be found from Exhibit 6.2 for a 75 mile/h free-flow speed.

Target the level of service is C, $MSF_C = 1830$ pc/h/ln;

Minimum acceptable level of D, $MSF_D = 2170$ pc/h/ln.

Step 3 Find number of lanes N

number of lanes N may be estimated using Equation (6-7):

$$N = \frac{DDHV}{PHF \cdot MSF_i \cdot f_{HV} \cdot f_p}$$

Where: $DDHV = 2700$ veh/h;

$PHF = 0.85$;

$MSF_C = 1830$ pc/h/ln;

$MSF_D = 2170$ pc/h/ln (in Step 2);

$f_p = 1.0$ (regular users assumed).

For level terrain and down grade:

$$f_{HV}(\text{level, down}) = \frac{1}{1 + P_T(E_T - 1) + P_R(E_R - 1)}$$

$$= \frac{1}{1 + 0.15 \times (1.5 - 1) + 0} = 0.930$$

$$N(\text{level, down}) = \frac{DDHV}{PHF \cdot MSF_i \cdot f_{HV} \cdot f_p} = \frac{2700}{0.85 \times 1830 \times 0.930 \times 1.00} = 1.87$$

For up-grade:

$$f_{HV}(\text{up}) = \frac{1}{1 + P_T \times (E_T - 1) + P_R \times (E_R - 1)}$$

$$= \frac{1}{1 + 0.15 \times (2.5 - 1) + 0} = 0.816$$

$$N(\text{up}) = \frac{2700}{0.85 \times 1830 \times 0.816 \times 1.00} = 2.13$$

The results of such an analysis most often result in fractional lanes. For the level and down grade section of facility it is suggested that the facility should be constructed as a four lane freeway. However, for upgrade part of facility, the facility should be constructed as four lane freeway with a truck-climbing lane on the sustained upgrade. While the results of the analysis provide the engineers or decision makers with a great deal of information to assist in making a final design decision on the upgrade section, it does not dictate such a decision. Economical, environmental, and social factors would also have to be considered.

6.3 Capacity Analysis for Two Lane Highway

6.3.1 Classification of Two Lane Highway

A two-lane highway is an undivided roadway with two lanes, one for use by traffic in each direction. Passing a slower vehicle requires use of the opposing lane as sight distance and gaps in the opposing traffic stream permit. As volumes and geometric restrictions increase the ability to pass decreases and platoons form. Two-lane highways in USA are categorized into three classes in Figure 6.11 for analysis by HCM as follows.

6.3.1.1 Class I

Class I Two-lane Highways are highways where motorists expect to travel at relatively high speeds. Two-lane highways that are major intercity routes, primary connectors of major traffic generators, daily commuter routes, or major links in state or national highway networks are generally assigned to Class I. These facilities serve mostly long-distance trips or provide the connections between facilities that serve long-distance trips.

6.3.1.2 Class II

Class II Two-lane highways are highways where motorists do not necessarily expect to travel at high speeds. Two-lane highways functioning as access routes to Class I facilities, serving as scenic or recreational routes (and not as primary arterials), or passing through rugged terrain (where high-speed operation would be impossible) are assigned to Class II. Class II facilities most-often serve relatively short trips, the beginning or ending portions of longer trips, or trips for which sightseeing plays a significant role.

6.3.1.3 Class III

Class III Two-lane highways are highways serving moderately developed areas. They may be portions of a Class I or Class II highway that pass through small towns or developed recreational areas. On such segments, local traffic often mixes with through traffic, and the density of unsignalized roadside access points is noticeably higher than in a purely rural area. Class III highways may also be longer segments passing through more-spread-out recreational areas, also with increased roadside densities. Such segments are often accompanied by reduced speed limits that reflect the higher activity level.

6.3.2 Capacity of Two-lane Highway

The base conditions for a two-lane highway include:

a) Examples of Class I Two-lane Highways

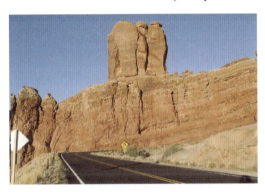 

b) Examples of Class II Two-lane Highways

c) Examples of Class III Two-lane Highways

Figure 6.11 Types of Two lane Highway

(1) Lane widths greater than or equal to 12 ft;
(2) Clear shoulders wider than or equal to 6 ft;
(3) No no-passing zones❶;
(4) All passenger cars;

---

❶ A no-passing zone is any zone marked for no passing or any section of road with a passing sight distance of 300 m or less.

(5) No impediments to through traffic, such as traffic control or turning vehicles; and

(6) Level terrain.

The capacity of two-lane highway for the base condition is 700 pc/h in one direction, 3200 pc/h for both directions.

6.3.3 LOS for Two-Lane Highway

There are two performance measures used to quantify the LOS of a two-lane highway. These are (1)(2). **Percent Time-Spent-Following**(跟车时间比), Average Travel Speed and (3) percent of Free-Flow Speed. LOS criteria for two-lane highways in HCM2000 are presented in Table 6.4.

Table 6.4 Levels of Service for Two-Lane Highways

Level of Service	Class I Highways		Class II Highways	Class III Highways
	ATS (mi/h)	PTSF (%)	PTSF (%)	PFFS (%)
A	>55	≤35	≤40	>91.7
B	>50~55	>35~50	>40~55	>83.3~91.7
C	>45~50	>50~65	>55~70	>75.0~83.3
D	>40~45	>65~80	>70~85	>66.7~75.0
E	≤40	>80	>85	≤66.7

Operating conditions for each LOS are described as follows:

At LOS A, motorists experience high operating speeds on Class I highways, and experience little difficulty in passing. Platoons of three or more vehicles are rare. On Class II highways, speed would be controlled primarily by roadway conditions. A small amount of platooning would be expected. On Class III highways, drivers should be able to maintain operating speeds close or equal to the free-flow speed of the facility.

At LOS B, the balance of passing demand and passing capacity approaches equivalence. On both Class I and Class II highways, the degree of platooning noticeably increases. Some speed reductions are present on Class I highways. On Class III highways, it becomes difficult to maintain free-flow speed operation, but the speed reduction is still relatively small.

At LOS C, platoon formation becomes a noticeable problem, and the degree of platooning increases sharply on Class I and II facilities. Speeds are noticeably curtailed on all three classes of highway.

At LOS D, platooning increases significantly. Passing demand is high on both Class I and II facilities, but passing capacity approaches zero. Most vehicles are now traveling in platoons, and general congestion is noticeable. On Class III highways, the fall-off from free-flow speed is now significant.

At LOS E, demand is approaching capacity. Passing on Class I and II highways is virtually impossible, and the degree of platooning is more than 80%. Speeds are seriously curtailed. On Class III highways, speed is less than two-thirds the free-flow speed. The lower limit of this LOS represents capacity.

LOS F exists whenever demand flow in one or both directions exceeds the capacity of the segment. Operating conditions are unstable, and heavy congestion exists on all classes of two-lane highway.

6.3.3.1 Average travel speed

Average travel speed reflects the mobility on a two-lane highway. It is the length of the highway segment divided by the average travel time of all vehicles traversing the segment in both directions during a designated interval.

The LOS for Class I highways on which efficient mobility is paramount is defined in terms of both average travel speed and percent time-spent-following.

$$ATS = FFS - 0.0125 v_p - f_{np} \qquad (6-8)$$

Where: ATS——average travel speed for both directions of travel combined (km/h);

f_{np}——adjustment for percentage of no-passing zones (see Exhibit 6.19);

v_p——passenger-car equivalent flow rate for peak 15-min period (pc/h, use Equation (6-9));

$$v_P = \frac{V}{PHF \cdot f_G \cdot f_{HV}} \qquad (6-9)$$

Where: v_p——passenger-car equivalent flow rate for peak 15-min period (pc/h);

V——demand volume for the full peak hour (veh/h);

PHF——peak-hour factor;

f_G——grade adjustment factor, accounts for the effect of the terrain on travel speeds and percent time-spent-following, even if no heavy vehicles are present (see Exhibit 6.20, 6.21);

f_{HV}——heavy-vehicle adjustment factor, f_{HV} applies to two types of vehicles: trucks and RVs. Buses should not be treated as a separate type of heavy vehicle but should be included with trucks (Equation (6-2), see Exhibit 6.22, 6.23).

6.3.3.2 Percent time-spent-following

Percent time-spent-following represents the freedom to maneuver and the comfort and convenience of travel. It is the average percentage of travel time that vehicles must travel in platoons behind slower vehicles due to the inability to pass.

Percent time-spent-following is difficult to measure in the field. However, the percentage of vehicles traveling with headways of less than 3 s at a representative location can be used as a surrogate measure. On Class II highways, since mobility is less critical, LOS is defined only in terms of percent time-spent-following.

$$PTSF = BPTSF + f_{d/np} \qquad (6\text{-}10)$$

Where: *PTSF*——percent-time-spent following;

  BPTSF—— base percent time-spent-following for both directions of travel combined (use Equation(6-9));

  $f_{d/np}$——adjustment for the combined effect of the directional distribution of traffic and of the percentage of no-passing zones on percent time-spent-following (see Exhibit 6.18);

$$BPTSF = 100(1 - e^{-0.000879\ v_p}) \qquad (6\text{-}11)$$

  v_p——passenger-car equivalent flow rate for peak 15-min period (pc/h, use Equation (6-9)).

6.3.3.3 Percent time-spent-following

Percent of Free-Flow Speed (PFFS) represents the ability of vehicles to travel at or near the posted speed limit.

On Class III highways, high speeds are not expected. Because the length of Class III segments is generally limited, passing restrictions are also not a major concern. In these cases, drivers would like to make steady progress at or near the speed limit. Therefore, on these highways, PFFS is used to define levels of service.

6.3.4 FFS for Two-lane Highway

A key step in the assessment of the LOS of a two-lane highway is to determine the free-flow speed (FFS). Two general methods can be used to determine the FFS for a two-lane highway: field measurement and estimation with the Equation(6-13).

Method 1 Field Measurement

The FFS of a highway can be determined directly from a speed study conducted in the field. No adjustments are made to the field-measured data. The field study should be conducted in periods of low traffic flow (up to a two-way flow of 200 pc/h) and should measure the speeds of all vehicles or of a systematic sampling (e.g., of every 10th vehicle).

$$FFS = S_{FM} + 0.0125 \frac{V_f}{f_{HV}} \qquad (6\text{-}12)$$

Where: *FFS*——estimated free-flow speed (km/h);

  S_{FM}——mean speed of traffic measured in the field (km/h);

  V_f——observed flow rate for the period when field data were obtained (veh/h);

  f_{HV}——heavy-vehicle adjustment factor, determined as shown in Equation (6-2).

Method 2 Estimating FFS

The FFS can also be estimated indirectly if field data are not available. To estimate FFS, the analyst must characterize the operating conditions of the facility in terms of a base free-flow speed (BFFS) that reflects the character of traffic and the alignment of the facility. Estimates of BFFS can be developed based on speed data and local knowledge of operating conditions on similar facilities. The design speed and posted speed limit of the facility may be considered in determining the BFFS; however, the design speeds and speed limits for many facilities are not based on current operating conditions. Once BFFS is estimated, adjustments can be made for the influence of lane width, shoulder width, and access-point density. The FFS is estimated using Equation(6-13).

$$FFS = BFFS - f_{LS} - f_{A} \qquad (6\text{-}13)$$

Where: *FFS*——estimated *FFS* (km/h);

BFFS——base *FFS* (km/h);

f_{LS}——adjustment for lane width and shoulder width, from 6.24;

f_{A}——adjustment for access point, from Exhibit 6.25.

6.3.5 Operation Analysis for Two-lane Highway

Example 6.5 Operational Analysis

The Highway: A Class I two-lane highway segment.

The Question: What is the two-way segment LOS for the peak hour?

The Facts:

- 1600veh/h (two-way volume);
- 50/50 directional split;
- 14 percent trucks and buses;
- 4 percent RVs;
- 0.95 *PHF*;
- 100km/h base *FFS*;
- Rolling terrain;
- 3.4m lane width;
- 1.2m shoulder width;
- 10km length, and;
- 50 percent no-passing zones;
- 12 access points/km.

Outline of Solution:

Two-way average travel speed and percent time-spent-following will be determined, and from these parameters, the LOS.

Steps

(1) Determine grade adjustment factor for average travel speed.

$f_G = 0.99$ (Exhibit 6.23, Rolling terrain, 1600 veh/h (two-way volume))

(2) Compute f_{HV} for average travel speed.

f_{HV} (adjustment factor for presence of heavy vehicles) may be estimated using Equation (6-2):

$$f_{HV} = \frac{1}{1 + P_T(E_T - 1) + P_R(E_R - 1)}$$

Where: $E_T = 1.5$ (Exhibit 6.22, Rolling terrain, 1600 veh/h (two-way volume));

$E_R = 1.1$ (Exhibit 6.23, Rolling terrain, 1600 veh/h (two-way volume));

$P_R = 0.04$ (4 percent RVs);

$P_T = 0.14$ (14 percent trucks and buses);

$$f_{HV} = \frac{1}{1 + 0.14 \times (1.5 - 1) + 0.04 \times (1.1 - 1)} = 0.931$$

(3) Compute v_p.

v_p (passenger-car equivalent flow rate for peak 15-min period (pc/h)) may be estimated using Equation (6-11):

$$v_p = \frac{V}{PHF \cdot f_G \cdot f_{HV}} = \frac{1600}{0.95 \times 0.99 \times 0.931} = 1827 \text{(pc/h)}$$

(4) Calculate highest directional flow rate.

$$v_p \times 0.50 = 1827 \times 0.50 = 914 \text{(pc/h)}$$

(5) Check the highest directional flow rate and two-way flow rate against capacity values of 1700 pc/h and 3200 pc/h, respectively.

$$914 \text{pc/h} < 1700 \text{pc/h}$$
$$1827 \text{pc/h} < 3200 \text{pc/h}$$

(6) Compute the *FFS*.

The free-flow speed of a two lane highway may be estimated using Equation (6-13):

$$FFS = BFFS - f_{LS} - f_A$$

Where: $BFFS = 100$ km/h (base *FFS*);

$f_{LS} = 2.8$ (Exhibit 6.24, 3.4m lane width, 1.2m shoulder width);

$f_A = 8.0$ (Exhibit 6.25, 12 access points/km);

$$FFS = BFFS - f_{LS} - f_A = 100 - 2.8 - 8.0 = 89.2 (\text{km/h}).$$

(7) Compute the average travel speed.

The Average Travel Speed of a two lane highway may be estimated using Equation(6-10):

$$ATS = FFS - 0.0125 v_p - f_{np}$$

Where: $FFS = BFFS - f_{LS} - f_A = 100 - 2.8 - 8.0 = 89.2 (\text{km/h})$ (see Step 6);

$$v_P = \frac{V}{PHF \cdot f_G \cdot f_{HV}} = \frac{1600}{0.95 \times 0.99 \times 0.931} = 1827 (\text{pc/h}) \text{ (see Step 3)};$$

$f_{np} = 1.3$ (Exhibit 6.19, 1600 veh/h (two-way volume), 50 percent no-passing zones);

$$ATS = 89.2 - 0.0125 \times 1827 - 1.5 = 64.9 (\text{km/h}).$$

(8) Determine grade adjustment factor for percent time-spent-following.

$f_G = 1.00$ (Exhibit 6.21, 1600 veh/h (two-way volume), Rolling terrain)

(9) Compute f_{HV} for time-spent-following.

f_{HV} (adjustment factor for presence of heavy vehicles) for time-spent-following may be estimated using Equation(6-2):

$$f_{HV} = \frac{1}{1 + P_T(E_T - 1) + P_R(E_R - 1)}$$

Where: $E_T = 1.0$ (Exhibit 6.23, Rolling terrain, 1600 veh/h (two-way volume));

$E_R = 1.0$ (Exhibit 6.23, Rolling terrain, 1600 veh/h (two-way volume));

$P_R = 0.04$ (4 percent RVs);

$P_T = 0.14$ (14 percent trucks and buses);

$$f_{HV} = \frac{1}{1 + 0.14(1.0 - 1) + 0.04(1.0 - 1)} = 1.000.$$

(10) Compute v_p.

v_p (passenger-car equivalent flow rate for peak 15-min period (pc/h)) may be estimated using Equation(6-11):

$$V_p = \frac{V}{PHF \cdot f_G \cdot f_{HV}} = \frac{1600}{0.95 \times 1.00 \times 1.000} = 1684 (\text{pc/h})$$

(11) Calculate the highest directional flow rate.

$$V_p \times 0.50 = 1684 \times 0.50 = 842 (\text{pc/h})$$

(12) Check the highest directional flow rate and two-way flow rate against the capacity values of 1700 pc/h and 3200 pc/h, respectively.

$$842 \text{ pc/h} < 1700 \text{ pc/h}$$
$$1684 \text{ pc/h} < 3200 \text{ pc/h}$$

(13) Compute base percent time-spent-following.

BPTSF (base percent time-spent-following) may be estimated using Equation (6-9):

$$BPTSF = 100(1 - e^{-0.000879 v_p}) = 100 \times (1 - e^{-0.000879 \times 1684}) = 77.2\%$$

(14) Compute percent time-spent-following.

PTSF (percent time-spent-following) may be estimated using Equation (6-8):

$$PTSF = BPTSF + f_{d/np} = 77.2 + 4.8 = 82.0(\%)$$

(15) Determine LOS.

Results: The two-lane highway operates at LOS E. (Table 6.4, $ATS = 65.1$ km/h and $PTSF = 82.0\%$).

Other Performance Measures

$$v/c = \frac{V_C}{3200} = \frac{1827}{3200} = 0.57$$

Steps are Summaried in Table 6.5.

Table 6.5 Operational Analysis steps of the Twolane Highway

1. Determine grade adjustment factor for average travel speed (use Exhibit 6.20).	$f_G = 0.99$
2. Compute f_{HV} for average travel speed (use Exhibit 6.25 and Equation(6-2)).	$f_{HV} = \frac{1}{1 + P_T(E_T - 1) + P_R(E_R - 1)}$ $f_{HV} = \frac{1}{1 + 0.14(1.5 - 1) + 0.04(1.1 - 1)} = 0.931$
3. Compute v_p (use Equation (6-11)).	$v_p = \frac{V}{PHF \cdot f_G \cdot f_{HV}}$ $v_p = \frac{1600}{0.95 \times 0.99 \times 0.931} = 1827 (\text{pc/h})$
4. Calculate highest directional flow rate.	$v_p \times 0.50 = 1827 \times 0.50 = 914 (\text{pc/h})$
5. Check the highest directional flow rate and two-way flow rate against capacity values of 1700 pc/h and 3200 pc/h, respectively.	914 pc/h < 1700 pc/h 1827 pc/h < 3200 pc/h
6. Compute the FFS (use Exhibits 6.24 and 6.25 and Equation (6-13)).	$FFS = BFFS - f_{LS} - f_A$ $FFS = 100 - 2.8 - 8.0 = 89.2 (\text{km/h})$
7. Compute the average travel speed (use Exhibit 6.22 and Equation (6-10)).	$ATS = FFS - 0.0125 v_p - f_{np}$ $ATS = 89.2 - 0.0125 \times 1827 - 1.3 = 65.1 (\text{km/h})$

	Continued table
8. Determine grade adjustment factor for percent time-spent-following (use Exhibit 6.21)	$f_G = 1.00$
9. Compute f_{HV} for time-spent-following (use Exhibit 6.26 and Equation (6-2))	$f_{HV} = \dfrac{1}{1+0.14\times(1.0-1)+0.04\times(1.0-1)} = 1.000$
10. Compute v_p (use Equation (6-11)).	$v_p = \dfrac{1600}{0.95\times1.000\times1.00} = 1684(\text{pc/h})$
11. Calculate the highest directional flow rate.	$v_p \times 0.50 = 1684 \times 0.50 = 842(\text{pc/h})$
12. Check the highest directional flow rate and two-way flow rate against the capacity values of 1700 pc/h and 3200 pc/h, respectively.	842pc/h < 1700pc/h 1684pc/h < 3200pc/h
13. Compute base percent time-spent-following (use Equation (6-9)).	$BPTSF = 100(1-e^{-0.000879 v_p})$ $BPTSF = 100(1-e^{-0.000879\times1684}) = 77.2\%$
14. Compute percent time-spent-following (use Exhibit 6.18 and Equation (6-8)).	$PTSF = BPTSF + f_{np}$ $PTSF = 77.2 + 4.8 = 82.0(\%)$
15. Determine LOS (use Exhibit 6.19).	$ATS = 65.1$ km/h and $PTSF = 82.0\%$ LOS E

It should be pointed out that the steps of the preceding analysis are purely based on the American experiences in dealing with two-lane highway. This discussion is site specific. These steps can only be considered as reference and can't be taken as the standard to follow.

6.4 Capacity & LOS Analysis for Weaving, Merging, and Diverging on Freeways and Multilane Highways

6.4.1 Basic Knowledge

6.4.1.1 Definition

Weaving is defined as the crossing of two or more traffic streams traveling in the same general direction along a significant length of highway without the aid of traffic control devices (with the exception of guide signs). Weaving segments are formed when a merge area is closely followed by a diverge area, or when an on-ramp is closely followed by an off-ramp and the two are joined by an auxiliary lane.

Diverge: A movement in which a single lane of traffic separates into two lanes without the aid of traffic control devices.

Merge: A movement in which two separate lanes of traffic combine to form a single lane without the aid of traffic signals or other right-of-way controls.

Based on HCM2010, The maximum length for which weaving analysis is conducted is 750 m for all configuration types. Beyond these lengths, merge and diverge areas are considered separately. Figure 6.12 shows the definition of ramp influence areas.

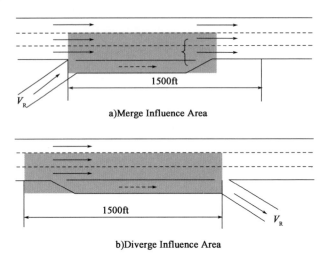

Figure 6.12 Merge and Diverge Influence Area

Crown line (路冠线) is defined as a lane line that joins the nose of the merge junction directly to the nose of the diverge junction. (直接连接进、出口三角区顶对顶的车道标线). Figure 6.13 illustrates trown line of Ramp-Weare.

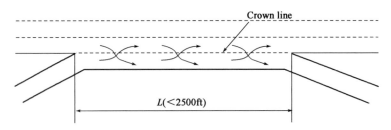

Figure 6.13 Ramp-Weave for Type A

Constrained operation: An operating condition in a weaving segment, involving geometric and traffic constraints, that prevents weaving vehicles from occupying a large portion of the lanes available to achieve balanced operation.

Unconstrained operation: An operating condition when the geometric constraints on a weaving segment do not limit the ability of weaving vehicles to achieve balanced operation.

6.4.1.2 Weaving Segment Configuration

Weaving segment configuration is based on the number of lane changes required of each weaving movement.

The three types of geometric configurations are defined as follows:

(1) Type A: Weaving vehicles in both directions must make one lane change to successfully complete a weaving maneuver as shown in Figure 6.14.

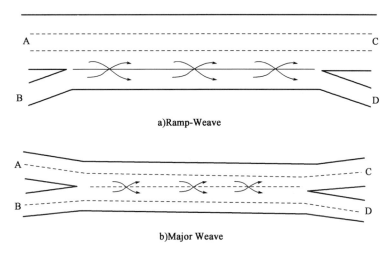

Figure 6.14 Type A Weaving Segments

(2) Type B: Weaving vehicles in one direction may complete a weaving maneuver without making a lane change, whereas other vehicles in the weaving segment must make one lane change to successfully complete a weaving maneuver as shown in Figure 6.15.

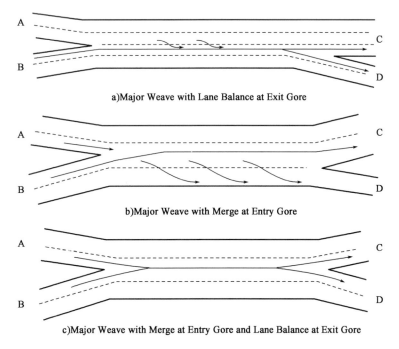

Figure 6.15 Type B Weaving Segments

(3) Type C: Weaving vehicles in one direction may complete a weaving maneuver without making a lane change, whereas other vehicles in the weaving segment must make two or more lane changes to successfully complete a weaving maneuver as shown in Figure 6.16.

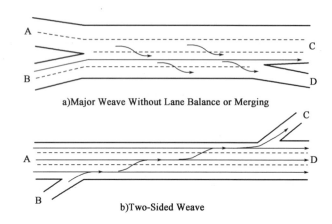

Figure 6.16　Type C Weaving Segments

There are seven configurations covering types of A, B and C. This Chapter focuses on type A (ramp-weave) only.

6.4.2　Capacity of Weaving Area

6.4.2.1　Weaving Segment

The capacity of a weaving segment is any combination of flows that causes the density to reach the LOS E/F boundary condition of 27.0 pc/km/ln for freeways or 25.0 pc/km/ln for multilane highways. Thus, capacity varies with a number of variables: configuration, number of lanes, free-flow speed of the freeway or multilane highway, length, and volume ratio. Capacity for various weaving segments is illustrated in Exhibit 6.26.

$$c_h = c_b \cdot f_{HV} \cdot f_p \cdot PHF \tag{6-14}$$

Where: c_h——capacity of the weaving area expressed as a full-hour under prevailing conditions;

c_b——capacity of the weaving area in equivalent pc/h under base conditions (see Exhibit 6.26).

6.4.2.2　Merge Area

The capacity of a merge area is determined primarily by the capacity of the downstream freeway segment. Thus, the total flow arriving on the upstream freeway and the on-ramp cannot exceed the basic freeway capacity of the departing downstream freeway segment. Exhibit 6.27 lists capacity values for this type of flow.

6.4.2.3 Diverge Area

In a diverge area, the total flow that can depart is generally limited by the capacity of freeway lanes approaching the diverge. In all appropriate diverge designs, the number of lanes leaving the diverge area is either equal to or one greater than the number entering. This flow (V_F) is as previously defined. Exhibit 6.31 provides capacity values for this type of flow.

6.4.3 Level of Service Criteria

Density is also used as measure of effectiveness to exhibit level of service as shown in Exhibit 6.29 (Metric)/Exhibit 6.30 (weaving segment), and Exhibit 6.31 (merge and diverge segment), respectively.

6.4.4 Analysis of Weaving Areas

In general there are four kinds of flows in weaving area.

(1) Weaving flow: This is the traffic movements in a weaving segment that are engaged in weaving movements.

(2) Non-weaving flow: That is the traffic movements in a weaving segment that are not engaged in weaving movements.

(3) Crossing-in weaving flow: That is the traffic movements in a weaving segment that are trying to maneuver to most-inner lane, involving a lot of lane change.

(4) Crossing-out weaving flow: That is the traffic movements in a weaving segment that are trying to exit, involving a lot of lane change.

The four weaving flows are given as shown in Figure 6.17.

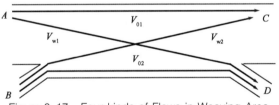

Figure 6.17 Four kinds of Flows in Weaving Area

Where: $V_w = V_{w1} + V_{w2}$ —— total weaving flow;

$V_{nw} = V_{o1} + V_{o2}$ —— total non-weaving flow;

$V = V_w + V_{nw}$ —— total demand flow;

$VR = \dfrac{V_w}{V}$ —— volume ratio; the ratio of weaving flow rate to total flow rate in the weaving segment;

$R = \dfrac{V_{w2}}{V_w}$ —— weaving ratio; the ratio of the smaller weaving flow rate to total weaving flow rate.

Calculation procedures for weaving area analysis:

Step 1　Specify all traffic and geometric conditions for the site.

Step 2　Convert all component demand volumes to peak flow rates in pc/h under equivalent base conditions, using Equation (6-15).

$$V_i = \frac{V_i}{PHF \cdot f_{HV} \cdot f_P} \tag{6-15}$$

Step 3　Assume that operations are unconstrained, and estimate the resulting speed of weaving and non-weaving vehicles in the weaving area.

When $N_w \leqslant N_w(\max)$, the operation is unconstrained;

When $N_w > N_w(\max)$, the operation is constrained.

Where: N_w——*number of lanes weaving vehicles* （交织平衡车道数）, it must occupy to achieve balanced equilibrium operation with non-weaving vehicles;

$N_w(\max)$——*maximum number of lanes* （最大交织平衡车道数） that can be used by weaving vehicles for a given configuration.

From Exhibit 6.32, You obtain the values of N_w and $N_w(\max)$.

Step 4　Using the results of Step c, determine whether actual operations are unconstrained or constrained. If they are constrained, re-estimate the speed of weaving and non-weaving vehicles assuming the constrained result.

Step 5　Compute the weighted average speed and density for all vehicles in the weaving area.

$$S = \frac{V_{nw} + V_w}{\dfrac{V_{nw}}{S_{nw}} + \dfrac{V_w}{S_w}} \tag{6-16}$$

Where: S——Weighted average space mean speed of all vehicle in weaving area;

$$S_i = 24 + \frac{FFS - 16}{1 + W_i} \quad (km/h) \tag{6-17}$$

(i = w for weaving; i = nw for non-weaving)

W_i——weaving intensity factor for weaving (i = w) and non-weaving (i = nw) flows;

$$W_i = \frac{a(1 + VR)^b \left(\dfrac{V}{N}\right)^c}{(3.28L)^d} \tag{6-18}$$

V——total flow rate in the weaving segment (pc/h);

VR——volume ratio;

N——total number of lanes in the weaving segment;

L——length of the weaving segment (m);

$a、b、c、d$——constants of calibration. They vary with different conditions: unconstrained and constrained (see Exhibit 6.33).

Step 6 Determine level of service from the estimated density in the weaving area based on criteria.

$$D = \frac{\frac{V}{N}}{S} \quad (6\text{-}19)$$

Sometimes, separate densities for weaving and non-weaving vehicles may be computed and compared, even it is not recommended to do so in HCM2010.

$$D_w = \frac{\frac{V_w}{N_{wA}}}{S_w} \quad D_{nw} = \frac{\frac{V_{nw}}{N_{nwA}}}{S_{nw}} \quad (6\text{-}20)$$

Where: D_w——average density of weaving vehicles;
D_{nw}——average density of non-weaving vehicles;
N_{wA}——number of lanes actually occupied by weaving vehicles;
N_{nwA}——number of lanes actually occupied by non-weaving vehicles.

$$\begin{cases} N_{wA} = N_w \\ N_{nwA} = N - N_w \end{cases} \quad (\text{under unconstrained}) \quad (6\text{-}21)$$

$$\begin{cases} N_{wA} = N_w(\max) \\ N_{nwA} = N - N_w(\max) \end{cases} \quad (\text{under constrained}) \quad (6\text{-}22)$$

It should be noted here that separate levels of service for weaving and non-weaving vehicles are used in terms of speed, instead of density. Density was introduced in 1997 and 2000. It was thought that the concept of separate densities would be confusing as weaving and non-weaving vehicles share lanes.

Step 7 Check input variables against limitations of the methodology.

Step 8 Determine the capacity of weaving section.

Example 6.6

Figure 6.18 illustrates a type A ramp-weave section on a six-lane freeway (three lanes in each direction). The analysis is to determine the expected level of service and capacity for the prevailing conditions shown.

Solution:

(1) Convert volume (veh/h) to flow rate (pc/h)

$$V_i = \frac{V_i}{PHF \cdot f_{HV} \cdot f_p}$$

Where: $PHF = 0.9$ (given)
$f_p = 1.0$ (assuming drivers are familiar with the site)

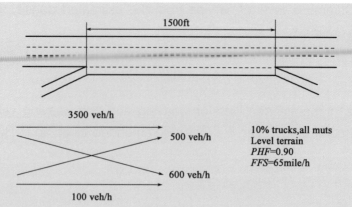

Figure 6.18 Figure of a Typical Ramp-Weave Section on a Six-lane Freeway

f_{HV} (adjustment factor for presence of heavy vehicles) may be estimated using Equation(6-2):

$$f_{HV} = \frac{1}{1 + P_T(E_T - 1) + P_R(E_R - 1)}$$

$E_T = 1.5$ (Exhibit 6.3, level terrain)

$E_R = 0$ (Exhibit 6.3, no RVs)

$$f_{HV} = \frac{1}{1 + P_T(E_T - 1) + P_R(E_R - 1)} = \frac{1}{1 + 0.10 \times (1.5 - 1) + 0} = 0.952$$

Four kinds of flow in weaving area are showed in Figure 6.17 as following.

$$V_{o1} = \frac{3500}{0.90 \times 0.952 \times 1.00} = 4085 (pc/h)$$

$$V_{o2} = \frac{100}{0.90 \times 0.952 \times 1.00} = 117 (pc/h)$$

$$V_{w1} = \frac{600}{0.90 \times 0.952 \times 1.00} = 700 (pc/h)$$

$$V_{w2} = \frac{500}{0.90 \times 0.952 \times 1.00} = 584 (pc/h)$$

(2) Determine weaving segment configuration type. : Type A.

(3) Compute critical variables.

$$V_w = V_{w1} + V_{w2} = 700 + 584 = 1284 (pc/h)$$

$$V_{nw} = V_{o1} + V_{o2} = 4085 + 117 = 4202 (pc/h)$$

$$V = V_w + V_{nw} = 1284 + 4202 = 5486 (pc/h)$$

$$V/N = 5486/4 = 1372 (pc/h/ln)$$

$$VR = \frac{V_w}{V} = 1284/5486 = 0.23$$

$$L = 1500 (ft)$$

(4) Compute weaving and non-weaving speeds assuming unconstrained operation (see Exhibit 6.33).

$$W_i = \frac{a(1+VR)^b \left(\frac{V}{N}\right)^c}{L^d} \quad (L \text{ is in feet})$$

$$W_w = \frac{0.15(1+0.23)^{22}(1372)^{0.97}}{1500^{0.8}} = 0.752$$

$$W_{nw} = \frac{0.0035(1+0.23)^{4.0}(1372)^{1.3}}{1500^{0.75}} = 0.398$$

$$S_i = 15 + \frac{FFS-10}{1+W_i} \quad (\text{mile/h})$$

$$S_w = 15 + \frac{65-10}{1+0.752} = 46.4 \quad (\text{mile/h})$$

$$S_{nw} = 15 + \frac{65-10}{1+0.398} = 54.3 \quad (\text{mile/h})$$

(5) Check type of operation.

Criteria for Unconstrained versus Constrained Operation of Weaving Segments (see Exhibit 6.35).

$$N_w = \frac{0.74 \times N \times VR^{0.571} \times L^{0.234}}{S_w^{0.438}} = \frac{0.74 \times 4 \times 0.23^{0.571} \times 1500^{0.234}}{46.4^{0.438}}$$

$$= 1.32 < 1.4 (N_w(\max))$$

Since operation is unconstrained, speed estimated is corrected.

(6) Compute weaving segment weighted average speed.

$$S = \frac{V_w + V_{nw}}{\frac{V_w}{S_w} + \frac{V_{nw}}{S_{nw}}} = \frac{1284 + 4202}{\frac{1284}{46.4} + \frac{4202}{54.3}} = 52.2 (\text{mile/h})$$

(7) Compute weaving segment density.

$$D = \frac{\frac{V}{N}}{S} = \frac{1372}{52.2} = 26.3 (\text{pc/mile/ln})$$

Comparing this with the criteria of Exhibit 6.30 it can be seen that the prevailing level of service is C.

(8) Determine weaving segment capacity.

The capacity of this weaving area (Type A, four lanes, 1500ft, $VR = 0.23$, $FFS = 65$ mile/h) is found from following Table 6.6.

Table 6.6 Type A Weaving Segments-65mile/h Free-Flow Speed

Volume Ratio, VR	Length of Weaving Segment(ft)				
	500	1000	1500	2000	2500
Four-Lane Segments					
0.10	7430	8310	8830	9190	9400[b]
0.20	6760	7660	8170	8550	8830
0.30	6180[c]	6970[c]	7470[c]	7830[c]	8110[c]
0.35[e]	5870[c]	6620[c]	7120[c]	7470[c]	7760[c]

Notes: Refer to the Exhibit 6.26.
    a. Weaving segments longer than 750 m are treated as isolated merge and diverge areas using the procedures of Chapter 25, "Ramps and Ramp Junctions."
    c. Capacity occurs under constrained operating conditions.
    e. Four-lane Type A segments do not operate well at volume ratios greater than 0.35. Poor operations and some local queuing are expected in such cases.

Using straight-line interpolation:
$c_b = 7470 + (0.30 - 0.23)/(0.30 - 0.20) \times (8170 - 7470) = 7960 (pc/h)$

This result is a maximum flow rate in terms of pc/h under equivalent base conditions. This may be converted to a full-hour maximum volume using equation 6-14 as follows:

$c_h = c_b \cdot f_{HV} \cdot f_p \cdot PHF = 7960 \times 0.952 \times 1.00 \times 0.90 = 6820 (veh/h)$

6.4.5 Analysis of Merge and Diverge Areas

The focus of merge and diverge analysis is on the two right-most lanes. The critical step in the methodology is the estimation of the lane distribution of traffic immediately upstream of the merge or diverge (Figure 6.19).

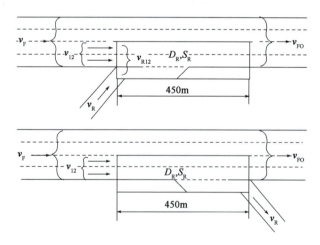

Figure 6.19 Critical Variables in Merge and Diverge Analysis

Calculation procedures for merge/diverge area analysis are as follows.

Step 1 Specify all traffic and geometric conditions for the site.

Step 2 Convert all component demand volumes to peak flow rates in pc/h under equivalent base conditions, using Equation (6-15)

Step 3 Estimate demand flow rates in lanes 1 and 2.

$$v_{12} = v_F \cdot P_{FM} \quad \text{(for merge area)} \quad (6\text{-}23)$$

$$v_{12} = v_R + (v_F - v_R) \cdot P_{FD} \quad \text{(for diverge area)} \quad (6\text{-}24)$$

where: v_{12}——freeway demand flow rate in lanes 1 and 2 of the freeway immediately upstream of the merge or diverge junctions, in pc/h under equivalent base conditions;

v_F——freeway demand flow rate immediately upstream of merge or diverge junction, in pc/h under equivalent base conditions;

P_{FM}—— proportion of approaching vehicles remaining in lanes 1 and 2 immediately upstream of the merge junction, in decimal form (see Exhibit 6.34 for details of estimation of P_{FM}).

Step 4 Capacity considerations.

The purpose of conducting capacity analysis is to determine whether the segment in study has failed (LOS = F) based upon a comparison of demand flow rates to the critical capacity values.

Criteria of capacity checkpoints can be summarized as below:

For merge areas, the maximum facility flow occurs downstream of the merge. Thus, the facility capacity is compared with the downstream facility flow, v_{FO} (see Exhibit 6.27 for details).

$$v_{FO} = v_F + v_R \quad (6\text{-}25)$$

For diverge areas, the maximum facility flow occurs upstream of the diverge. Thus, the facility capacity is compared to the approaching upstream facility flow, v_F (see Exhibit 6.28 for details).

All ramp flows must be checked against the ramp capacities given in Exhibit 6.36.

Step 5 Determination of density and level of service in the ramp influence area.

$$D_R = 3.402 + 0.00456 \times v_R + 0.0048 \times v_{12} - 0.001278 L_A \quad \text{(for merge)} \quad (6\text{-}26)$$

Where: D_R——density of merge influence area (pc/km/ln);

v_R——on-ramp peak 15-min flow rate (pc/h);

v_{12}——flow rate entering ramp influence area (pc/h);

L_A——length of acceleration lane (m).

$$D_R = 2.642 + 0.0053 v_{12} - 0.0183 L_D \quad \text{(for diverge)} \quad (6\text{-}27)$$

Where: L_D——length of deceleration lane (m);
v_{12}——flow rate in lane 1 and 2 of freeway immediately upstream of diverge (pc/h).

Step 6 Determination of expected speed (Table 6.7)

Table 6.7 Average Speeds in Vicinity of Freeway-Ramp Terminals

	Average Speed in Ramp Influence Area (km/h)	Average Speed in Outer Lanes of Ramp Influence Area (km/h)
Merge Areas (on-ramps)	$S_R = S_{FF} - (S_{FF} - 67)M_S$ $M_S = 0.321 + 0.0039e^{(v_{R12}/1000)} - 0.004$ $(L_A S_{FR}/1000)$	$S_o = S_{FF}$ Where: $v_{oA} < 500$ (pc/h) $S_o = S_{FF} - 0.0058(v_{oA} - 500)$ Where: $v_{oA} = 500$ to 2300 (pc/h) $S_o = S_{FF} - 10.52 - 0.01(v_{oA} - 2300)$ Where: $v_{oA} > 2300$ (pc/h)
Diverge Areas (off-ramps)	$S_R = S_{FF} - (S_{FF} - 67)D_S$ $D_S = 0.883 + 0.00009v_R - 0.008S_{FR}$	$S_o = 1.06 S_{FF}$ Where: $v_{oA} < 1000$ (pc/h) $S_o = 1.06 S_{FF} - 0.0062(v_{oA} - 1000)$ Where: $v_{oA} \geq 1000$ (pc/h)

The average per-lane flow rate in outer lanes (v_{oA}) is found according to Equation (6-28).

$$v_{oA} = \frac{v_F - v_{12}}{N_o} \tag{6-28}$$

Where: v_{oA}——average per-lane demand flow in outer lanes (pc/h/ln);
N_o——number of outside lanes in one direction (not including acceleration or deceleration lanes or Lane 1 and 2);
v_F——total approaching freeway flow rate (pc/h);
v_{12}——demand flow rate approaching ramp influence area (pc/h).

Once S_R and S_o are determined, the space mean speed for all vehicles within the 450m length range of the ramp influence area may be computed as the harmonic mean of the two according to Equation (6-29) for merge areas or Equation (6-30) for diverge areas.

$$S = \frac{v_{R12} + v_{oA}N_o}{\frac{v_{R12}}{S_R} + \frac{v_{oA}N_o}{S_o}} \quad \text{(merge areas)} \tag{6-29}$$

$$S = \frac{v_{12} + v_{oA}N_o}{\frac{v_{12}}{S_R} + \frac{v_{oA}N_o}{S_o}} \quad \text{(diverge areas)} \tag{6-30}$$

Where: v_{R12}, v_{12}——Maximum total flow entering the ramp influence area (v_{R12} for merge areas, $v_{R12} = v_R + v_{12}$ and v_{12} for diverge areas).

Example 6.7

An on-ramp to a busy eight-lane urban freeway is illustrated in Figure 6.20. An analysis of this merge area is to determine the likely level of service under the prevailing conditions shown.

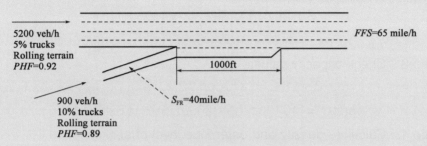

Figure 6.20　Merge Area for Example 6.7

Step 1　Convert all demand volumes to Flow Rates in pc/h under. equivalent base conditions:

$$v_i = \frac{V_i}{PHF \cdot f_{HV} \cdot f_P}$$

$$f_{HV}(\text{ramp}) = \frac{1}{1 + P_T \cdot (E_T - 1) + P_R \cdot (E_R - 1)}$$

$$= \frac{1}{1 + 0.10 \times (2.5 - 1) + 0} = 0.870$$

$$f_{HV}(\text{freeway}) = \frac{1}{1 + P_T \cdot (E_T - 1) + P_R \cdot (E_R - 1)}$$

$$= \frac{1}{1 + 0.05 \times (2.5 - 1) + 0} = 0.930$$

$$v_R(\text{ramp}) = \frac{V_R}{PHF \cdot f_{HV} \cdot f_P} = \frac{900}{0.89 \times 0.870 \times 1.00} = 1162(\text{pc/h})$$

$$v_F(\text{freeway}) = \frac{V_F}{PHF \cdot f_{HV} \cdot f_P} = \frac{5200}{0.92 \times 0.930 \times 1.00} = 6078(\text{pc/h})$$

Step 2　Determine the demand flow remaining in lanes 1 and 2 immediately upstream of the merge v_{12}.

P_{FM} = Proportion of approaching freeway flow remaining in Lane 1 and 2 immediately upstream of merge(see Exhibit 6.34).

$$L_A = 1000\text{ft} = 1000 \times 0.3048 = 304.8(\text{m})$$

$$S_{FR} = 40\text{mile/h} = 40 \times 1.60934 = 64.4(\text{km/h})$$

$$P_{FM} = 0.2178 - 0.000125 \times V_R + 0.05887 \times L_A/S_{FR}$$
$$= 0.2178 - 0.000125 \times 1162 + 0.05887 \times 304.8/64.4$$
$$= 0.3512$$
$$V_{12} = V_F \cdot P_{FM} = 6078 \times 0.3512 = 2135 (pc/h)$$
$$S_{FF} = 65 mile/h = 65 \times 1.60934 = 104.6 km/h, \text{From}$$
$$\text{Exhibit 6.30}, \text{Max} V_{R12} = 4600 pc/h$$
$$V_{R12} = V_R + V_{12} = 1162 + 2135 = 3297 (pc/h) < 4600 (pc/h)$$

Step 3 Check capacity values.
$$V_{FO} = V_F + V_R = 6078 + 1162 = 7240 (pc/h) < 9400 (pc/h) (\text{Exhibit 6.27})$$
$$V_R(\text{ramp}) = 1162 (pc/h) < 2000 (pc/h) (\text{Exhibit 6.36})$$

Step 4 Calculate density and determine level of service.
$$D_R = 3.402 + 0.00456 \times v_R + 0.0048 \times v_{1,2} - 0.001278 \times L_A$$
$$= 3.402 + 0.00456 \times 1162 + 0.0048 \times 2135 - 0.001278 \times 304.8$$
$$= 15.0 (pc/km/ln)$$

From the criteria in Exhibit 6.31, this is Level of Service C.

Step 5 Determine expected speed.

According to the equation in Table 6.7, estimating average speeds in merge areas:

$$M_s = 0.321 + 0.0039 e^{(V_{R12}/1000)} - 0.004 \times (L_A \cdot S_{FR}/1000) = 0.348$$
$$S_R = S_{FF} - (S_{FF} - 67) \cdot M_s$$
$$= 104.6 - (104.6 - 67) \times 0.348 = 91.5 (km/h)$$
$$V_{oA} = \frac{V_F - V_{12}}{N_o} = \frac{6078 - 2135}{2} = 1972 (pc/ln)$$
$$S_o = S_{FF} - 0.0036 \times (V_{oA} - 500)$$
$$= 64.4 - 0.0036 \times (1972 - 500) = 59.1 (km/h)$$
$$S = \frac{V_{R12} + V_{oA} N_o}{\frac{V_{R12}}{S_R} + \frac{V_{oA} N_o}{S_o}} = \frac{3297 + 3943}{\frac{3297}{91.5} + \frac{3943}{59.1}} = 70.5 (km/h)$$

The processing of capacity analysis for merge/diverge areas looks tedious and time consuming from the above example. The lane distribution of the incoming freeway flow v_F should be checked for reasonableness. In this case 2135pc/h use lanes 1 and 2, while 3943 pc/h use lanes 3 and 4. This is not unexpected, given the large ramp flow entering at the on-ramp. Apart from that it is also very useful to check the level of service on the downstream basic segment of freeway. It carries a total of 7240 pc/h in four lanes, or 1810 pc/h/ln in average. It can be seen that the level of service on the downstream freeway is D, meaning that the total freeway flow is the determining element in overall level of service.

6.5　Exhibit for Chapter 6

Exhibit 6.1　LOS Criteria for Basic Freeway Segments(Metric) ·················· 136
Exhibit 6.2　LOS Criteria for Basic Freeway Segments ·················· 137
Exhibit 6.3　Passenger-Car Equivalents on Extended Freeway Segments ······· 138
Exhibit 6.4　Passenger-Car Equivalents for Trucks and Buses on Upgrades ··· 138
Exhibit 6.5　Passenger-Car Equivalents for RVs on Upgrades ·················· 139
Exhibit 6.6　Passenger-Car Equivalents for Trucks and Buses on Downgrades ··· 140
Exhibit 6.7　Speed-Flow Curves and LOS for Basic Freeway Segments ·········· 140
Exhibit 6.8　Adjustment to Free-Flow Speed for Lane Width on a Freeway ······ 141
Exhibit 6.9　Adjustment to Free-Flow Speed for Lateral Clearance on a
　　　　　　　Freeway ·················· 141
Exhibit 6.10　Adjustment to Free-Flow Speed for Number of Lanes on a
　　　　　　　 Freeway ·················· 141
Exhibit 6.11　Adjustment to Free-Flow Speed for Interchange Density on a
　　　　　　　 Freeway ·················· 142
Exhibit 6.12　LOS Criteria for Multilane Highways ·················· 142
Exhibit 6.13　Speed-Flow Curves With LOS Criteria ·················· 143
Exhibit 6.14　Adjustment to Free-Flow Speed for Lane Width on a Multilane
　　　　　　　 Highway ·················· 144
Exhibit 6.15　Adjustment to Free-Flow Speed for Total Lateral Clearance on
　　　　　　　 a Multilane Highway ·················· 144
Exhibit 6.16　Adjustment to Free-Flow Speed for Median Type on a Multilane
　　　　　　　 Highway ·················· 144
Exhibit 6.17　Access-Point Density Adjustment on a Multilane Highway ·········· 144
Exhibit 6.18　Adjustment ($f_{d/np}$) for Combined Effect of Directional
　　　　　　　 Distribution of Traffic and Percentage of No-Passing
　　　　　　　 Zones on Percent Time-Spent-Following on Two-Way
　　　　　　　 Segments ·················· 144

Exhibit 6.19　Adjustment (f_{np}) for Effect of No-Passing Zones on Average Travel Speed on Two-Way Segments ·················· 145

Exhibit 6.20　Grade Adjustment Factor (f_g) to Determine Speeds on Two-Way and Directional Segments ····················· 145

Exhibit 6.21　Grade Adjustment Factor (f_G) to Determine Percent Time-Spent-Following on Two-Way and Directional Segments ··· 146

Exhibit 6.22　Passenger-Car Equivalents for Trucks and RVs to Determine Speeds on Two-Way and Directional Segments ····················· 146

Exhibit 6.23　Passenger-Car Equivalents for Trucks and RVs to Determine Percent Time-Spent-Following on Two-Way and Directional Segments ·· 146

Exhibit 6.24　Adjustment (f_{LS}) for Lane Width and Shoulder Width ··············· 147

Exhibit 6.25　Adjustment (f_A) for Access-Point Density ····························· 147

Exhibit 6.26　Capacity for Various Weaving Segments ······························· 147

Exhibit 6.27　Capacity Values for Merge Areas ··· 149

Exhibit 6.28　Capacity Values for Diverge Areas ······································· 149

Exhibit 6.29　LOS Criteria for Weaving Segments (Metric) ·························· 149

Exhibit 6.30　LOS Criteria for Weaving Segments ····································· 149

Exhibit 6.31　LOS Criteria for Merge and Diverge Areas ···························· 150

Exhibit 6.32　Criteria for Unconstrained Versus Constrained Operation of Weaving Segments ·· 150

Exhibit 6.33　Constants for Computation of Weaving Intensity Factors ·········· 150

Exhibit 6.34　Models for Predicting v_{12} at On-Ramps ······························· 150

Exhibit 6.35　Models for Predicting v_{12} at Off-Ramps ······························· 151

Exhibit 6.36　Approximate Capacity for Ramp Roadways ···························· 151

Exhibit 6.1　LOS Criteria for Basic Freeway Segments (Metric)

Criteria	LOS				
	A	B	C	D	E
FFS =120km/h					
Maximum Density(pc/km/ln)	7	11	16	22	28
Minimum Speed(km/h)	120.0	120.0	114.6	99.6	85.7
Maximum v/c	0.35	0.55	0.77	0.92	1.00
Maximum Service Flow Rate(pc/h/ln)	840	1320	1840	2200	2400
FFS =110km/h					
Maximum Density(pc/km/ln)	7	11	16	22	28
Minimum Speed(km/h)	110.0	110.0	108.5	97.2	83.9

Continued table

Criteria	LOS				
	A	B	C	D	E
FFS =110km/h					
Maximum v/c	0.33	0.51	0.74	0.91	1.00
Maximum Service Flow Rate(pc/h/ln)	770	1210	1740	2135	2350
FFS =100km/h					
Maximum Density(pc/km/ln)	7	11	16	22	28
Minimum Speed(km/h)	100.0	100.0	100.0	93.8	82.1
Maximum v/c	0.30	0.48	0.70	0.90	1.00
Maximum Service Flow Rate(pc/h/ln)	700	1100	1600	2065	2300
FFS =90km/h					
Maximum Density(pc/km/ln)	7	11	16	22	28
Minimum Speed(km/h)	90.0	90.0	90.0	89.1	80.4
Maximum v/c	0.28	0.44	0.64	0.87	1.00
Maximum Service Flow Rate(pc/h/ln)	630	990	1440	1955	2250

Exhibit 6.2 LOS Criteria for Basic Freeway Segments

Criteria	LOS				
	A	B	C	D	E
FFS =75mile/h					
Maximum Density(pc/mile/ln)	11	18	26	35	45
Minimum Speed(mile/h)	75.0	74.8	70.6	62.2	53.3
Maximum v/c	0.34	0.56	0.76	0.90	1.00
Maximum Service Flow Rate(pc/h/ln)	820	1350	1830	2170	2400
FFS =70mile/h					
Maximum Density(pc/mile/ln)	11	18	26	35	45
Minimum Speed(mile/h)	70.0	70.0	68.2	61.5	53.3
Maximum v/c	0.32	0.53	0.74	0.90	1.00
Maximum Service Flow Rate(pc/h/ln)	770	1260	1770	2150	2400
FFS =65mile/h					
Maximum Density(pc/mi/ln)	11	18	26	35	45
Minimum Speed(mile/h)	65.0	65.0	64.6	59.7	52.2

Continued table

Criteria	LOS				
	A	B	C	D	E
FFS =65mile/h					
Maximum v/c	0.30	0.50	0.71	0.89	1.00
Maximum Service Flow Rate(pc/h/ln)	710	1170	1680	2090	2350
FFS =60mile/h					
Maximum Density(pc/mile/ln)	11	18	26	35	45
Minimum Speed(mile/h)	60.0	60.0	60.0	57.8	51.1
Maximum v/c	0.29	0.47	0.68	0.88	1.00
Maximum Service Flow Rate(pc/h/ln)	630	990	1440	1955	2250
FFS =55mile/h					
Maximum Density (pc/mile/ln)	11	18	26	35	45
Minimum Speed(mile/h)	55.0	55.0	55.0	54.7	50.0
Maximum v/c	0.27	0.44	0.64	0.85	1.00
Maximum Service Flow Rate(pc/h/ln)	600	990	1430	1910	2250

Exhibit 6.3 Passenger-Car Equivalents on Extended Freeway Segments

Factor	Type of Terrain		
	Level	Rolling	Mountainous
E_T(trucks and buses)	1.5	2.5	4.5
E_R(RVs)	1.2	2.0	4.0

Note: HCM 2000, Exhibit 23-8.

Exhibit 6.4 Passenger-Car Equivalents for Trucks and Buses on Upgrades

Upgrade (%)	Length (km)	E_T								
		Percentage of Trucks and Buses								
		2	4	5	6	8	10	15	20	25
<2	All	1.5	1.5	1.5	1.5	1.5	1.5	1.5	1.5	1.5
≥2 ~3	0.0 ~0.4	1.5	1.5	1.5	1.5	1.5	1.5	1.5	1.5	1.5
	>0.4 ~0.8	1.5	1.5	1.5	1.5	1.5	1.5	1.5	1.5	1.5
	>0.8 ~1.2	1.5	1.5	1.5	1.5	1.5	1.5	1.5	1.5	1.5
	>1.2 ~1.6	2.0	2.0	2.0	2.0	1.5	1.5	1.5	1.5	1.5
	>1.6 ~2.4	2.5	2.5	2.5	2.5	2.0	2.0	2.0	2.0	2.0
	>2.4	3.0	3.0	2.5	2.5	2.0	2.0	2.0	2.0	2.0

Continued table

Upgrade (%)	Length (km)	E_T Percentage of Trucks and Buses								
		2	4	5	6	8	10	15	20	25
>3~4	0.0~0.4	1.5	1.5	1.5	1.5	1.5	1.5	1.5	1.5	1.5
	>0.4~0.8	2.0	2.0	2.0	2.0	2.0	2.0	1.5	1.5	1.5
	>0.8~1.2	2.5	2.5	2.0	2.0	2.0	2.0	2.0	2.0	2.0
	>1.2~1.6	3.0	3.0	2.5	2.5	2.5	2.5	2.0	2.0	2.0
	>1.6~2.4	3.5	3.5	3.0	3.0	3.0	3.0	2.5	2.5	2.5
	>2.4	4.0	3.5	3.0	3.0	3.0	3.0	2.5	2.5	2.5
>4~5	0.0~0.4	1.5	1.5	1.5	1.5	1.5	1.5	1.5	1.5	1.5
	>0.4~0.8	3.0	2.5	2.5	2.5	2.0	2.0	2.0	2.0	2.0
	>0.8~1.2	3.5	3.0	3.0	3.0	2.5	2.5	2.5	2.5	2.5
	>1.2~1.6	4.0	3.5	3.5	3.5	3.0	3.0	3.0	3.0	3.0
	>1.6	5.0	4.0	4.0	4.0	3.5	3.5	3.0	3.0	3.0
>5~6	0.0~0.4	2.0	2.0	1.5	1.5	1.5	1.5	1.5	1.5	1.5
	>0.4~0.5	4.0	3.0	2.5	2.5	2.0	2.0	2.0	2.0	2.0
	>0.5~0.8	4.5	4.0	3.5	3.0	2.5	2.5	2.5	2.5	2.5
	>0.8~1.2	5.0	4.5	4.0	3.5	3.0	3.0	3.0	3.0	3.0
	>1.2~1.6	5.5	5.0	4.5	4.0	3.0	3.0	3.0	3.0	3.0
	>1.6	6.0	5.0	5.0	4.5	3.5	3.5	3.5	3.5	3.5
>6	0.0~0.4	4.0	3.0	2.5	2.5	2.5	2.5	2.0	2.0	2.0
	>0.4~0.5	4.5	4.0	3.5	3.5	3.5	3.0	2.5	2.5	2.5
	>0.5~0.8	5.0	4.5	4.0	4.0	3.5	3.0	2.5	2.5	2.5
	>0.8~1.2	5.5	5.0	4.5	4.5	4.0	3.5	3.0	3.0	3.0
	>1.2~1.6	6.0	5.5	5.0	5.0	4.5	4.0	3.5	3.5	3.5
	>1.6	7.0	6.0	5.5	5.5	5.0	4.5	4.0	4.0	4.0

Exhibit 6.5 Passenger-Car Equivalents for RVs on Upgrades

Upgrade (%)	Length (km)	E_R Percentage of RVs								
		2	4	5	6	8	10	15	20	25
<2	All	1.2	1.2	1.2	1.2	1.2	1.2	1.2	1.2	1.2
>2~3	0.0~0.8	1.2	1.2	1.2	1.2	1.2	1.2	1.2	1.2	1.2
	>0.8	3.0	1.5	1.5	1.5	1.5	1.5	1.2	1.2	1.2
>3~4	0.0~0.4	1.2	1.2	1.2	1.2	1.2	1.2	1.2	1.2	1.2
	>0.4~0.8	2.5	2.5	2.0	2.0	2.0	2.0	1.5	1.5	1.5
	>0.8	3.0	2.5	2.5	2.5	2.0	2.0	2.0	1.5	1.5

Continued table

Upgrade (%)	Length (km)	E_R Percentage of RVs							
		2	4	5	6	8	10	15	20	25
>4~5	0.0~0.4	2.5	2.0	2.0	2.0	1.5	1.5	1.5	1.5	1.5
	>0.4~0.8	4.0	3.0	3.0	3.0	2.5	2.5	2.0	2.0	2.0
	>0.8	4.5	3.5	3.0	3.0	3.0	2.5	2.5	2.0	2.0
>5	0.0~0.4	4.0	3.0	2.5	2.5	2.5	2.0	2.0	2.0	1.5
	>0.4~0.8	6.0	4.0	4.0	3.5	3.0	3.0	2.5	2.5	2.0
	>0.8	6.0	4.5	4.0	4.5	3.5	3.0	3.0	2.5	2.0

Exhibit 6.6 Passenger-Car Equivalents for Trucks and Buses on Downgrades

Downgrade(%)	Length(km)	E_T Percentage of Trucks			
		5	10	15	20
<4	All	1.5	1.5	1.5	1.5
4~5	≤6.4	1.5	1.5	1.5	1.5
4~5	>6.4	2.0	2.0	2.0	1.5
>5~6	≤6.4	1.5	1.5	1.5	1.5
>5~6	>6.4	5.5	4.0	4.0	3.0
>6	≤6.4	1.5	1.5	1.5	1.5
>6	>6.4	7.5	6.0	5.5	4.5

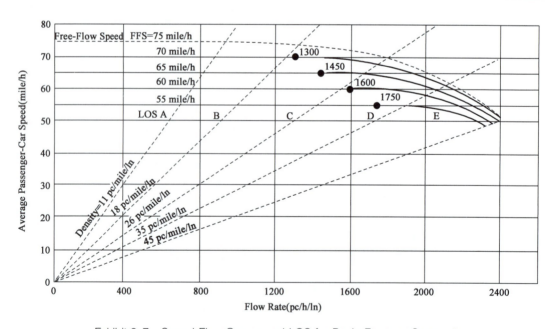

Exhibit 6.7 Speed-Flow Curves and LOS for Basic Freeway Segments

Note:1. Capacity varies by free-flow speed. Capacity is 2400,2350,2300,and 2250 pc/h/ln at free-flow speeds of 70 and greater,65,60,and 55 mile/h,respectively.

for $70 < FFS \leqslant 75$,
$(3400 - 30FFS) < v_p \leqslant 2400$

$$S = FFS - \left[\left(FFS - \frac{160}{3}\right)\left(\frac{v_p + 30FFS - 3400}{30FFS - 1000}\right)^{26}\right]$$

for $55 \leqslant FFS \leqslant 70$ and for flow rate (v_p),
$(3400 - 30FFS) < v_p \leqslant (1700 + 10FFS)$

$$S = FFS - \left[\frac{1}{9}(7FFS - 340)\left(\frac{v_p + 30FFS - 3400}{40FFS - 1700}\right)^{26}\right]$$

for $55 \leqslant FFS \leqslant 75$ and $v_p \leqslant (3400 - 30FFS)$,

$$S = FFS$$

2. HCM 2000, Exhibit 23-3.

Exhibit 6.8 Adjustment to Free-Flow Speed for Lane Width on a Freeway

Lane Width (ft)	Reduction in Free-Flow Speed, f_{LW} (mile/h)	Lane Width (ft)	Reduction in Free-Flow Speed, f_{LW} (mile/h)
≥12	0.0	10	6.6
11	1.9		

Note: HCM 2000, Exhibit 23-4, p. 23-6.

Exhibit 6.9 Adjustment to Free-Flow Speed for Lateral Clearance on a Freeway

Right Shoulder Lateral Clearance (ft)	Reduction in Free-Flow Speed, f_{LC} (mile/h)			
	Lanes in One Direction			
	2	3	4	≥5
≥6	0.0	0.0	0.0	0.0
5	0.6	0.4	0.2	0.1
4	1.2	0.8	0.4	0.2
3	1.8	1.2	0.6	0.3
2	2.4	1.6	0.8	0.4
1	2.0	2.0	1.0	0.5
0	3.6	2.4	1.2	0.6

Note: HCM 2000, Exhibit 23-5, p. 23-6.

Exhibit 6.10 Adjustment to Free-Flow Speed for Number of Lanes on a Freeway

Number of Lanes (in one direction)	Reduction in Free-Flow Speed, f_N (mile/h)
≥5	0.0
4	1.5
3	3.0
2	4.5

Note: ❶For all rural highways, $f_N = 0.0$ mile/h.
HCM 2000, Exhibit 23-6, p. 23-6.

---

❶ Lateral clearance:
(1) The total left-and right-side clearance from the outside edge of travel lanes to fixed obstructions on a multilane highway;
(2) the right-side clearance distance from the rightmost travel lane to fixed obstructions on a freeway.

Exhibit 6.11 Adjustment to Free-Flow Speed for Interchange Density on a Freeway

Interchanges Per Mile	Reduction in Free-Flow Speed, f_{ID} (mile/h)
≤0.50	0.0
0.75	1.3
1.00	2.5
1.25	3.7
1.50	5.0
1.75	8.3
2.00	7.5

Note: HCM 2000, Exhibit 23-7, p.23-7.

Exhibit 6.12 LOS Criteria for Multilane Highways

Free-Flow Speed (km/h)	Criteria	LOS				
		E	A	B	C	D
100	Maximum density (pc/km/ln)	7	11	16	22	25
	Average speed (km/h)	100.0	100.0	98.4	91.5	88.0
	Maximum volume to capacity ratio v/c	0.32	0.50	0.72	0.92	1.00
	Maximum service flow rate (pc/h/ln)	700	1100	1575	2015	2200
90	Maximum density (pc/km/ln)	7	11	16	22	26
	Average speed (km/h)	90.0	90.0	89.8	84.7	80.8
	Maximum v/c	0.30	0.47	0.68	0.89	1.00
	Maximum service flow rate (pc/h/ln)	630	990	1435	1860	2100
80	Maximum density (pc/km/ln)	7	11	16	22	27
	Average speed (km/h)	80.0	80.0	80.0	77.6	74.1
	Maximum v/c	0.28	0.44	0.64	0.85	1.00
	Maximum service flow rate (pc/h/ln)	560	880	1280	1705	2000
70	Maximum density (pc/km/ln)	7	11	16	22	28
	Average speed (km/h)	70.0	70.0	70.0	69.6	67.9
	Maximum v/c	0.26	0.41	0.59	0.81	1.00
	Maximum service flow rate (pc/h/ln)	490	770	1120	1530	1900

Note: The exact mathematical relationship between density and volume to capacity ratio (v/c) has not always been maintained at LOS boundaries because of the use of rounded values. Density is the primary determinant of LOS. LOS F is characterized by highly unstable and variable traffic flow. Prediction of accurate flow rate, density, and speed at LOS F is difficult.

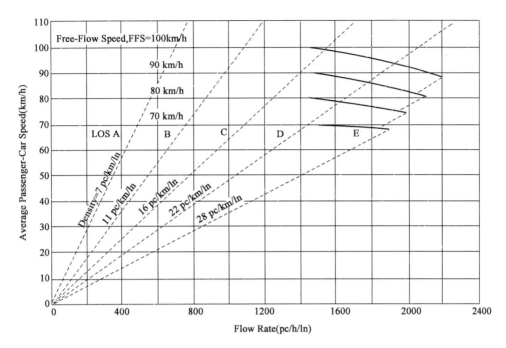

Exhibit 6.13 Speed-Flow Curves with LOS Criteria

Note: Maximum densities for LOS E occur at a v/c ratio of 1.0. They are 25, 26, 27, and 28 pc/km/ln at FFS of 100, 90, 80, and 70km/h, respectively. Capacity varies by FFS. Capacity is 2200, 2100, 2000, and 1900pc/h/ln at FFS of 100, 90, 80, and 70km/h; respectively.

for flow rate(v_0), $v_p > 1400$ and $90 < FFS \leq 100$ then

$$S = FFS - \left[\left(\frac{9.3}{25} FFS - \frac{630}{25} \right) \left(\frac{v_p - 1400}{15.7 FFS - 770} \right)^{1.31} \right]$$

for $v_p > 1400$ and $80 < FFS \leq 90$ then

$$S = FFS - \left[\left(\frac{10.4}{26} FFS - \frac{696}{26} \right) \left(\frac{v_p - 1400}{15.6 FFS - 704} \right)^{1.31} \right]$$

for $v_p > 1400$ and $70 < FFS \leq 80$ then

$$S = FFS - \left[\left(\frac{11.1}{27} FFS - \frac{728}{27} \right) \left(\frac{v_p - 1400}{15.9 FFS - 672} \right)^{1.31} \right]$$

for $v_p > 1400$ and $FFS = 70$ then

$$S = FFS - \left[\left(\frac{3}{28} FFS - \frac{75}{14} \right) \left(\frac{v_p - 1400}{25 FFS - 1250} \right)^{1.31} \right]$$

for $v_p \leq 1400$ then

$$S = FFS$$

Exhibit 6.14 Adjustment to Free-Flow Speed for Lane Width on a Multilane Highway

Lane Width (ft)	Reduction in Free-Flow Speed, f_{LW} (mile/h)	Lane Width (ft)	Reduction in Free-Flow Speed, f_{LW} (mile/h)
≥12	0.0	10	6.6
11	1.9		

Note: HCM 2000, Exhibit 21-4, p.21-5.

Exhibit 6.15 Adjustment to Free-Flow Speed for Total Lateral Clearance on a Multilane Highway

4-Lane Multilane Highway		6-Lane Multilane Highway	
Total Lateral Clearance (ft)	Reduction in Free-Flow Speed, f_{LC} (mile/h)	Total Lateral Clearance (ft)	Reduction in Free-Flow Speed, f_{LC} (mile/h)
≥12	0.0	≥12	0.0
10	0.4	10	0.4
8	0.9	8	0.9
6	1.3	6	1.3
4	1.8	4	1.7
2	3.6	2	2.8
0	5.4	0	3.9

Note: HCM 2000, Exhibit 21-5, p.21-6.

Exhibit 6.16 Adjustment to Free-Flow Speed for Median Type on a Multilane Highway

Median Type	Reduction in Free-Flow Speed, f_M (mile/h)	Median Type	Reduction in Free-Flow Speed, f_M (mile/h)
Undivided	1.6	Divided	0.0
TWLTL's❶	0.0		

Note: HCM 2000, Exhibit 21-6, p.21-6.

Exhibit 6.17 Access-Point Density Adjustment on a Multilane Highway

Access-Point(mile)	Reduction in Free-Flow Speed, f_A (mile/h)	Access-Point/(mile)	Reduction in Free-Flow Speed, f_A (mile/h)
0	0.0	30	7.5
10	2.5	≥40	10.0
20	5.0		

Note: HCM 2000, Exhibit 21-6, p.21-6.

Exhibit 6.18 Adjustment ($f_{d/np}$) for Combined Effect of Directional Distribution of Traffic and Percentage of No-Passing Zones on Percent Time-Spent-Following on Two-Way Segments

Two-Way Flow Rate v_p (pc/h)	Increase in Percent Time-Spent-Following(%)					
	No-Passing Zones(%)					
	0	20	40	60	80	100
	Directional Split =50/50					
≤200	0.0	10.1	17.2	20.2	21.0	21.8

❶TWLTL: Two-Way Left Turn Lane (median treatment on roadways that allows left turns from both directions).

Continued table

Two-Way Flow Rate v_p (pc/h)	Increase in Percent Time-Spent-Following (%)					
	No-Passing Zones (%)					
	0	20	40	60	80	100
Directional Split =50/50						
400	0.0	12.4	19.0	22.7	23.8	24.8
600	0.0	11.2	16.0	18.7	19.7	20.5
800	0.0	9.0	12.3	14.1	14.5	15.4
1400	0.0	3.6	5.5	6.7	7.3	7.9
2000	0.0	1.8	2.9	3.7	4.1	4.4
2600	0.0	1.1	1.6	2.0	2.3	2.4
3200	0.0	0.7	0.9	1.1	1.2	1.4

Note: HCM 2000, Exhibit 20-12.

Exhibit 6.19 Adjustment (f_{np}) for Effect of No-Passing Zones on Average Travel Speed on Two-Way Segments

Two-Way Demand Flow Rate, v_p (pc/h)	Reduction in Average Travel Speed (km/h)					
	No-Passing Zones (%)					
	0	20	40	60	80	100
0	0.0	0.0	0.0	0.0	0.0	0.0
200	0.0	1.0	2.3	3.8	4.2	5.6
400	0.0	2.7	4.3	5.7	6.3	7.3
600	0.0	2.5	3.8	4.9	5.5	6.2
800	0.0	2.2	3.1	3.9	4.3	4.9
1000	0.0	1.8	2.5	3.2	3.6	4.2
1200	0.0	1.3	2.0	2.6	3.0	3.4
1400	0.0	0.9	1.4	1.9	2.3	2.7
1600	0.0	0.9	1.3	1.7	2.1	2.4
1800	0.0	0.8	1.1	1.6	1.8	2.1
2000	0.0	0.8	1.0	1.4	1.6	1.8
2200	0.0	0.8	1.0	1.4	1.5	1.7
2400	0.0	0.8	1.0	1.3	1.5	1.7
2600	0.0	0.8	1.0	1.3	1.4	1.6
2800	0.0	0.8	1.0	1.2	1.3	1.4
3000	0.0	0.8	0.9	1.1	1.1	1.3
3200	0.0	0.8	0.9	1.0	1.0	1.1

Note: HCM 2000, Exhibit 20-11.

Exhibit 6.20 Grade Adjustment Factor (f_G) to Determine Speeds on Two-Way and Directional Segments

Range of Two-Way Flow Rates (pc/h)	Range of Directional Flow Rates (pc/h)	Type of Terrain	
		Level	Rolling
0~600	0~300	1.00	0.71
>600~1200	>300~600	1.00	0.93
>1200	>600	1.00	0.99

Note: HCM 2000, Exhibit 20-7.

Exhibit 6.21 Grade Adjustment Factor (f_G) to Determine Percent Time-Spent-Following on Two-Way and Directional Segments

Range of Two-Way Flow Rates (pc/h)	Range of Directional Flow Rates (pc/h)	Type of Terrain	
		Level	Rolling
0~600	0~300	1.00	0.77
>600~1200	>300~600	1.00	0.94
>1200	>600	1.00	1.00

Note: HCM 2000, Exhibit 20-8.

Exhibit 6.22 Passenger-Car Equivalents for Trucks and RVs to Determine Speeds on Two-Way and Directional Segments

Vehicle Type	Range of Two-Way Flow Rates (pc/h)	Range of Directional Flow Rates (pc/h)	Type of Terrain	
			Level	Rolling
Trucks, E_T	0~600	0~300	1.7	2.5
	>600~1200	>300~600	1.2	1.9
	>1200	>600	1.1	1.5
RVs, E_R	0~600	0~300	1.0	1.1
	>600~1200	>300~600	1.0	1.1
	>1200	>600	1.0	1.1

Note: HCM 2000, Exhibit 20-9.

Exhibit 6.23 Passenger-Car Equivalents for Trucks and RVs to Determine Percent Time-Spent-Following on Two-Way and Directional Segments

Vehicle Type	Range of Two-Way Flow Rates (pc/h)	Range of Directional Flow Rates (pc/h)	Type of Terrain	
			Level	Rolling
Trucks, E_T	0~600	0~300	1.1	1.8
	>600~1200	>300~600	1.1	1.5
	>1200	>600	1.0	1.0
RVs, E_R	0~600	0~300	1.0	1.0
	>600~1200	>300~600	1.0	1.0
	>1200	>600	1.0	1.0

Note: HCM 2000, Exhibit 20-10.

Exhibit 6.24 Adjustment(f_{LS}) for Lane Width and Shoulder Width

Lane Width(m)	Reduction in FFS(km/h)			
	Shoulder Width(m)			
	≥0.0, <0.6	≥0.6, <1.2	≥1.2, <1.8	≥1.8
2.7 <3.0	10.3	7.7	5.6	3.5
≥3.0 <3.3	8.5	5.9	3.8	1.7
≥3.3 <3.6	7.5	4.9	2.8	0.7
≥3.6	6.8	4.2	2.1	0.0

Note: HCM 2000, Exhibit 20-5.

Exhibit 6.25 Adjustment (f_A) for Access-Point Density

Access Point per kilometer	Reduction in FFS (km/h)	Access Point per kilometer	Reduction in FFS (km/h)
0	0.0	18	12.0
6	4.0	≥24	16.0
12	8.0		

Note: HCM 2000, Exhibit 20-6.

Exhibit 6.26 Capacity for Various Weaving Segments

Volume Ratio	(A) Type A Weaving Segments – 120km/h Free-Flow Speed				
	Length of Weaving Segment(m)				
	150	300	450	600	750[a]
Three-Lane Segments					
0.10	6050	6820	7200[c]	7200[c]	7200[c]
0.20	5490	6260	6720	7050	7200[b]
0.30	5040	5780	6240	6570	6830
0.40	4660	5380	5530	5800[c]	6050[c]
0.45[d]	4430	5000[c]	5270[c]	5550[c]	5800[c]
Four-Lane Segments					
0.10	8060	9010	9600[b]	9600[b]	9600[b]
0.20	7320	8340	8960	9400	9600[b]
0.30	6710	7520[c]	8090[c]	8510[c]	8840
0.35[e]	6370[c]	7160[c]	7700[c]	8000[f]	8000[f]
Five-Lane Segments					
0.10	10080	11380	12000[b]	12000[b]	12000[b]
0.20[g]	9150	10540[c]	11270[c]	11790[c]	12000[b]

Continued table

Volume Ratio	(B) Type A Weaving Segments – 110km/h Free-Flow Speed				
	Length of Weaving Segment(m)				
	150	300	450	600	750[a]
Three-Lane Segments					
0.10	5770	6470	6880	7050[b]	7050[b]
0.20	5250	5960	6280	6680	6900
0.30	4830	5520	5940	6240	6480
0.40	4480	5150	5250[c]	5530[c]	5760[c]
0.45[d]	4190	4790[c]	5020[c]	5310[c]	5530[c]
Four-Lane Segments					
0.10	7690	8630	9180	9400[b]	9400[b]
0.20	7000	7940	8500	8900	9200
0.30	6440	7180[c]	7710[c]	8090[c]	8390[c]
0.35[e]	6080[c]	6830[c]	7360[c]	7730[c]	8030[c]
Five-Lane Segments					
0.10	9610	10790	11470	11750[b]	11750[b]
0.20[g]	8750	10030[c]	10690[c]	11160[c]	11520[c]

Note: Used with permission of Transportation Research Board, National Research Council, HCM 2000, Exhibit 24-8, p24-10.
  a. Weaving segments longer than 750 m are treated as isolated merge and diverge areas using the procedures of Chapter 25, "Ramps and Ramp Junctions."
  b. Capacity constrained by basic freeway capacity.
  c. Capacity occurs under constrained operating conditions.
  d. Three-lane Type A segments do not operate well at volume ratios greater than 0.45. Poor operations and some local queuing are expected in such cases.
  e. Four-lane Type A segments do not operate well at volume ratios greater than 0.35. Poor operations and some local queuing are expected in such cases.
  f. Capacity constrained by maximum allowable weaving flow rate: 2800 pc/h (Type A), 4000 (Type B), 3500 (Type C).
  g. Five-lane Type A segments do not operate well at volume ratios greater than 0.20. Poor operations and some local queuing are expected in such cases.
  h. Type B weaving segments do not operate well at volume ratios greater than 0.80. Poor operations and some local queuing are expected in such cases.
  i. Type C weaving segments do not operate well at volume ratios greater than 0.50. Poor operations and some local queuing are expected in such cases.

Exhibit 6.27 Capacity Values for Merge Areas

Freeway Free-Flow Speed (km/h)	Maximum Downstream Freeway Flow v (pc/h)				Max Desirable Flow Entering Influence Area, v_{R12} (pc/h)
	Number of Lanes in One Direction				
	2	3	4	>4	
120	4800	7200	9600	2400/ln	4600
110	4700	7050	9400	2350/ln	4600
100	4600	6900	9200	2300/ln	4600
90	4500	6750	9000	2250/ln	4600

Note: HCM 2000, Exhibit 25-7, p25-9.

Exhibit 6.28 Capacity Values for Diverge Areas

Freeway Free-Flow Speed (km/h)	Maximum Upstream, v_{F1} or Downstream Freeway Flow v (pc/h)				Max Flow Entering Influence Area, v_{12} (pc/h)
	Number of Lanes in One Direction				
	2	3	4	>4	
120	4800	7200	9600	2400/ln	4400
110	4700	7050	9400	2350/ln	4400
100	4600	6900	9200	2300/ln	4400
90	4500	6750	9000	2250/ln	4400

Note: (1) For capacity of off-ramp roadways, see Exhibit 25-3.
(2) HCM 2000, Exhibit 25-14, p.25-14.

Exhibit 6.29 LOS Criteria for Weaving Segments (Metric)

LOS	Density (pc/km/ln)	
	Freeway Weaving Segment	Multilane and Collector-Distributor Weaving Segments
A	≤6.0	≤8.0
B	>6.0 ~12.0	>8.0 ~15.0
C	>12.0 ~17.0	>15.0 ~20.0
D	>17.0 ~22.0	>20.0 ~23.0
E	>22.0 ~27.0	>23.0 ~25.0
F	>27.0	>25.0

Note: HCM 2000, Exhibit 24-2, p. 24-3.

Exhibit 6.30 LOS Criteria for Weaving Segments

LOS	Density (pc/mi/ln)	
	Freeway Weaving Segment	Multilane and Collector-Distributor Weaving Segments
A	≤10.0	≤12.0
B	>10.0 ~20.0	>12.0 ~24.0
C	>20.0 ~28.0	>24.0 ~32.0
D	>28.0 ~35.0	>32.0 ~36.0
E	>35.0 ~43.0	>36.0 ~40.0
F	>43.0	>40.0

Exhibit 6.31 LOS Criteria for Merge and Diverge Areas

LOS	Density(pc/km/ln)	LOS	Density(pc/km/ln)
A	≤6.0	D	>17~22
B	>6~12	E	>22
C	>12~17	F	Demand exceeds capacity

Note: HCM 2000, Exhibit 25-4, p.25-5.

Exhibit 6.32 Criteria for Unconstrained Versus Constrained Operation of Weaving Segments
[L is length of the weaving segment (m)]

Configuration	Number of Lanes Required for Unconstrained Operation N_w	$N_W(max)$
Type A	$1.21(N)V_R^{0.571}L^{0.234}/S_w^{0.438}$	1.4
Type B	$N[0.085+0.703V_R+(71.57/L)-0.0112(S_{nw}-S_w)]$	3.5
Type C	$N[0.761+0.047V_R-0.00036L-0.0031(S_{nw}-S_w)]$	3.0[a]

Note: HCM 2000, Exhibit 24-7, p.24-8.
a. For two-sided weaving segments, all freeway lanes may be used by weaving vehicles.

Exhibit 6.33 Constants for Computation of Weaving Intensity Factors

General Form								
$W_i = \dfrac{a(1+V_R)^b \left(\dfrac{v}{N}\right)^c}{(3.28L)^d}$ (L is in meter)				$W_i = \dfrac{a(1+V_R)^b \left(\dfrac{v}{N}\right)^c}{L^d}$ (L is in feet)				
	Constants for Weaving Speed, S_w				Constants for Nonweaving Speed, S_{nw}			
	a	b	c	d	a	b	c	d
Type A Configuration								
Unconstrained	0.15	2.2	0.97	0.80	0.0035	4.0	1.3	0.75
Constrained	0.35	2.2	0.97	0.80	0.0020	4.0	1.3	0.75
Type B Configuration								
Unconstrained	0.08	2.2	0.70	0.50	0.0020	6.0	1.0	0.50
Constrained	0.15	2.2	0.70	0.50	0.0010	6.0	1.0	0.50
Type C Configuration								
Unconstrained	0.08	2.3	0.80	0.60	0.0020	6.0	1.1	0.60
Constrained	0.14	2.3	0.80	0.60	0.0010	6.0	1.1	0.60

Note: HCM 2000, Exhibit 24-6, p24-6.

Exhibit 6.34 Models for Predicting v_{12} at On-Ramps

$v_{12}=v_F \cdot P_{FM}$	
v_F, v_R, v_{12}, and v_D are in pc/h; L_A, L_{up}, and L_{down} are in meters; S_{FR} is in km/h	
For 4-lane freeways (2 lanes each direction)	$P_{FM}=1.000$
For 6-lane freeways (3 lanes each direction)	$P_{FM}=0.5775+0.000092L_A$ (Equation1) $P_{FM}=0.7289-0.0000135(v_F+v_R)-0.002048S_{FR}+0.0002L_{UP}$ (Equation2) $P_{FM}=0.5478+0.0801v_D/L_{down}$ (Equation3)
For 8-lane freeways (4 lanes each direction)	$P_{FM}=0.2178-0.000125v_R+0.05887L_A/S_{FR}$ (Equation4)

Note: HCM 2000, Exhibit 25-5, p.25-6.

Exhibit 6.35 Models for Predicting v_{12} at Off-Ramps

$$v_{12} = v_R + (v_F - v_R)P_{FD}$$
v_F, v_R, v_{12}, and v_D are in pc/h; L_D, L_{up} and L_{down} are in meters

For 4-lane freeways (2 lanes each direction)	$P_{FD} = 1.00$	
For 6-lane freeways (3 lanes each direction)	$P_{FD} = 0.760 - 0.000025 v_F - 0.00004 v_R$ $P_{FD} = 0.717 - 0.000039 v_F + 0.184 v_U/L_{up}$ $P_{FD} = 0.616 - 0.000021 v_F + 0.038 v_D/L_{down}$	(Equation 5) (Equation 6) (Equation 7)
For 8-lane freeways (4 lanes each direction)	$P_{FD} = 0.436$	(Equation 8)

Note: HCM 2000, Exhibit 25-12, p.25-12.

Exhibit 6.36 Approximate Capacity for Ramp Roadways

Free-Flow Speed of Ramp, S_{FR}(km/h)	Capacity (pc/h)	
	Single-Lane Ramps	Two-Lane Ramps
>80	2200	4400
>65~80	2100	4100
>50~65	2000	3800
≥30~50	1900	3500
<30	1800	3200

Note: HCM 2000, Exhibit 25-3, p.25-4.

Key points of the chapter

1. Definitions of capacity and level of service and their relationship.

2. Define the basic segment of freeway, and what measure of effectiveness is used to determine the level of service?

3. The concept of v/c ratio and its implication.

4. What is free flow speed? Indicate the factors influencing the free flow speed (for freeway and multilane highway).

5. Why has maximum service flow rate been proposed?

6. What are the basic steps of conducting operational analysis (estimation of level of service) and design analysis (estimation of number of lanes)?

7. Analytical procedure of capacity for two-lane highway.

8. Be aware of the basic segment, merge, diverge and weaving areas of freeways.

本章要点

1. 如何定义通行能力和服务水平？两者之间有何关系？
2. 高速公路的基本路段定义是什么？其服务水平的度量指标有哪些？
3. 叙述负荷度的概念。
4. 自由流速度定义是什么？影响自由流速度的因素有哪些？（对应高速公路和多车道公路）。
5. 为什么提出最大服务流率(流量)指标？
6. 简述运营分析(得出服务水平)和设计分析(计算车道数)的基本步骤。
7. 简述双车道公路的通行能力分析步骤。
8. 简述合流、分流及交织区的概念。

Chapter 7 Fundamentals of Intersection Design

Intersections are considered the most important part of roadway network. Intersection control plays key role to guarantee the safe and smooth movement of conflicting traffic. In this chapter the hierarchy of the intersection controls is first elaborated, followed by introducing capacity and level of service of unsignalized intersections. Basic concept of intersection signalization and general steps of signal timing are briefly discussed at the end of this chapter.

Intersection is regarded as the bottleneck in urban street network. Based on definition given in Green Book (USA), an intersection is the general area where two or more highways join or cross, including the roadway and roadside facilities for traffic movements within it. The critical task of the traffic engineer is to manage the conflicts occurred at intersections in a manner that ensures safety and provides for efficient movement through the intersection for both motorists and pedestrians. Three topics will be discussed in this chapter including: types of intersection control; basic principles of intersection signalization; fundamentals of signal timing and design. The intersection we are going to discuss is *at-grade intersection* (平面交叉口).

7.1 Introduction to Intersection Control

7.1.1 Types of Intersection

Generally, intersections can be divided into following three types.

7.1.1.1 *At-grade Intersection*(平交)

At-grade intersection is an intersection where two or more highways meet at the same level. If there are N highways meeting at an intersection this intersection is called N-leg intersection. There are two types of at-grade intersection: unsignalized and signalized. Figure 7.1 provides a photo of a typical four-legs signalized intersection.

Figure 7.1 At-grade intersection (four legs)

7.1.1.2 Grade Separation or Interchange(立交)

Grade separation or interchange refers to an intersection where two or more highways meet at different level. This kind of intersection can, to the greatest extent, segregate the traffic conflicts from different directions. An interchange can have many forms depending on the design and layout of its ramps. Figure 7.2 presents an interchange without ramp and with ramps, respectively.

Figure 7.2 Interchange without ramp (left) and interchange with ramp (right)

7.1.1.3 *Roundabout* (or *circle* 环岛)

Roundabout is a circular intersection that provides a circular traffic pattern with significant reduction in the crossing conflict points. This type of intersection is popularly used in United Kingdom. Figure 7.3 shows a small sized roundabout and a mini-roundabout.

Figure 7.3 Roundabout(left:Dual mini-roundabouts)

7.1.2 Hierarchy of At-grade Intersection Control

There are three levels in the determination of hierarchy of an at-grade intersection control.

(1) Level I: basic rules of the road.

(2) Level II: direct assignment of right-of-way using YIELD or STOP signs.

(3) Level III: traffic signalization.

7.1.2.1 Level I——*Basic Rule of Road*(基本通行规则)

For level I intersection control there is no any form of control devices provided at the approaches of intersection and drivers have to pass intersection based on the following rules.

(1) Drivers on the left must yield to the driver on the right;
(2) Through vehicles have the right-of-way over turning vehicles;
(3) *Concept of sight triangle* (视距三角形)(Figure 7.4).

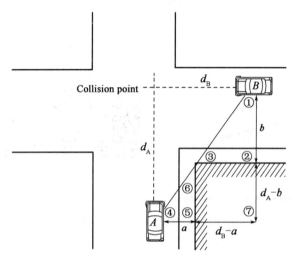

Figure 7.4 Sight Triangle at an Intersection

It is worth noticing that sight triangle is dynamic. AASHTO suggests that both drivers should be able to stop before reaching the collision point when they first see each other.

$$d_A (\text{and } d_B) \geqslant d = 0.278 S_i t + \frac{S_i^2 - S_f^2}{254(F \pm G)} \quad (7\text{-}1)$$

This type of intersection is only used when the traffic is very light or very few pedestrians cross the intersection. From traffic design perspective this type of intersection is not recommended, otherwise.

7.1.2.2 Level II ——YIELD & STOP Control

For level II intersection control there are three types: two-way STOP, YIELD and full-way STOP.

(1) Two-way STOP sign control (TWSC)

Two-way STOP(二路停车) is applied at an unsignalized intersection where a major road and a minor road meet. STOP signs are installed on the minor road only as shown in Figure 7.5. Vehicles on the major road have right-of-way to pass the intersection, while vehicles on the minor road need to stop at stop line waiting for the available gaps. Warrants for the two-way STOP sign are based MUTCD (Manual on Uniform Traffic Control Devices) as indicated in Table 7.1.

Table 7.1 Warrants for Two-Way STOP Control

STOP signs should not be used unless engineering judgment indicates that one or more of the following conditions are met:
a. Intersection of a less important road with a main road where application of the normal right-of-way rule would not be expected to provide reasonably safe operation.
b. Street entering a through highway or street.
c. Unsignalized intersection in a signalized area.
d. High speeds, restricted view, or crash records indicate a need for control by the STOP sign.

Note: U.S Dept. of Transportation, Manual on Uniform Traffic Control Devices, Millennium Edition, Washington DC, 2000, p.2B-8.

Two-way STOP sign has following features.

①It is the most popular-used control method at unsignalized intersections where major and minor roadways are met.

②The STOP signs are installed at approaches on minor street.

③Vehicles on major street pass intersection without stopping, while vehicles on minor street have to stop first and then use gap to pass intersection.

It should be pointed out that there is still no similar warranty used in dictating the application of two-way STOP signs in China and it is hoped that MUTCD with Chinese characteristics will be published.

(2) YIELD sign control

YIELD sign is only used for the major-minor roadway by assigning right-of-way to the major uncontrolled street. YIELD signs are installed at approaches on minor streets vehicles on major street pass intersection without stopping, while vehicles on minor street have to slow down first and then use gap to pass intersection.

Sight distance, when using a YIELD sign, should be at least as good as those required for application of basic rules of the road. Warrants for YIELD sign is contained in Table 7.2.

Table 7.2 Warrants for YEILD Control

YIELD signs may be installed:
a. When the ability to see all potentially conflicting traffic is sufficient to allow a road use traveling at the posted speed, 85th percentile speed, or the statutory speed to pass through the intersection or stop in a safe manner.
b. If controlling a merge-type movement on the entering roadway where acceleration geometry or sight distance is not adequate for merging traffic operations.
c. At a second crossroad of a divided highway, where the median width is 30ft or grater. A STOP sign may be installed at the entrance to the first roadway of a divided highway, and a YIELD sign may be installed at the entrance to the second roadway.
d. At an intersection where a special problem exists and where engineering judgment indicates that the problem is susceptible to correction by use of a YIELD sign

Note: U.S. Dept. of Transportation, Manual on Uniform Traffic Control Devices, Millennium Edition, Washington DC, 2001, p. 2B-12.

(3) *Multi-way* (*Full-way*, or *All-way*) (全路停车) STOP sign control

In general, a full-way STOP sign control is applied where all same-level roadways meet. STOP signs are installed on the approaches of all roadways. Any vehicle from any roadway approaching intersection must stop first, then driver follows first-come-first-go rule to pass intersection. Warranty for the installation of full-way STOP sign is given in Table 7.3. The criteria used in warranty come from interim measure for signal control, crash history, and volumes.

Table 7.3 Warrants for Multi-way STOP Control

The following criteria should be considered in the engineering study for a multi-way STOP sign:
a. Where traffic control signals are justified, the multi way STOP is an interim measure that can be installed quickly to control traffic while arrangements are being made for the installation of the traffic control signal.
b. A crash problem, as indicated by five or more reported crashes in a 12 month period that are susceptible to correction by a multi way STOP installation. Such crashes include right and left turn collisions as well as right-angle collisions.
c. Minimum volumes: 1. The vehicular volume entering the intersection from the major street approaches (total of both approaches) averages at least 300 veh/h for any eight hours of an average day.   2. The combined vehicular, pedestrian, and bicycle volume entering the intersection from the minor street approaches (total of both approaches) averages at least 200 units/h for the same eight hours, with an average delay to minor street vehicular traffic of at least 30 s/veh during the highest hour.   3. If the 85th percentile approach speed of the major highway exceeds 40 mile, the minimum vehicular volume warrants are 70% of the above values.
d. Where no single criterion is satisfied, but where criteria *B*, *C*1, and *C*2 are all satisfied to 80% of the minimum values. Criterion *C*3 is excluded from this condition.

Note: U.S Dept. of Transportation, Manual on Uniform Traffic Control Devices, Millennium Edition, Washington DC, 2001, p. 2B-10.

Figure 7.5 shows all-way STOP signs. For two-way STOP sign there is no word under the octagonal board. For all-way STOP sign "4-Way" or "All Way" can be worded.

Figure 7.5 All Way STOP Signs at Intersection

7.1.2.3 Level III——Traffic Control Signals

The ultimate form of intersection control is the traffic signal. Because signal can alternately assign right-of-way to specific movements, it can substantially reduce the number of conflicts between vehicles. However, signal has demerit compared to other control form. The following is given to demonstrate the advantages and disadvantages of installing traffic signals at intersections.

The advantages are:

(1) provide orderly movement;

(2) enhance traffic-handling capacity;

(3) reduce frequency and severity of crashes;

(4) coordinate continuous movement along arterial;

(5) protect pedestrians and bikers.

The disadvantages are:

(1) excessive delay;

(2) disobedience of the signal indications if not properly designed;

(3) encourage *cut-through traffic*(穿行交通);

(4) increase of rear-end collisions.

The warrants for traffic signals are as follows:

It is required in MUTCD that a comprehensive engineering study be conducted to determine whether or not installation of a signal is justified. In addition, an engineering judgment also plays an important role in the determination of signal installation. It should be noted that signals should be installed only where no other solution or form of control would be effective in assuring safety and efficiency at the intersection.

Some basic principles are summarized as follows:

(1) Volume principle:

①twelve-hour volume(in China);

②eight-hour volume;

③four-hour volume;

④peak hour volume.

(2) Pedestrian and cyclist principle;

(3) School crossing principle;

(4) System coordination principle;

(5) Crash principle.

7.1.2.4　Volume Principle

Vehicular volume at intersection is considered the main element that dictates the installation of signal. When the volume reaches a certain level it is necessary to consider installation of a signal. Twelve-hour volume in a day is one warrant to applied in China; whereas eight-hour, four-hour and peak hour volume is used in the USA as the warrant of signal installation.

7.1.2.5 Pedestrian and Cyclist Principle

When the vehicular traffic volume on a major is so heavy that pedestrians or bicycle riders experience excessive delay in passing the intersection, signal installation is warranted from safety perspective.

7.1.2.6 School Crossing Principle

In many places of the USA school zones are designated with provision of flashing beacon and speed limit sign to ensure safe crossing for school kids.

7.1.2.7 System Coordination Principle

Progressive movement in a coordinated signal system often requires that a traffic signal be installed at intersections where they would not otherwise be needed based on volume or other principles in order to maintain proper platooning of vehicles. In a word, signal may be installed at an unwarranted intersection based on requirement of system coordination.

7.1.2.8 Crash Principle

Traffic accident data can be used to determine if intersection is warranted to place a signal. This principle indicates that when accident frequency or severity has failed to decline by management and enforcement at the intersection a signal would be considered.

In conclusion, no signal should be placed without an engineering study, indicating that the criteria of at least one of the warrants are met. However, meeting one or more of these warrants does not necessitate signalization. Engineering judgment should be exercised at any rate in case studies.

7.1.3 Capacity Analysis of TWSC Intersection

Unlike the definition of capacity for basic segment of freeway the capacity of TWSC intersection refers to possible maximum flow of traffic movement that can pass the intersection. This maximum flow varies depending on the traffic flow rate of higher-priority movement. Therefore, capacity of TWSC intersection denotes to the potential maximum flow rate for a specific movement that can pass intersection. This specific movement includes: left turns from major roadway and all movements from minor roadways. This potential maximum flow rate is often called potential capacity.

To estimate capacity of unsignalized intersection it is necessary to identify the priority of movement of unsignalized intersection, come up with equation, and determine related parameters in the equation.

7.1.3.1 Priority of Movements

The priority of movements of TWSC intersection is defined as the ranking of right-of-way among all movements at intersection as indicated in Figure 7.6. From Figure 7.6 it is seen that through traffic on the major roadways enjoys the highest ranking of right-of-way, whereas left turns on the minor roadways have the lowest ranking of right-of-way.

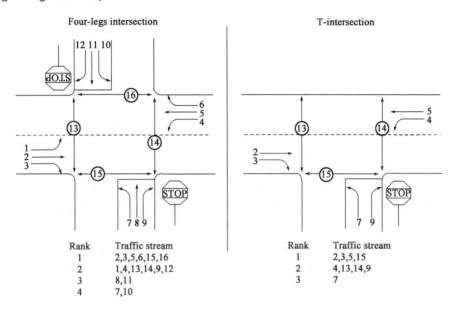

Figure 7.6 Ranking of Traffic Streams at a TWSC Intersection

Note:HCM 2000, Exhibit 17-3.

7.1.3.2 Potential Capacity Equation

Traditionally, traffic flow approaching intersection is in accord with Poisson distribution. The potential capacity of lower-ranking movement X can be estimated based on the following equation.

$$c_{px} = v_{cx} \left[\frac{e^{-(v_{cx} \times t_{cx}/3600)}}{1 - e^{-(v_{cx} \times t_{fx}/3600)}} \right] \tag{7-2}$$

Where: c_{px}——potential capacity of movement x(veh/h);

v_{cx}——conflicting flow for movement x (veh/h);

t_{cx}——critical gap for movement x(s);

t_{fx}——follow-up time for movement x(s).

Equation(7-2) is justified under the assumption that all conflicting flows arrive at intersection in accord with Poisson distribution.

It is needed to discuss conflicting volume, critical gap and follow-up time in order to calculate capacity of movement.

Conflicting volume is defined as the traffic that will conflict with movements of interest. The more the conflicting volume for a particular movement is, the less the potential capacity of that movement because of fewer available critical gaps. The determination of conflicting volume for any movement of interest is given in Table 7.4.

Table 7.4 Computation of Conflicting Volumes

Subject Movement	Subject and Conflicting Movements Conflicting Traffic Flows, $v_{c,s}$	
Major LT (1,4)	$V_{c1} = V_5 + V_6^{(a)} + V_{16}$	$V_{c4} = V_2 + V_3^{(a)} + V_{15}$
Minor RT (9,12)	$V_{c9} = \dfrac{V_2^{(b)}}{N} + 0.5 V_3^{(c)} + V_{14} + V_{15}$	$V_{c12} = \dfrac{V_5^{(b)}}{N} + 0.5 V_5^{(c)} + V_{13} + V_{16}$
Minor TH (8,11)	Stage I $V_{c8I} = 2V_1 + V_2 + 0.5 V_3^{(c)} + V_{15}$ $V_{c8II} = 2V_4 + V_5 + 0.56 V_6^{(a)} + V_{16}$	$V_{c11I} = 2V_4 + V_5 + 0.5 V_6^{(c)} + V_{16}$ Stage II $V_{c11II} = 2V_1 + V_2 + V_3^{(a)} + V_{15}$
Major LT (J,10)	Stage I $V_{c7I} = 2V_1 + V_2 + 0.5 V_3^{(c)} + V_{15}$ Stage II $V_{c7II} = 2V_4 + \dfrac{V_5}{N} + 0.5 V_6^{(d)} + 0.5 V_{12}^{(e,f)} + 0.5 V_{11} + V_{13}$	$V_{c10I} = 2V_4 + V_5 + 0.5 V_6^{(c)} + V_{16}$ $V_{c10II} = 2V_1 + \dfrac{V_5}{N} + 0.5 V_3^{(d)} + 0.5 V_9^{(e,f)} + 0.5 V_8 + V_{14}$

Note:1. Highway Capacity Manual, 4th Edition, Washington DC, 2000, Exhibit 17-2, p. 17-2.
2. If right-turning traffic from the major street is separated by a triangular island and has to comply with a YIELD or STOP sign, v_6 and v_3 need not be considered.
3. If there is more than one lane on the major street, the flow rates in the right lane are assumed to be v_2/N or v_5/N where N is the number of though lanes. The user can specify a different lane distribution if field data is available.
4. If there is a right-turn lane on the major street, v_3 or v_6 should not be considered.
5. Omit the farthest right turn, v_3, for Subject M_{vt} 7 or v_6 for subject M_{vt} 7 if the major street is multilane.
6. If right-turning traffic from the minor street is separated by a triangular island and has to comply with a YIELD or STOP sign, v_9 and v_{12} need not be considered.
7. Omit v_9 and v_{12} for multilane sites, or use 1/2 their values if the minor approach is flared.

The critical gap(临界间隙 t_{cx}) is defined as the minimum average acceptable gap that allows intersection entry for one minor-street (or major-street left turn) vehicle. The gap is measured as the clear time in the traffic stream defined by all of the conflicting movements.

The follow-up time(随车时距 t_{fx}) is defined as the minimum average acceptable time for a second queued minor-street vehicle to use a gap large enough to admit two or more vehicles to transverse.

Table 7.5 shows base or unadjusted values of the critical gap and follow-up time for various movements.

Table 7.5 Base Critical Gap and Follow-Up Times

Vehicle Movement	Base Critical Gap, t_{cb}(s)		Base Follow-Up Times, t_{fb}(s)
	Two-Lane Major Street	Four-Lane Major Street	
LT from Major Street	4.1	4.1	2.2
RT from Minor Street	6.2	6.9	3.3
TH from Minor Street	6.5	6.5	4.0
LT from Minor Street	7.1	7.5	3.5

Note: HCM 2000, Exhibit 17-5 p. 17-7.

It should be noted here that critical gaps and follow-up time are obtained from field observations. Either Raff's or Logit model can be used to determined critical gap. Raff's model needs to measure the two kinds of gap, which are rejected gap and accepted gap. The point of intersection of cumulative rejected and accepted curve is the point of critical gap(Figure 7.7). However, Logit model only needs accepted gap data. The critical gap is located on cumulative accepted curve of the 50% cumulative probability(Figure 7.8).

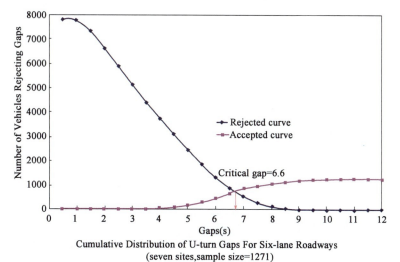

Cumulative Distribution of U-turn Gaps For Six-lane Roadways
(seven sites, sample size=1271)

Figure 7.7 Critical Gap Determined by Raff's Model

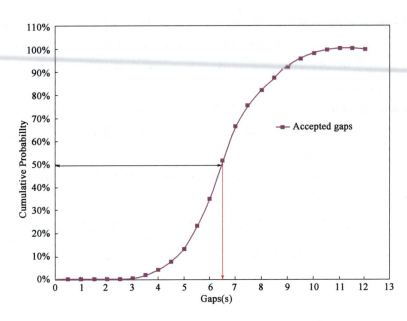

Figure 7.8 Critical Gap Determined by Logit Model

Base critical gaps and follow-up times as presented in Table 7.5 must be adjusted to account for a number of conditions, including heavy-vehicle presence, grade, and the existence of two-stage gap acceptance.

$$t_{cx} = t_{cb} + t_{cHV}P_{HV} + t_{cG}G - t_{cT} - t_{3LT}$$
$$t_{fx} = t_{fb} + t_{fHV}P_{HV}$$
(7-3)

Where: t_{cx}——critical gap for movement x(s);

t_{fx}——follow-up time for movement x(s);

t_{cb}——base critical gap from Table 7.5;

t_{cHV}——critical gap adjustment factor for heavy vehicles(s);

P_{HV}——Proportion of heavy vehicles;

t_{cG}——critical gap adjustment factor for grade(s);

G——grade, decimal or percent/100;

t_{cT}——critical gap adjustment factor for two-stage gap acceptance(s);

t_{3LT}——critical gap adjustment factor for intersection geometry(s);

t_{fb}——base follow up time from Table 7.5;

t_{fHV}——follow up time adjustment factor for heavy vehicles(s).

Adjustment factors are summarized in table 7.6.

Table 7.6 Adjustment factors for Base Critical Gap and Follow-Up Times

Adjustment Factor		Values(s)
t_{cHV}	1.0	Two-lane major streets
	2.0	Four-lane major streets

Cont inued table

Adjustment Factor		Values(s)
t_{cG}	0.1	Movements 9 and 12
	0.2	Movements 7,8,10 and 11
	1.0	Otherwise
t_{cT}	1.0	First or second stage of two-stage process
	0.0	For one-stage process
t_{3LT}	0.7	Minor-street LT at T-intersection
	0.0	Otherwise
t_{fHV}	0.9	Two-lane major streets
	1.0	Four-lane major streets

Note: Two-stage gap acceptance occurs where the major street has a median wide enough to store one or more vehicles. In such case, drivers treat crossing the directional roadways as separate operations, and the amount of median storage affects overall operation.

Example 7.1 For TWSC Intersection Analysis

AT-intersection is STOP-controlled as shown in Figure 7.9. Calculate the potential capacity of the T-intersection.

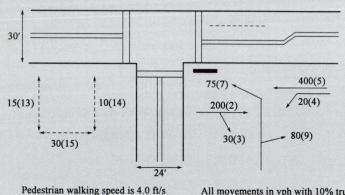

Pedestrian walking speed is 4.0 ft/s
Movement numbers are in parentheses.
There are no signals within 0.25 miles.

All movements in vph with 10% trucks.
No grades.
Peak 15-min flow rates shown.

Figure 7.9 A STOP-controlled T-intersection

Solution:

Step 1 Calculate the Potential Capacity of the T-intersection.

From Table 7.9 it can be seen that:

(1) Major street left turn (Rank 2, v_4) conflicts with vehicle movements 2 and 3 and pedestrian movement 15.

(2) Minor-street right turn (Rank 2, v_9) conflicts with vehicle movements 2 and 3 and pedestrian movements 14 and 15.

(3) Minor-street left turn (rank 3, v_7) conflicts with vehicle movements 2, 3, 4, and 5 and pedestrian movements 13 and 15.

Using Table 7.4:

$v_{c4} = v_2 + v_3 + v_{15} = 200 + 30 + 30 = 260 \text{(veh/h)}$

$v_{c9} = v_2/N + 0.5v_3 + v_{14} + v_{15} = 200/1 + 0.5 \times 30 + 10 + 30 = 255 \text{(veh/h)}$

$v_{c7} = 2v_4 + v_5/N + v_{13} + v_2 + 0.5v_3 + v_{15}$

$= 2 \times 20 + 400/1 + 15 + 200 + 0.5 \times 30 + 30 = 700 \text{(veh/h)}$

Note that in the computation of v_{c7} for a T-intersection, the values of v_1, v_6, v_{11}, and v_{12} are "0," causing these terms to disappear from the computation.

Step 2 Find Critical Gaps and Follow-Up Times for Each Movement.

Critical gaps are as follows:

$$t_c = t_{cb} + t_{cHV}P_{HV} + t_{cG}G - t_{cT} - t_{3LT}$$

Base critical gaps are found in Table 7.5; adjustments are found in Table 7.6.

t_{cb} = 4.1s (movement 4); 6.2s (movement 9); 7.1s (movement 7)

t_{cHV} = 1.0 for all movements (two-lane major street)

P_{HV} = 0.10 for all movements

t_{cG} = 0.1 for movement 9; 0.2 for movement 7; 1.0 for movement 4

G = 0.0 for all movements

t_{cT} = 0.0 for all movements (only one-stage gap acceptance present)

t_{3LT} = 0.7 for movement 7; 0.0 for movements 4 and 9

$t_{c4} = 4.1 + 1.0(0.10) + 1.0(0.0) - 0.0 - 0.0 = 4.2(s)$

$t_{c9} = 6.9 + 1.0(0.10) + 0.1(0.0) - 0.0 - 0.0 = 6.3(s)$

$t_{c7} = 7.1 + 1.0(0.10) + 0.2(0.0) - 0.0 - 0.7 = 6.5(s)$

Following-up times are as follows:

$$t_f = t_{fb} + t_{fHV}P_{HV}$$

Base follow-up times are found in Table 7.5; adjustments are found in Table 7.6.

t_{fb} = 2.2s (movement 4); 3.3s (movement 9); 3.5s (movement 7)

t_{fHV} = 0.9 for all movements

P_{HV} = 0.10 for all movements

$t_{c4} = 2.2 + 0.9(0.10) = 2.29(s)$

$t_{c9} = 3.3 + 0.9(0.10) = 3.39(s)$

$t_{c7} = 3.5 + 0.9(0.10) = 3.59(s)$

Step 3 Compute Potential Capacities.

Potential capacities are then computed by plugging conflicting volumes, critical gaps, and follow-up times in Equation (7-2),

$$C_{px} = V_{cx} \frac{e^{-(V_{cx}t_{cx}/3600)}}{1 - e^{-(V_{cx}t_{fx}/3600)}}$$

This computation is carried out in Table 7.7.

Table 7.7 Potential Capacities Results for Example 7.1

Movement	v_{cx}(veh/h)	t_c(s)	t_f(s)	v_{px}(veh/h)
4	260	4.2	2.29	1259
9	255	6.3	3.39	765
7	700	6.5	3.59	394

Thus, the potential capacities of left turn from major road, right turn from minor road and left turn from minor are 1259, 765, and 394, respectively.

7.1.3.3 Level-of-Service

Level-of-service criteria of TWSC intersection are based on control delays of vehicles of lower-ranking movements and are shown in Table 7.8.

Table 7.8 Level-of-Service Criteria for TWSC Intersections

Level of Service	Average Control Delay (s/veh)
A	0 ~ 10
B	>10 ~ 15
C	>15 ~ 25
D	>25 ~ 35
E	>35 ~ 50
F	>50

Note: HCM 2000, Exhibit 17-2 p. 17-2.

Control delays are computed by plugging flow rate of movement, capacity of movement, and analysis time period in Equation (7-4).

$$d = \frac{3600}{c_{m,x}} + 900T \left[\frac{v_x}{c_{m,x}} - 1 + \sqrt{\left(\frac{v_x}{c_{m,x}} - 1\right)^2 + \frac{\left(\frac{3600}{c_{m,x}}\right)\left(\frac{v_x}{c_{m,x}}\right)}{450T}} \right] + 5 \quad (7-4)$$

where: d——control delay (s/veh);

v_x——flow rate for movement x (veh/h);

$c_{m,x}$——capacity of movement x (veh/h);

T——analysis time period (h) (T=0.25 for a 15-min period).

The constant value of 5 s/veh is included in Equation (7-4) to account for the deceleration of vehicles from free-flow speed to the speed of vehicles in queue and the acceleration of vehicles from the stop line to free-flow speed.

7.2　Basic Principles and Steps of Intersection Signalization

Traffic signal is regarded as the ultimate form of at-grade intersection control due to the fact that it can greatly reduce the number and nature of intersection conflicts as no other form of control can. The operation of signalized intersections is often complex, involving competing vehicular and pedestrian movements. Methodologies for the signal timing and for the operational analysis of signalized intersections require that the behavior of driver and pedestrians be modeled in a form that can be easily manipulated and optimized. In the following section basic principles and steps of signal timing are described.

7.2.1　Terms and Definitions

Before introducing basic principle and steps of signal timing for intersections, it is necessary to provide definitions of often-used terms in signal timing.

(1) *Cycle*(周期) is defined one complete rotation through all of the indications provided.

(2) *Cycle length*(周期长度) is the time that it takes to complete one full cycle of indications, expressed in second.

(3) *Interval*(时段) is a period of time during which no signal indication changes. It is the smallest unit of time described within a signal cycle and has many forms within a signal cycle as follows.

①*Change interval* is the "yellow" indication functioning as part of the transition from "green" to "red".

②*Clearance interval* is also part of the transition from "green" to "red" for a given set of movements with "all red" indication.

③*Green interval* is the period of time during which the movements permitted have a "green" light, while all other movements have a "red" light.

④*Red interval* is the period of time during which all movements not permitted have a "red" light, while those permitted to move have a "green" light.

(4) *Phase*(相位) is defined a set of intervals that allows a designated movement or set of movements to flow and to be safely *halted*(停止) before release of conflicting set of movements, number of phase can be from 2 to 9.

Phase consists of a green interval, plus the change and clearance intervals that follow. It is a set of intervals that allows a designated movement or set of movements to flow and to be safely halted before release of conflicting set of movements.

7.2.2 Saturation flow rate, lost times and capacity

(1) ***Saturation headway***(饱和车头时距) is defined as the headway by which a queue of traffic stream at intersection is discharged in a stable and saturated way. (This can be achieved after the first 3 or 4 vehicles in the queue.)

(2) ***Saturation flow rate***(饱和流率) is the flow rate in an hour under saturation headway and its mathematical format is $S = \frac{3600}{h}$, h is the saturation headway.

(3) ***Start-up lost time***(起动时损,绿损) is the additional time involved in each of initial headways (large than saturation headway), symbolized by l_1.

(4) ***Clearance lost time***(清空时损) is defined as the time interval between the last vehicle's front wheels crossing the stop line and the initiation of the GREEN for the next phase, symbolized by l_2.

(5) ***Effective green time***(有效绿灯时间) is the amount of time that vehicles are moving and expressed as:

$$g_i = G_i + Y_i - t_{li} \tag{7-5}$$

Where: g_i——effective green time for movement i(s);

G_i——actual green time for movement i(s);

Y_i——sum of yellow and all rad intervals for movement i(s);

t_{li}——total lost time for movement i(s).

It is the addition of start-up lost time and clearance lost time, namely $t_{Li} = l_1 + l_2$

(6) ***Capacity of an intersection lane or lane group***(车道组的通行能力) is the representation of the saturation flow rate.

$$c_i = s_i \cdot \frac{g_i}{C} \tag{7-6}$$

Where: c_i——capacity of lane or lane group i(veh/h);

s_i——saturation flow rate for lane or lane group i(veh/h);

g_i——effective green time for lane or lane group i(s);

C——signal cycle length in second.

7.2.3 The critical lane and time budget

These two concepts are closely related in signal analysis.

(1) The ***time budge***(绿灯时间分配) is defined as the allocation of green time to various vehicular and pedestrian movements at an intersection through signal control.

(2) The ***critical lane***(关键车道) is the identification of specific lane movements that will control the timing of a given signal phase. It is the lane with the most *intense traffic demand*, not the lane with the highest volume.

There is a critical lane and a critical-lane flow for each discrete signal phase provided.

(1) Except for lost times, when no vehicles move, there must be one and only one critical lane moving during every second of effective green time in the signal cycle.

(2) Where there are overlapping phases, the potential combination of lane flows yielding the highest sum of critical lane flows.

Example 7.2 For Critical Lane & Budget Time Determination

The following example demonstrates the process of determining critical lane and green time of each direction for a signalized intersection. The traffic volumes of the intersection are shown in Figure 7.10.

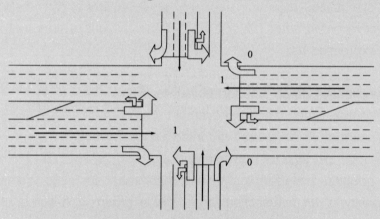

Figure 7.10 Critical Lane Determination

The signal timing conditions are:
Cycle length = 120 seconds; Red plus Yellow time = 5 seconds
The phase plan is assumed as follows:
Phase 1: protected left turn for east-west direction.
Phase 2: through plus right turn for east-west direction.
Phase 3: protected left turn for south-north direction.
Phase 4: through plus right turn for south-north direction.

Thus critical-lane volume for each phase is as follows.

$$\text{Phase 1} = 400/2 = 200 \text{ (veh/h)}$$
$$\text{Phase 2} = 1600/4 = 400 \text{ (veh/h)}$$
$$\text{Phase 3} = 110/1 = 110 \text{ (veh/h)}$$
$$\text{Phase 4} = 700/2 = 350 \text{ (veh/h)}$$
$$V_c = 200 + 400 + 110 + 350 = 1060 \text{ (veh/h)}$$

It is known that the total green time for each cycle equals to cycle length minus the total lost time, namely total green time is 100 seconds in a cycle. Therefore, the green time assigned for each phase is calculated as follows.

$$g_1 = (200/1060) \times 100 = 19(s)$$
$$g_2 = (400/1060) \times 100 = 38(s)$$
$$g_3 = (110/1060) \times 100 = 10(s)$$
$$g_4 = (350/1060) \times 100 = 33(s)$$

(3) Maximum sum of critical-lane volumes:

$$V_c(\max) = \frac{1}{h}\left[3600 - N \times t_L\left(\frac{3600}{C}\right)\right] \tag{7-7}$$

Where: $V_c(\max)$——maximum sum of critical lane volumes(veh/h);

h——saturation headway(s);

N——number of phases in the cycle;

t_L——total lost time per phase(s).

In general, as the cycle length increases, the capacity of the intersection also increases. This is because of lost times that are constant per cycle. However, capacity can rarely be increased significantly by only increasing the cycle length. The relationship between sum of critical-lane volumes and cycle length is shown in Figure 7.11.

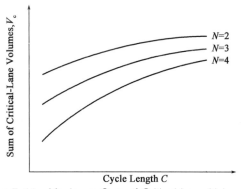

Figure 7.11   Maximum Sum of Critical-Lane Volumes

(4) Determination of cycle length:

①Minimum acceptable cycle length $C_{\min}$

$$C_{\min} = \frac{N \cdot t_L}{1 - \left(\dfrac{V_c}{3600/h}\right)} \tag{7-8}$$

②Desirable cycle length C_{des}

$$C_{des} = \frac{N \times t_L}{1 - \left[\dfrac{V_c}{3600/h \times PHF \times (v/c)}\right]} \tag{7-9}$$

Where: v/c——desired volume to capacity ratio.

Due to the stochastic variations in demand on a cycle-by-cycle and daily basis, some excess capacity must be provided to avoid failure of individual cycles or peak periods on a specific day. Therefore, desired volume to capacity ratio is the given information. The relationship between a desirable cycle length, the maximum critical-lane volumes, and the target v/c ratio is illustrated in Figure 7.12.

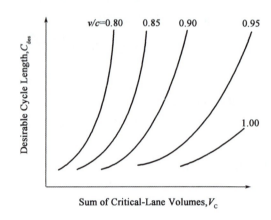

Figure 7.12　Desirable Cycle Length vs. Sum of Critical-Lane Volumes

7.2.4　Concept of *Left-turn and Right-turn Equivalence*(左转/右转当量)

The key point of equivalence of left turn is based on the fact that the effective green time consumed by a left-turn vehicle is E_{LT} times the effective green time consumed by a similar through vehicle. The value of E_{LT} implies converting factor of left turn versus through vehicle. Table 7.9 provides left-turn equivalence values.

Table 7.9　Left-turn equivalence, ELT

Opposing Flow V_o (veh/h)	Number of Opposing Lanes, N_o		
	1	2	3
0	1.1	1.1	1.1
200	2.5	2.0	1.8
400	5.0	3.0	2.5
600	10.0*	5.0	4.0
800	13.0*	8.0	6.0
1000	15.0*	13.0*	10.0*
≥1200	15.0*	15.0*	15.0*
E_{LT} for all protected left turns = 1.05			

Note: * indicates that the LT capacity is only available through "sneakers".

Likewise, the right-turn equivalence E_{RT} implies converting factor of right turn versus through movement. Right turn movement is greatly affected by the pedestrians. Table 7.10 provides right-turn equivalence values.

Table 7.10 Right-turn equivalence, E_{RT}

Pedestrian Volume In Conflicting Crosswalk (peds/h)	Equivalent
None (0)	1.18
Low (50)	1.21
Moderate (200)	1.32
High (400)	1.52
Extreme (800)	2.14

7.2.5 Delay as a Measure of Effectiveness

As defined and discussed in chapter 4 delays are the main factor to measure the performance of intersection. There are many models to describe how to estimate delays of vehicles at intersection. However, Webster's model is considered the most popular one in the intersection delay studies. Webster's delay models are discussed as below.

(1) Uniform delay model:

$$UD = \frac{0.5 \times C(1-g/C)^2}{1-(g/C)X} \quad (7\text{-}10)$$

Where: UD——average uniform delay per vehicle(s/veh);

C——cycle length(s);

g——effective green time(s);

X——v/c ratio, or degree of saturation.

It should be noted that this average delay includes the vehicles that arrive and depart on green, accruing no delay. The maximum value of X is 1.00.

(2) Random delay model:

$$RD = \frac{X^2}{2 \times v(1-X)} \quad (7\text{-}11)$$

Where: RD——average random delay per vehicle(s/veh);

X——v/c ratio, or degree of saturation.

(3) Delay models in HCM2000:

$$d = d_1 \cdot PF + d_2 + d_3 \quad (7\text{-}12)$$

$$d_1 = \left(\frac{C}{2}\right)\left\{\frac{(1-g/C)^2}{1-[\min(1,X) \cdot (g/C)]}\right\}$$

$$d_2 = 900 \times T\left[(X-1) + \sqrt{(X-1)^2 + \left(\frac{8 \times K \cdot I \cdot X}{c \cdot T}\right)}\right]$$

Where: d——control delay(s/veh);

d_1——uniform delay component(s/veh);

PF——progression adjustment factor;

d_2——overflow delay component(s/veh);
d_3——delay due to pre-existing queue(s/veh);
T——analysis period(h);
X——v/c ratio;
C——cycle length(s);
K——incremental delay factor for actuated controller 0.50 for all pre-timed controllers;
I——upstream filtering/metering adjustment factor; 1.00 for all individual intersection analysis.

7.3 Fundamentals of Signal Timing and Design

The objective of signal timing is to guarantee the safe and efficient movements of traffic flows within intersection. While most signal timings are developed for vehicles and checked for pedestrian needs, it is critical that signal timings provide safety and relative efficiency for both. Engineering judgment is important for the signal timing.

7.3.1 Development of Phase Plan

This is the critical aspect of signal design and timing, which in most cases needs engineering judgment and applies a number of commonly used guidelines in MUTCD. It is widely believed that once phase plan is done, many other aspects of the signal timing can be analytically treated in a deterministic fashion. In general the minimum number of phase is two and maximum number of phase can be as high as nine. However, it is widely believed that the fewer the number of phase, the lower the delays at intersection.

7.3.1.1 Treatment of Left Turns

(1) *Permitted left-turn phase*(许可型相位)

This type of phase has been widely used at signalized intersection where two-phase or three-phase plan is applied. Under this condition left turn movement is allowed to cross through the opposing flow, but should yield to the opposing traffic until appropriate gap in the opposing flow occurs. In practice it has been easily noticed that two or three left turn vehicles can make a turning movement just before the opposing traffic fleet reaches conflict point. These left turn drivers are often called *sneakers*(抢行者) in traffic engineering. It should be noted that permitted left-turn phase is only used when the opposing traffic flow provides reasonable amount of gaps for left turn vehicle to cross. This type of control is not recommended, otherwise. Normally, the signal indication is green ball.

(2) *Protected left-turn phase*(保护型相位)

This type of control can be seen at signalized intersection where the number of left turn vehicles is very high or the opposing traffic flow can't come up with reasonable amount of gaps. Under the protected left-turn phase the opposing through traffic stops. Left turn movements go through intersection without conflict. This type of control leads to multiphase plan, resulting in three, four, even more number of phases. Generally, the green arrow signalization is applied for the protected left-turn phase.

Criteria of protected left-turn phase in the USA are as follows:
$$v_{LT} \geqslant 200 (\text{veh/h}) \qquad (7\text{-}13)$$
$$v_{LT} \cdot \left(\frac{v_0}{N_0}\right) \geqslant 50000 (\text{veh/h})$$

Where: v_{LT}——left-turn flow rate (veh/h);

v_0——opposing through movement flow rate(veh/h);

N_0——number of lanes for opposing through movement.

Apart from these two criteria, there are some criteria used when protected left-turn phase is put into operation such as: opposing through flow rate, number of lanes of opposing through traffic, speed limit, left-turn crash rate.

(3) *Compound left-turn phase*(组合型相位)

Sometimes, combination of the permitted and protected can be used based on the traffic conditions at intersection. The Compound left-turn phase refers to either protected-plus-permitted phase or permitted-plus-protected phase. The protected-plus-permitted phase is designed to allow left turn movements to cross intersection under the green arrow indication (protected) for a portion of the signal cycle and then the signal indication changes to green ball to permit left turn movements to cross intersection by yielding to the opposing flow. Caution should be made in design of this type of control because collisions can happen when drivers don't understand the meaning of this phase or ignore the rules. This type of phasing is rarely seen in China.

(4) *Ban of left turns*(禁左)

Prohibition of left turns is rarely a practical option for traffic engineers to use as a tool. If this option can't be avoided some other alternatives such as jug handle (most seen in New Jersey) and U-turn must be provided. Regarding jug handle and U-turn approaches please read other related references.

7.3.1.2 General Considerations in Signal Phase

(1) More phasing can eliminate conflicts, but increases efficiency of intersection

operation. Therefore, tradeoff is needed in determining the number of phase in signal timing

(2) Phase plans should be consistent with the criteria in MUTCD and must be accompanied by the necessary signs, markings, and signal hardware needed to identify appropriate lane usage.

(3) Phase plans must also comply with the intersection geometry, lane-use assignments, volumes and speeds, and pedestrian crossing requirements.

7.3.1.3 Phase and Ring Diagrams

A phase diagram shows all movements being made in a given phase within a single block of the diagram. A ring diagram shows which movements are controlled by which "ring" on a signal controller. They are shown in Figure 7.13 and Figure 7.14 respectively.

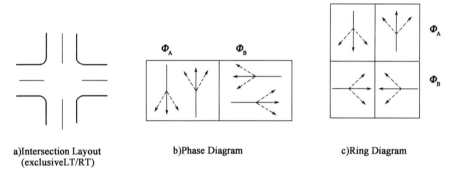

a) Intersection Layout (exclusiveLT/RT) b) Phase Diagram c) Ring Diagram

Figure 7.13 Illustration of a Two-Phase Signal

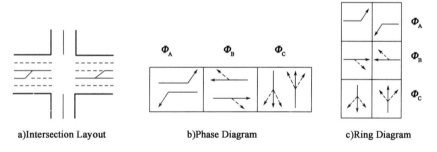

a) Intersection Layout b) Phase Diagram c) Ring Diagram

Figure 7.14 An Exclusive Left-Turn Phase Illustrated

Common phase plans and their use are as follows.

(1) Basic two-phase plan: This plan is applicable for an intersection where traffic is low, particularly when the left turn volume is relatively low.

(2) Exclusive left-turn phase plan: Unlike two-phase plan, this plan provides protected phase for left turn movement. When this plan is applied the green arrow should be indicated.

(3) **Leading**(先行) and **lagging**(滞后) plans: Leading or lagging plan refers to the protective left turn phase. When left turn signal indication goes first, followed by through traffic signal indication, this plan is called leading phase plan, or called lagging phase plan if otherwise.

(4) **Right-turn-on-red**(灯控右转): This plan requires that the motorist stop before executing right-turn movement on red.

7.3.2　Determination of vehicular signal parameters.

(1) Determination of change and clearance intervals.

The ITE recommends the following for methodology for determining the Length yellow.

$$y = t + \frac{1.47 \times S_{85}}{2a + (64.4 \times 0.01G)} \tag{7-14}$$

Where: y——length of yellow interval(s);

　　　　t——driver's reaction time(s);

　　S_{85}——85th percentile speed of approaching vehicles, or speed limit(mile/h);

　　　　a——deceleration rate of vehicles(ft/s^2);

　　　　G——grade of approach;

　　64.4——twice the acceleration rate due to gravity, which is 32.2 ft/s^2.

(2) Determination of All-Red clearance interval.

The ITE also recommends the following policy for determining the Length of all-red clearance intenal.

when there is no pedestrian:

$$ar = \frac{w + L}{1.47 \times S_{15}} \tag{7-15}$$

when there is significant pedestrian traffic:

$$ar = \frac{P + L}{1.47 \times S_{15}} \tag{7-16}$$

when there is moderate pedestrian traffic:

$$ar = \max\left[\left(\frac{w+L}{1.47 \times S_{15}}\right), \left(\frac{P}{1.47 \times S_{15}}\right)\right] \tag{7-17}$$

Where: ar——length of the all-red interval (phase) (s);

　　　　w——distance from the departure STOP line to the far side of the farthest conflicting traffic lane (ft);

　　　　P——distance from the departure STOP line to the far side of the farthest conflicting crosswalk (ft);

　　　　L——length of a standard vehicle (ft);

　　S_{15}——15th percentile speed of approaching vehicles, or speed limit(mile/h).

(3) Determination of lost times.

Lost times vary with the length of the yellow and all-red phases in the signal timing. Therefore, it is no longer suitable to use a constant default value for lost times.

(4) Determination of the sum of critical-lane volumes.

The basic step is to convert all demand volumes to equivalent through vehicle units (tvus), then do comparison. Table 7.8 and table 7.9 give through vehicle equivalents for left and right turns, respectively.

(5) Determination of the desired cycle length.

$$C_{des} = \frac{L}{1 - \left[\frac{V_c(max)}{1615 \times PHF \cdot (v/c)}\right]} \quad (7\text{-}18)$$

(6) Determination of split of green time (time budget).

The total effective green time in the cycle is allocated to the various phases or sub-phases of the signal plan in proportion to the critical lane volumes for each phase or sub-phase.

$$g_i = g_{TOT} \times \left(\frac{V_{ci}}{V_c}\right) \quad (7\text{-}19)$$

Where: g_i——effective green time for phase i (s);

g_{TOT}——total effective green time in the cycle(s), different between cycle length and total lost time $g_{TOT} = C - L$;

V_{ci}——critical lane volume for phase i (veh/h);

V_c——sum of critical lane volumes.

7.3.3 Determination of Pedestrian Signal Parameters The 2010 edition of Highway Capacity Nanual Suggests the following minimum green-time requirements for pedestrians.

$$G_p = 3.2 + \frac{L}{S_p} + 2.7 \times \frac{N_{ped}}{W_E} \quad \text{when } W_d > 10 \text{ ft} \quad (7\text{-}20)$$

$$G_p = 3.2 + \frac{L}{S_p} + 2.7 \times N_{ped} \quad \text{when } W_d \leq 10 \text{ ft} \quad (7\text{-}21)$$

Where: G_p——minimum pedestrian crossing time (s);

L——length of the crosswalk (ft);

S_p——average walking speed of pedestrians (ft/s);

N_{ped}——number of pedestrians crossing per phase in a single crosswalk;

W_d——effective width of crosswalk (ft).

It should be pointed out that what has been discussed in this chapter is a fleece of signalization of intersection. This chapter has provided very basic knowledge in the signal timing. Detailed procedures and techniques of signal timing should be studies in other references.

7.4 Computer Software Related to Intersection Signal Timing

There a lot software to be available for signal timing such as: HCS2000, HCM/cinema, SIGNAL2000, TRANSYT-7F and SYNCHRO. It is encouraged that students go to lab to use these packages to exercise.

Key points of the chapter

1. What are the differences between STOP sign and YIELD sign?
2. Be aware of the ranking of traffic stream of TWSC intersection.
3. What are the critical gap and follow-up time?
4. How to determine critical lane?
5. Familiar with the terms and their implications used in signal timing.
6. What is difference between permissive and protected phase for left turn?

本章要点

1. STOP 与 YIELD 在使用上有何区别?
2. 了解二路停车交叉口交通流通行级别。
3. 什么是临界可接受间隙和随车时距?
4. 如何确定关键(临界)车道?
5. 熟悉并掌握信号灯配时中的相关术语及其含义。
6. 对于左转车,许可型和保护型相位的区别是什么?

Chapter 8 Traffic Control Devices

Traffic control devices are considered vital elements in traffic control and management. In this chapter traffic markings, signs, and traffic signals are discussed. The purpose of providing traffic control devices is also described. In addition some photos to show these devices and their usages in real situation are presented, along with the comparison of traffic control devices between China and the USA.

Traffic control devices are important factors in traffic management and enforcement. Traffic control devices are considered powerful means by which traffic engineers communicate with road users to make sure that their ideas of design are fully and correctly understood by the road users.

8.1　Definition and categories of traffic control devices

Traffic control devices are defined as the media by which traffic engineers communicate with road users. A good communication between traffic engineers and road users can ensure the safe and efficient traffic operations. This chapter presents MUTCD and three kinds of traffic control devices:

(1) Traffic markings.

(2) Traffic signs.

(3) Traffic signals.

Purpose of Traffic control devices——communicating with the driver

The driver is accustomed to being given certain messages in clear, standard ways, often with great redundancy. A number of mechanisms are used to convey messages. These mechanisms make use of and recognize human limitations. From traffic control device perspective, there are four ways to convey messages to the road users: color, shape, pattern, and legend.

Color. Color is the most easily seen characteristic of a device. A color is recognizable long before even a general shape is recognizable, and well before legend can be read and understood. The principal colors used in traffic control devices are red, yellow, green, orange, black, blue, and brown. These are used to code certain devices, and to reinforce specific messages whenever possible.

Pattern. Pattern is used in the application of traffic markings. In general, double solid, solid, dashed, and broken lines are used. Each conveys a type of meaning with which drivers are familiar. The frequent and consistent use of similar patterns in similar applications contributes greatly to their effectiveness, and to the instant recognition of their meanings.

Shape. After color, the shape of a device is the next element to be discerned by the driver. Particularly in signing, shape is an important element of the message, either identifying a particular type of information that the sign is transmitting, or conveying a unique message on its own.

Legend. The last element of a device that the driver comprehends during driving is the specific legend on the device. Signals and markings, for example, convey their entire messages without the use of legend. Signs, however, often use specific legend to transmit the details of the message being conveyed. Legend must be kept simple and short, so that drivers do not divert their attention from the driving task, yet are able to see and understand the specific messages being given.

Redundancy (重复) of message can be achieved in a number of ways. The STOP sign (shown in Figure 8.1) is a good example. This device has a unique shape [*octagon*(八边形)], a unique color (red), and a unique one-word message (STOP). Any of the three elements alone is sufficient to convey the message. Each provides redundancy for the others.

Figure 8.1   The STOP sign

A left-turn lane is reinforced with a left-turn signal, an arrow and some word markings on the pavement. Here, all three categories of control devices are used together to reinforce a single message.

The information of traffic control devices conveyed to the driver must be in uniform and consistent ways. Redundancy of message is useful, and often necessary to properly convey a message. The MUTCD is the federal standard of the USA providing for this necessary uniformity in use, design, and placement of devices.

The following sections of this chapter introduce some of the standards of critical traffic control devices. Again, the traffic engineers must consult current editions of the MUTCD for a complete version of all standards for all devices.

8.2   Introduction of the MUTCD

8.2.1   History and background of the MUTCD (Figure 8.2)

Manual on Uniform Traffic Control Devices can be considered another milestone in traffic engineering development, whid can parallel with HCM in terms of significance. The first complete version was in 1935, evolving 70 years of revisions. The objectives of the MUTCD are to provide *uniformity* (一致性) *and warranty* (依据)

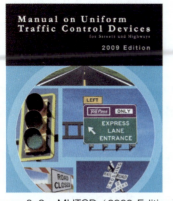

Figure 8.2 MUTCD (2009 Edition)

for the installation, design and placement of traffic control devices. One of the principal objectives of the MUTCD is to establish uniformity in the use, placement, and design of traffic control devices. Communication is greatly enhanced when the same message is delivered in the same way and in similar circumstances at all times. Consider the confusion caused if all the STOP signs have different shapes, colors and legends. Early traffic control devices were developed in various locales with little or no coordination on their design. Traffic control devices appeared on streets and highways in the USA. as early as the 1910s. The first centerline appeared in Michigan in 1911. The first electric signal installation was thought to have occurred in Cleveland, Ohio in 1914. The first STOP sign was installed in Detroit in 1915, whereas the first three-color traffic signal was installed in 1920.

The Table 2.6 demonstrates the evolution of the MUTCD in its development.

The first version attempted to create the US national standards for traffic control device occurred during the 1920s. Two organizations developed two manuals in this period. In 1927 the AASHTO published *Manual and Specification for the Manufacture, Display, and Erection of US Standard Road Marking and Signs*. This manual addressed only rural signing and marking applications. In 1930 the National Conference on Street and Highway Safety (NCSHS) published *Manual on Street Traffic Signs, Signals, and Markings*. This manual focused on urban applications. In 1932, the two groups formed a merged Joint *Committee on Uniform Traffic Control Devices*, and published the first complete MUTCD in 1935. This group continued to have responsibility for subsequent editions until 1972, when the Federal Highway Administration formally assumed responsibility for the manual.

8.2.2 General principles of the MUTCD

The MUTCD defines five requirements for a traffic control device. To be effective, a device must:

(1) Fulfill a need.
(2) Command attention.
(3) Convey a clear, simple meaning.
(4) Command respect of road users.
(5) Give adequate time for proper response.

In addition to the obvious meanings of these requirements, some ***subtleties*** (细

微差别) should be carefully observed. The first implies that superfluous devices are NOT to be used. Each device must has a specific purpose, and must be needed for the safe and efficient flow of traffic. The fourth requirement reinforces this. Respect is commanded only when drivers are conditioned to expect that all devices carry meaningful and important messages. Abuse or misuse of devices encourages drivers to ignore them. When this happens, drivers will then not pay full attention to those devices that are needed.

Items 2 and 3 affect the design of a device. Commanding attention requires proper visibility and a distinctive design that attracts the drivers' attention. Clarity and simplicity of message critical if the message is to be understood in the short time a driver has to consider an individual device. Use of color and shape as codes are important in this regard. Legend, the hardest element of a device to be understood, must be kept short and simple.

Item 5 affects the placement of devices. A STOP sign, for example, while always placed at the stop line of the intersection, must be visible for at least one safe stopping distance from the stop line. Guide signs requiring drivers to make lane changes, such as on a freeway, must be placed well in advance of the diverge gore area.

8.2.3 Contents of the MUTCD

In general there are three parts in the MUTCD including:

(1) Detailed standards for the physical design of the device, specifying shape, size, colors, legend types and sizes, and specific legend.

(2) Detailed standards and guidelines at the plase where devices should be located with respect to the traveled way.

(3) Warrants, or conditions, that justify the use of a particular device.

The most detailed and definitive standards are for the design of the device. Here, little is left to judgment, and virtually every detail of the design is fully specified. Variance is generally not permitted. The standards sometimes allow for the use of several different sized devices depending on the particular situation and need.

Placement standards and guidelines are also relatively definitive, but often allow for some variation within specified limits.

Warrants are given with various levels of specificity and clarity. Signal warrants, for example, are relatively detailed and precise. Warrants for STOP and YIELD signs, on the other hand, are relatively general. Because of the expense involved in signalization, much study has been devoted to defining conditions which require their use, resulting in more quantitative warrants than other devices. The content in chapter 15 of the MUTCD deals in details with warrants related to various forms of intersection control. Proper implementation of warrants in the MUTCD requires appropriate engineering studies to be made to determine the need for a particular device or devices.

Three words within the MUTCD require special attention, as they describe the relative force with which each standard or criterion is given:

(1) SHALL. The use of the word "shall" or "shall not" denoted a mandatory condition. Where the MUTCD imposed this word, such conditions must be met. Failure to observe conditions imposed with the "shall" or "shall not" qualification may create legal liability for the implementing agency.

(2) SHOULD. The use of the word "should" or "should not" denotes an advisory, but not mandatory condition. The criteria given are recommended. When it is not being observed, some documentation explaining why there is no compliance should be maintained. The logic for non-compliance should be clear and convincing.

(3) MAY. The use of the word "may" or "may not" denotes a permissive condition. No requirement on design or application is intended.

These words have enormous legal **connotations** (涵义), as indicated failure to observe a mandatory condition exposes the presiding agency to lawsuits. Advisory conditions are usually followed unless there is an extraordinary reason not to do so. Such reasons must always be carefully documented.

Warrants are rarely given as a mandatory condition. Thus, there is considerable latitude in the use and application of particular devices. When the devices are used, however, design and placement criteria are most often mandatory. Ironically, a jurisdiction will be more legally exposed when it places a device that does not follow design and placement conditions than it is when it fails to place a device which might be indicated, but with advisory or permissive criteria.

Legal aspects of the MUTCD

There are four aspects related to the legal activity.

(1) Standard: A standard is a statement of a required, mandatory, or specifically prohibitive practice regarding a traffic control device.

(2) Guidance: A guidance is a statement of recommended, but not mandatory, practice in typical situations. Deviation, to some extent, from the guidance is allowed.

(3) Option: An option is a statement of practice which is under a permissive condition, carrying no implication of requirement or recommendation.

(4) Support: This is a purely information statement provided to supply additional information to the traffic engineer.

8.3　Traffic markings

Traffic markings are defined as lines or line drawings, which are painted on the roadway surface using paint and thermoplastic. Traffic markings involve lane lines, edge markings, *gore area* (三角区) and other specialized markings used for channelizing.

8.3.1　Longitudinal markings

Longitudinal markings are parallel to the direction of travel to provide guidance for the placement of vehicles on the road. The function of longitudinal markings is to organize flow and optimize use of the pavement width.

The MUTCD gives nine key principals concerning longitudinal pavement markings which shall be observed at all times (mandatory conditions):

(1) Yellow lines delineate the separation of traffic flows in opposing directions, or mark the left edge of the pavement of divided highways and one-way roads.

(2) White lines delineate the separation of traffic flows in the same direction or mark the right edge of the pavement.

(3) Red markings delineate roadways that shall not be entered or used by the viewer of those markings.

(4) Broken lines are permissive in character.

(5) Solid lines are restrictive in character.

(6) Width of line indicates the degree of emphasis.

(7) Double lines indicate maximum restrictions.

(8) Markings which must be visible at night shall be *reflectorized* (反光) unless *ambient* (附近的) illumination assures adequate visibility.

(9) Raised pavement markers may serve as position guides for, or may supplement, or in some cases may be substituted for other types of markings.

According to above principles, centerlines can be in following shapes (Figure 8.3):

(1) Double-solid yellow line.

(2) Double-dashed yellow line (for passing).

(3) Double-dashed yellow lines (reversible lane).

Single or double dashed yellow lines are often seen on the rural highway to allow overtaking.

Lane markings are single white dashed line and double-dashed white lines separate lanes of traffic in the same direction. Double-dashed white lines are used for reversible lane in Figure 8.4a).

Figure 8.3　Three kinds of centerlines

Edge markings select different color to differ left or right edge of traffic lane. Right-edge markings are in the form of a single normal solid white line; left-edge markings are in the form of a single normal solid yellow line as indicated in Figure 8.4b).

a)　　　　　　　　　　　　　　　　b)

Figure 8.4　Lane markings and edge markings

8.3.2　Transverse markings

Transverse markings, as their name implies, include any and all markings with a component that cuts across a portion or all of the traveled way. When used, all transverse markings are white.

Stop lines are almost always used where cross walks are marked. Crosswalk markings are used at all intersections where "substantial" conflict between vehicles and pedestrians occurs as shown in Figure 8.5.

Figure 8.5　Stop lines and crosswalk markings

Parking space markings contain both longitudinal and transverse lines. Parking space markings are officially categorized as transverse markings in the MUTCD. They are always optional and are used to encourage efficient use of parking spaces. Such markings can also help prevent encroachment of parked vehicles into fire-hydrant zones, loading zones, taxi stands and bus stops, and other specific locations at which parking is prohibited. They are also useful on arterials with curb parking, as they also clearly demark the parking lane, and separate it from travel lanes. They can increase efficient use of parking space. A typical parking lot under Berlin Railway Station is given in Figure 8.6.

Figure 8.6　Parking space markings in Berlin, German

8.3.3　Object markers and delineators

Roadway delineators are reflectorized devices mounted at the roadside to demark roadway alignment. Generally mounted in series at a distance between 2ft (1ft =0.3048m) and 8ft from the edge of the shoulder, delineators are aids to night driving and are considered to be guidance devices, not warning devices. They may be used continuously along the roadway, or may be used to delineate changes in the roadway alignment, such as changes in horizontal or vertical alignment, or changes in the width of lunes or number of lanes. The color of the delineator matched the edge line of the roadway being delineated,i.e., delineators for the left side of a one-way roadway are yellow; delineators for the right side of a one-way roadway are white.

Object markers are used to denote obstructions either in or adjacent to the traveled way. Delineators are particularly useful during *inclement*(恶劣) weather, where pavement edge marking may not be visible (Figure 8.7).

8.3.4　Word and symbol markings

The MUTCD prescribes a number of words and symbol marking that may be used, often in conjunction with signs and/or signals(show in Figure 8.8). These (including arrow with accompanying signs) are mandatory where a through lane becomes a left-or right-turn-only lane approaching an intersection.

Word marking include "ONLY" used in conjunction with lane use arrows, and "STOP" which can be used only in conjunction with a STOP line and a STOP sign. "SCHOOL" markings are often used in conjunction with signs to demark school and school-crossing zones. The MUTCD contains a listing of all authorized word markings and allows for discretionary use of unique messages where needed.

Figure 8.7　Delineators

Figure 8.8　Word and symbol markings used in the USA

8.4 Traffic signs

Traffic sings are used to regulate, warn and guide roadway users in the traffic operations to guarantee the safe and efficient movements of people and goods. In general there are three types of traffic signs: regulatory, warning and guide signs.

8.4.1 Regulatory signs

Regulatory signs are used to convey information related to specific traffic regulations such as right-of-way, speed limit, lane usage, parking and others.

(1) Right-of-way. The right-of-way series include two unique signs: STOP and YIELD signs (show Figure 8.9).

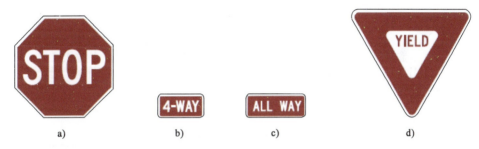

Figure 8.9 Regulatory signs (right-of way)

(2) Speed limit. There are five types of speed limits: linear speed limits, area-wide speed limits, night speed limits, truck speed limits (Figure 8.10) and minimum speed limits (Figure 8.11).

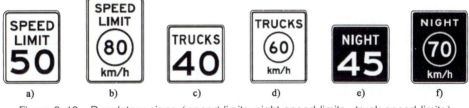

Figure 8.10 Regulatory signs (speed limits, night speed limits, truck speed limits)

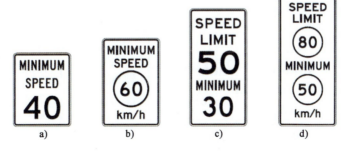

Figure 8.11 Regulatory signs (minimum speed limit)

(3) Turn prohibition signs are used where right and /or left turns are prohibited (Figure 8.12).

Figure 8.12　Turn prohibition signs

(4) Lane-use signs are used at which a given movement or movements are restricted and /or prohibited from designated lanes. Such situations include left-turn- and right-turn-only lanes, two-way left-turn lanes on arterials, and reversible lanes (Figure 8.13 and Figure 8.14).

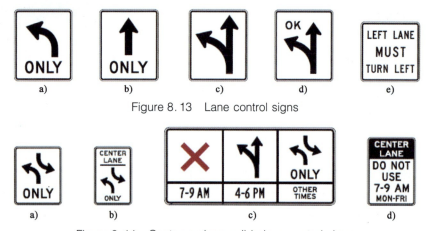

Figure 8.13　Lane control signs

Figure 8.14　Center and reversible lane control signs

(5) Parking control signs(Figure 8.15).

Figure 8.15　No parking signs

Parking signs may also indicate prohibition of "standing" or "stopping". While each state defines these terms in their vehicle and traffic codes, the most common interpretations are:

(1) Parking is generally defined as a vehicle in a stopped position without the motor running.

(2) Standing is generally defined as a vehicle in a stopped position, attended by a driver, with the motor running.

(3) Stopping is generally defined as a motor vehicle in a stopped position.

Parking signs should display the following information from top to bottom of the sign, in the order listed:

(1) The restriction or prohibition.

(2) The times of the day that it is applicable, if not at all hours.

(3) The days of the week that it is applicable, if not every day.

If the parking restriction applies to a limited area or zone, the limits of the restriction should be shown by arrows or supplemental plaques. If arrows are used and if the sign is at the end of a parking zone, there should be a single-headed arrow pointing in the direction that the regulation is in effect. If the sign is at an intermediate point in a zone, there should be a double-headed arrow pointing both ways. When a single sign is used at the transition point between two parking zones, it should display a right and left arrow pointing in the direction that the respective restrictions apply.

8.4.2 Warning signs

Warning signs try to inform drivers about upcoming hazards that they might not see or otherwise discern in time to safely react. Warning signs call attention to conditions that generally require additional vigilance, a decline in speed, or a maneuver on the part of the driver. While warning signs are valuable aids to the safe and efficient movement of traffic, overuse should be avoided. Warning signs are not placed where conditions are apparent and easily discerned by the driver. Their use is most and easily discerned by the driver. Their use is most valuable where a condition is not likely to be observed without calling attention to it. Like any control device, overuse will breed disrespect for all devices.

Warning signs are usually diamond shaped, with black legend or symbols on a yellow background.

The MUTCD lists 11 types of conditions for which warning signs may generally be placed:

(1) Changes in horizontal alignment (Figure 8.16).

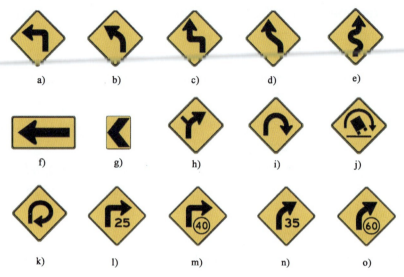

Figure 8.16　Warning signs (horizontal alignment)

(2) Intersections (Figure 8.17).

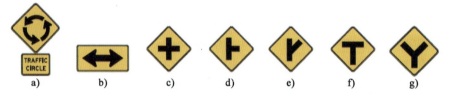

Figure 8.17　Warning signs (Intersections)

(3) Advance warning of control devices (Figure 8.18).

Figure 8.18　Warning signs (Intersections)

(4) Converging traffic lanes (Figure 8.19).

Figure 8.19　Warning signs (merging)

(5) Narrow roadway (Figure 8.20).

(6) Changed in highway design.

(7) Grades (Figure 8.21).

Figure 8.20 Warning signs (narrow roadway)   Figure 8.21 Warning signs (hill signs)

(8) Roadway surface conditions (Figure 8.22).

(9) Railroad crossings.

(10) Entrances and crossings.

(11) Miscellaneous (Figure 8.23).

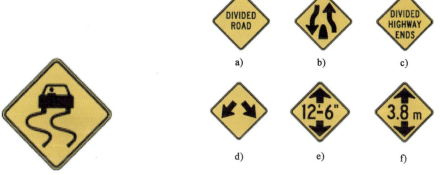

Figure 8.22 Warning signs (the slippery when wet sign)   Figure 8.23 Warning signs (miscellaneous)

8.4.3 Guide signs

Guide signs provide information on routes, destinations, services and historical/recreational facilities. Guide signs include the following four type signs.

(1) Route marker (Figure 8.24).

Figure 8.24 Guide signs (route marker)

(2) Destination signs (Figure 8.25).

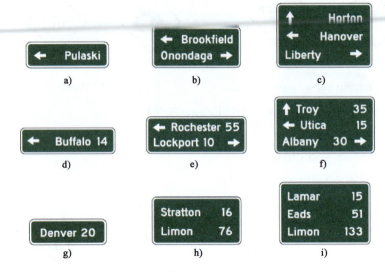

Figure 8.25　Guide signs (destination signs)

(3) Service guide signs (Figure 8.26).

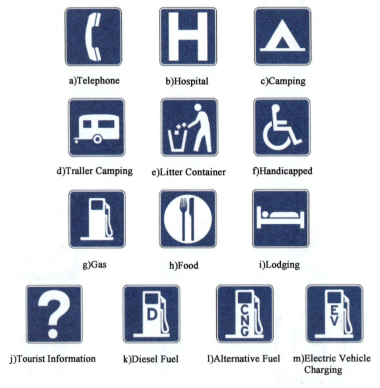

Figure 8.26　Guide signs (service guide signs)

(4) Mile posts (Figure 8.27).

Guide signs used in China are shown in Figure 8.28.

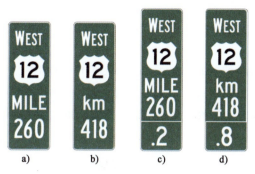

Figure 8.27 Guide signs (mile posts)

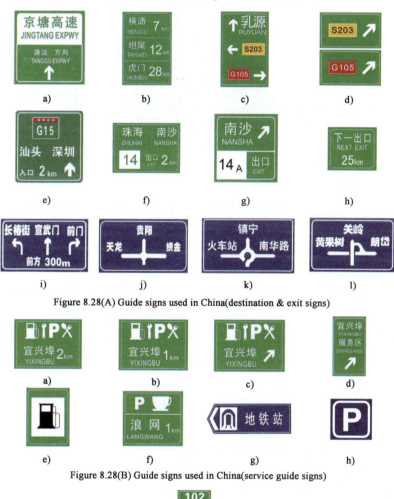

Figure 8.28(A) Guide signs used in China(destination & exit signs)

Figure 8.28(B) Guide signs used in China(service guide signs)

Figure 8.28(C) Guide signs used in China(mileposts)

Figure 8.28 Guide signs used in China

197

8.5 Traffic signals

The function of traffic signals is to assign the right-of-way for the conflicting traffic streams. Their objective is to ensure the safe and efficient movement of traffic flow. There are varieties of traffic signals with respect to different locations and different functionalities in managing traffic(Figure 8.29).

Figure 8.29　The earliest traffic signal used in USA

8.5.1　Characteristics of traffic signals

Traffic signals, when properly installed and operated at appropriate locations, provide a number of significant benefits.

(1)With appropriate physical designs, control measures, and signal timing, the capacity of critical intersection movements will increases.

(2)The frequency and severity of accidents reduced for certain types of crashed, including right-angle, turn, and pedestrian accidents.

(3)When properly coordinated, signals can provide for nearly continuous movement through traffic along an arterial at a designated speed under favorable traffic conditions.

(4)They provide for interruptions in heavy traffic streams to permit crossing vehicular and pedestrian traffic to safely cross.

At the same time, misapplied or poorly designed signals can cause excessive delay, signal violations, increased accidents (particularly rear-end accidents), and drivers' rerouting their trips to less appropriate routes.

(1)Signal indications.

The MUTCD defines the meaning of each traffic control signal indication as follows:

①*Green ball*(全绿).

A steady green circular indication allows vehicular traffic facing the ball to enter the intersection to travel straight through the intersection or to turn right or left, except when prohibited by lane-use control or physical design. Turning vehicles must yield the right-of-way to opposing through vehicles and to pedestrians legally in a conflicting crosswalk. In the absence of pedestrian signals, pedestrians may proceed to cross the roadway within a legally marked or unmarked crosswalk

②*Yellow ball*(全黄).

The steady yellow circular indication is a transition between the Green Ball and the Red Ball indication. It warns drivers that the related green movement is being terminated or that a red indication will immediately follow. In general, drivers are permitted to enter the intersection on the "red" that follows it. In the absence of pedestrian signals, pedestrians may not begin to cross the street on a "yellow" indication.

③*Red ball*(全红).

The steady red circular indication requires all traffic (vehicular and pedestrian) facing it to stop at the STOP line, crosswalk line (if no STOP line exists), or at the conflicting pedestrian path (if no crosswalk or STOP line exists). All states allow right-turning traffic to proceed with caution after stopping, unless specifically prohibited by signing or statute. Some states allow left-turners from one-way street turning into another to proceed with caution after stopping. However, this is far from a universal statute.

④*Flashing ball* (全闪).

A flashing "yellow" allows traffic to proceed with caution through the intersection. A flashing "red" has the same meaning as a STOP sign, implying that the driver may proceed with caution after coming to a complete stop.

⑤Arrow. Arrow indications Green, yellow, and red arrow indications have the same meanings as ball indications, except that they apply only to the movement designated by the arrow.

A green left-turn arrow is only used to indicate a protected left turn (i.e., a left turn made on a green arrow will not encounter an opposing vehicular through movement). Such vehicles, however, may encounter pedestrians legally in the conflicting crosswalk. The right-turn arrow is shown only when there are no pedestrians legally in the conflicting crosswalk.

Yellow arrows warn drivers that the green may be followed by a green ball indication where the protected left- and/or right-turning movement is followed by a permitted movement. A "permitted" left turn is made against an opposing vehicular flow. A "permitted" right turn is made against a conflicting pedestrian flow. It is followed by a red arrow where the movement must stop.

(2) Signal lenses, heads, faces and visibility

①*Signal lenses* (信号灯透镜) are part of the signal section that redirects the light coming directly from the light source and its reflector.

②*Signal head* (信号灯灯头) is an assembly of one or more signal sections. It is composed of signal lens, LED (light-emitting diode) and lens cap.

③*Signal face* (信号灯组), defined as signal board composed of a series of signal lenses, is part of a traffic control signal provided for controlling one or more traffic movements on a single approach. In general, a signal face should have three to five signal lenses as presented in Figure 8.30, with some exceptions allowing for a sixth to be shown. For one approach of an intersection, there would be one signal face, two signal faces, even three signal faces, depending on conditions at intersection (Figure 8.31).

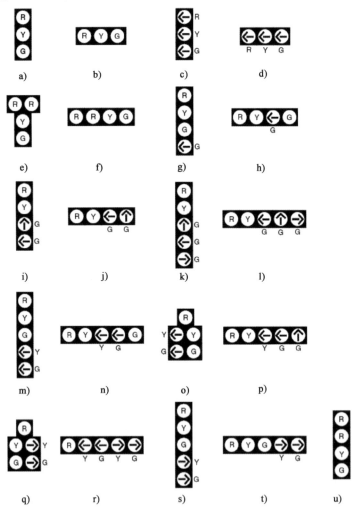

Figure 8.30 Typical arrangement of signal lenses in USA

Figure 8.31 Signals with one, two and three faces used in Beijing, China

Two lens sizes are provided for: 8-in diameter and 12-in lenses (1in = 0.0254m). The manual requires that 12-in lenses be used when any of the following conditions is met.

(1) Where road users view both traffic control and lane-use control signal heads simultaneously.

(2) Where the nearest signal face is between 120 ft and 150 ft beyond the STOP line, unless a nearside supplemental signal face is provided.

(3) Where signal faces are located more than 150 ft from the STOP line.

(4) Where minimum sight distances (Table 8.1) can't be met.

(5) For all arrow signal indications.

Table 8.1 Minimum sight distances for signal faces

85 th Percentile Speed (mi/h)	Minimum Sight Distance (ft)	85 th Percentile Speed (mi/h)	Minimum Sight Distance (ft)
20	175	45	460
25	215	50	540
30	270	55	625
35	325	60	715
40	390		

Note: 1mile = 1.609km.

It further recommends that 12-in-lenses should be used when one of the following conditions is met.

(1) Where 85th percentile approach speeds exceed 40 mi/h.

(2) Where the traffic control signal might be unexpected

(3) On all approached without curbs and gutters where only post-mounted signals are used.

(4) Where there is a significant percentage of elderly drivers.

The red signal lens must be the same size or larger than other lenses (see Figure 8.32). Thus, a 12-in red lens can be used in conjunction with 8-in green and yellow lenses. However, where green and yellow lenses are 12 inches, the red lens

Figure 8.32 Signals with large size than other lenses (in Italy)

must also be 12 inches.

Table 8.1 shows the minimum visibility distances required for signal faces. A minimum of two signal faces must be provided when the major movement is a turning movement. This requirement provides some measure of redundancy in case of an unexpected bulb failure. Where the minimum visibility distance of cannot be provided, 12-in lenses must be used, and placement of appropriate "Signal Ahead" warning signs is required. The warning signs may be supplemented by a "hazard identification beacon."

The arrangement of lenses on a signal face is also limited to approve sequences. In general, the red ball must be at the top of a vertical signal face or at the left of a horizontal signal face, followed by the yellow and green. Where arrow indications are on the same signal face as all indications, they are located on the bottom of a vertical display or right of a horizontal display. Figure 8.29 shows the most commonly used lens arrangements. The MUTCD contains detailed discussion of the applicability of various signal face designs.

8.5.2 Traffic signals warranty

The MUTCD provides very specific warrants for the use of traffic control signals. These warrants are far more detailed than those for other devices, due to their very high cost (relative to other control devices) and the negative impacts of their misapplication. Thus, the manual is clear that traffic control signals shall be installed only at locations where an engineering study has indicated that one or more of the specified warrants has been met, and that application of signals will improve safety and/or capacity of the intersection. The manual goes further; if a study indicates that an existing signal is in place at a location that does not meet any of the warrants, it should be removed and replaced with a less severe form of control.

The millennium Edition of the MUTCD details following eight different warrants. Any one among these warrants may indicate that the installation of a traffic control signal is appropriate.

Warrant 1, Eight-Hour Vehicular Volume(Table 8.2).

Warrant 2, Four-Hour Vehicular Volume(Figure 8.33).

Warrant 3, Peak Hour(Figure 8.34).

Warrant 4, Pedestrian Volume.

Warrant 5, School Crossing.

Warrant 6, Coordinated Signal System.

Warrant 7, Crash Experience.

Warrant 8, Roadway Network.

Table 8.2 Warrant 1, Eight-Hour Vehicular Volume

Condition A: Minimum Vehicular Volume									
Number of Lanes for moving traffic on each approach		Vehicles per hour on major street (total of both approaches)				Vehicles per hour on higher-volume minor-street approach (one direction only)			
Major Street	Major Street	100%[a]	80%[b]	70%[c]	56%[d]	100%[a]	80%[b]	70%[c]	56%[d]
1......	1......	500	400	350	280	150	120	105	84
2 or more...	1......	600	480	420	336	150	120	105	84
2 or more...	2 or more...	600	480	420	336	200	160	140	112
1......	2 or more...	500	400	350	280	200	160	140	112
Condition B: Interruption of Continuous Traffic									
Number of Lanes for moving traffic on each approach		Vehicles per hour on major street (total of both approaches)				Vehicles per hour on higher-volume minor-street approach (one direction only)			
Major Street	Major Street	100%[a]	80%[b]	70%[c]	56%[d]	100%[a]	80%[b]	70%[c]	56%[d]
1......	1......	750	600	525	420	75	60	53	42
2 or more...	1......	900	720	630	504	75	60	53	42
2 or more...	2 or more...	900	720	630	504	100	80	70	56
1......	2 or more...	750	600	525	420	100	80	70	56

Note: a. basic minimum hourly volume.

　　　b. used for combination of Conditions A and B after adequate trial of other remedial measures.

　　　c. may be used when the major-street speed exceeds 70 km/h or exceeds 40 mph or in an isolated community with a population of less than 10000.

　　　d. may be used for combination of Conditions A and B after adequate trial or other remedial measures when the major-street speed exceeds 70 km/h or exceeds 40 mph or in an isolated community with a population of less than 10000.

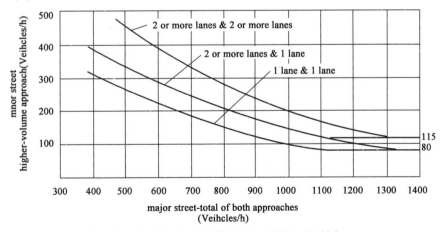

Figure 8.33 Warrant 2, Four-Hour Vehicular Volume

Note: 150 veihcles/h applies as the lower threshold volume for a inor-street approach with two or more lanes and 80 vph applies as the lower threshold volume for a minor-street approach with one lane.

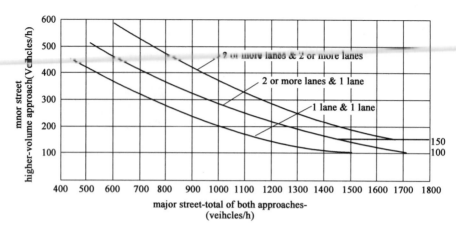

Figure 8.34 Warrant 3, Peak Hour

Note:150 veihcles/h applies as the lower threshold volume for a inor-street approach with two or more lanes and 100 veihcles/h applies as the lower threshold volume for a minor-street approach with one lane.

Engineering study datas may include the following items:

(1) The number of vehicles entering the intersection in each hour from each approach during 12 hours of an average day. It is desirable that the hours selected contain the greatest percentage of the 24-hour traffic volume.

(2) Vehicular volumes for each traffic movement from each approach, classified by vehicle type (heavy trucks, passenger cars and light trucks, public-transit vehicles, and, in some locations, bicycles), during each 15-minute period of the 2 hours in the morning and 2 hours in the afternoon during which the total traffic entering the intersection is greatest.

(3) Pedestrian volume counts on each crosswalk during the same period and during hours of highest pedestrian volume. Where young, elderly, and/or persons with physical or visual disabilities need specialconsideration, the pedestrians and their crossing times may be classified by general observation.

(4) Information about nearby facilities and activity centers that serve the young, elderly, and/or persons with disabilities, including requests from persons with disabilities for accessible crossing improvements at the location which is under study. These persons might not be adequately reflected in the pedestrian volume count if the absence of a signal restrains their mobility.

(5) The posted or statutory speed limit or the 85th-percentile speed on the uncontrolled approaches to the location.

(6) A condition diagram showing details of the physical layout, including such features as intersection geometrics, channelization, grades, sight-distance restrictions, transit stops and routes, parking conditions, pavement markings, roadway lighting,

driveways, nearby railroad crossings, distance to nearest traffic control signals, utility poles and fixtures, and adjacent land use.

(7) A collision diagram showing crash experience by type, location, direction of movement, severity, weather, time of day, date, and day of week for at least 1 year.

8.5.3 Pedestrian signals

The millennium edition of the MUTCD has mandated the use of new pedestrian signals (Figure 8.35) that had been introduced as options over the past several years. The use of the older "WALK" and "DON'T WALK" designs has been discontinued in favor of the following indications:

(1) Walking man (steady). The new "WALK" indication is the image of a walking person in the color white. This indicates that it is permissible for a pedestrian to enter the crosswalk to begin crossing the street.

(2) Upraised hand (flashing). The new "DON'T WALK" indication is an upraised hand in the color Portland orange. In the flashing mode, it indicates that no pedestrian may enter the crosswalk to begin crossing the street but that those already crossing the street may continue safely.

(3) Upraised hand (steady). In the steady mode, the upraised hand indicates that no pedestrian should begin crossing and that no pedestrian should still be in the crosswalk.

Figure 8.35 Signals for pedestrians in UK (left) and USA (right)

8.5.4 Other traffic signals

The MUTCD provides specific criteria for the design, placement, and use of a number of other types of signals, including:

(1) Beacons.

(2) In-roadway lights.

(3) Lane-use control signals.

(4) Ramp control signals (or ramp meters).

Beacons are generally used to identify a hazard or call attention to a critical control device, such as a speed limit sign, a STOP or YIELD sign, or a DO NOT ENTER sign.

In-roadway lights (可移动式信号灯) are a special types of highway traffic signals installed in the roadway surface to warn road users that they are approaching a condition on or adjacent to the roadway that might not be readily apparent and might require the road users to slow down and/or come to a stop. This type of signal can be seen at work zone as indicated in Figure 8.36.

Lane-use control signals are special overhead signals that permit or prohibit the use of specific lanes of a street or highway or that indicate the impending prohibition of their use. Lane-use control signals are distinguished by placement of special signal faces over a certain lane or lanes of the roadway and by their distinctive shapes and symbols. Lane-use control signals are most commonly used for reversible-lane control as demonstrated in Figure 8.37, but are also used in nonreversible freeway lane applications.

Figure 8.36　In-roadway light used at UK roadway

Figure 8.37　Lane-use control signals used in Shanghai (reversible-lane)

Ramp control signals are traffic control signals that control the flow of traffic entering the freeway facility.

Freeway entrance ramp control signals are sometimes used if controlling traffic entering the freeway could reduce the total expected delay to traffic in the freeway corridor, including freeway ramps and local streets, and so on.

Key points of the chapter

1. What is the objective of traffic control devices?

2. By which means do traffic control devices convey messages to road users?
3. Be aware of the functionality of markings, signs and signals.
4. What is the difference between solid line and dashed line in general?
5. What are the volume warrants for the signal installation defined in MUTCD?
6. Why are redundant messages needed?

本章要点

1. 设置交通控制设施的目标是什么?
2. 交通控制设施通过哪些方式向道路使用者传递信息?
3. 理解标志、标线以及信号灯的作用。
4. 交通标线中的实线与虚线的区别是什么?
5. MUTCD 中对信号设置的流量是如何定义的?
6. 交通信息为什么要重复设置?

GLOSSARY

A

AADT（Average Annual Daily Traffic）年平均日交通量
AAWT（Average Annual Weekday Traffic）年平均工作日交通量
Accessibility 可达性
Access Management 出入口管理
ADT（Average Daily Traffic）平均日交通量
All Walks of Life 各界人士
Approach 进口
Arterial 主干道
AWT（Average Weekday Traffic）平均工作日交通量

B

Basic Rule of Road 基本通行规则
Beijing Municipal Committee of Communications 北京市交通委员会
Bernoulli Distributions 伯努利分布
Binomial Distributions 二项分布

C

Capacity 通行能力
Capacity of an Intersection Lane or Lane Group 车道组的通行能力
Car-following Approach 跟车法
Central Tendency 集中趋势
Channelize 渠化
Chi-square Distributions 卡方分布
Climbing Capability 爬坡能力
Clearance Intervals 清空时间
Clearance Lost Time 清空时损
Classification of Roadways 道路分类
Cloverleaf Interchange 全苜蓿叶立交
Color Blindness 色盲
Commission of Transport 交通委员会

Contour Lines 等时线
Control Delay 控制延误
Coefficient of Variation 变异系数
Crash 事故
Crawl Speeds 爬行速度
Critical Lane 关键车道
Critical Gap 临界间隙
Cross Section 横断面
Crown Line 路冠线
Curb Parking 路侧停车
Cross Section 横断面
Cul-de-sac
Cut-through Traffic 抄近道
Cycle 周期
Cycle Length 周期长度

D

Data Grouping 数据分组
DDHV (Directional Design Hour Volume) 设计小时流量
Decision Sight Distance 决策视距
Delineator 道钉
Dilemma Zone 犹豫区
Degree of Confidence 置信度
Design Analysis 道路设计分析
Diamond Interchange 菱形立交
Discrete Versus Continuous 离散与连续
Dispersion 离散
Diverge 分流
Double-dash Yellow Line 双黄虚线
Double-solid Yellow Line 双黄实线
Double-stream Door 双扇车门
Doppler Effect 多普勒效应
Draw Bridges 开启桥
Driving Behavior 驾驶行为
Drive-through 得来速
Driveways 接入道

DSD（Decision Sight Distance）决策视距
DUI（Driving Under Influence）酒后驾车
DWI（Driving While Intoxicated）醉酒驾车
Dynamic Visual Acuity 动视力

E

Effective Green Time 有效绿灯时间
Enforcement 执法
Entrance Ramp 入口匝道
Evenness 均匀程度
Exit Ramp 出口匝道
Exclusive Bus Lane 公交专用道
Exclusive Turn Lane 专用转向车道
Exponential Distributions 负指数分布

F

Federal-Aid Highway Act 联邦公路法
Field of Vision 视野
Flared Approach 拓宽型进口
Flashing Ball 全闪
Flashing Beacon 闪灯
Floating-car Approach 浮动车法
Fluctuation 波动
FFS（Free-flow Speed）自由流速度
Follow-up Time 随车时距
Fractional Lanes 非整车道
Frontage road 辅路
Fully Actuated Control 全感应式控制

G

Gap Acceptance 可接受间隙
Gore Area 三角区
Geometric Designs 几何设计
Grade Separation 立交
Green Ball 全绿
Green Time 绿灯时间

Green Time Ratio 绿信比
Guide Signs 指路标志

H

Harmonic Mean 调和中项
Headway 车头时距
Heavy Rail 重型轨道交通
Heavy Vehicle 重型车
Hippocratic Oath 希波克拉底誓言
Horizontal Alignment 平曲线
HOV（High-Occupancy Vehicle）高载率车辆

I

Incident 事故
Incremental Delay 增量延误
Interchanging Space 立交间距
Intermodality 多模式
Interrupted Flows 间断流
Interrupted Flow Facilities 间断流道路设施
Intersections at Grade 平面交叉口
Interval 时段
ISTEA（Intermodal Surface Transportation Efficiency and Transportation Equity Act）冰茶法案
ITS（Intelligent Transportation System）智能交通系统

J

Jam Density 阻塞密度

K

Kiss and Ridden 送站换乘

L

Lane-use Control Signal 车道灯
Lateral clearances 侧向净空
Left Equivalent 左转当量
Level of Confidence 置信水平

Level of Service 服务水平
Level Terrain 平原地形
License-plate Approach 牌照法
Linear Loading Area 联合公交站
Load Factor 载客率
Longitudinal Marking 纵向标线
Loop Detector 线圈探测器
Loop Ramp 环形匝道
LRT (Light Rail Transit) 轻轨公交

M

Mean 均值
Mean Speed 平均速度
Measure of Dispersion 离散
Median 中位值；中央分隔带
Median Speed 中位速度
Merge 合流
Microwaved-detector 微波探测器
Ministry of Transport 交通运输部
Minor Arterial 次干道
Minor Street 支路
MSF (Maximum Service Flow rates) 最大服务流率
MOE (Measure of Effectiveness) 效率指标
Mode 众值
Mode Speed 众速度
Mode Split 方式分担
Modes of Transportation 运输方式
Mobility 机动性
Mountainous Terrain 山岭地形
Multilane Highway 多车道公路
Multimodal 多模式交通
Multi-way STOP 全路停车

N

Near-side Stop 右侧停车
No-passing Zones 非超车区域

Normal Distribution 正态分布

O

Object Markers Delineators 物标
Occupancy 占有率
Off-ramp 出口匝道
Offset 相位差
Off-street Path 辅道
On-ramp 进口匝道
Open Fare Collection System 开放式收费系统
Operation Analysis 道路运行状态分析
Opposing Approach 对向进口道
Over-lapping Phase 重叠相位
Overflow Queue 滞留车队

P

Pace 速度差幅度
Paratransit 辅助客运系统
Park and Ride 驻车换乘
Parkway 公园路(是指道路两侧绿化较好的城市道路)
Partial Cloverleaf Interchange/ Parclo 半苜蓿叶立交
Partial Diamond Interchange 半菱形立交
Passing Lane 超车道
Passing Sight Distance 超车视距
PCU/PCE (Passenger Car Unit/Passenger Car Equivalent) 标准小汽车当量
Peak Hour Factor 高峰小时系数
Peripheral Vision 周边视力
Percentile Speed 百分位速度
Permitted Plus Protected 许可型加保护型相位
Permitted Turn 许可型转向
Phase 相位
Platoon 队列
Poisson Distribution 泊松分布
Population 全体
Potential Capacity 可能通行能力
Pretimed Control 定周期控制

Principal Arterial 主干道
Professional Ethics 职业道德
Protected Plus Permitted 保护型加许可型相位
Protected Turn 保护型转弯
PRT（Perception-Reaction Time）反应时间

Q

Queue Carryover 滞留车队
Queue Discharge 排队消散
Queue Storage Ratio 排队溢出率

R

Ramp 匝道
Rapid Bus 快速公共汽车
Rapid Transit 快速轨道交通
Rate of Flow 流率
Reaction Process 反应过程
Red Ball 全红
Red Time 红灯时间
Regular Signs 法令标志
Relationship of SF 服务流率
Reversible Lane 潮汐车道
Right Equivalent 右转当量
Right-of-way 通行权
PRT（Perception-reaction Time）反应时间
RV（Recreational Vehicle）房车
Rolling Terrain 丘陵地形
Roundabout/Circle 环形交叉口

S

Sample 样本
Saturation Headway 饱和车头时距
Saturation Flow Rate 饱和流率
Schools 学派
Segment 路段
Semiactuated Control 半感应式控制

Service Volume 服务流量
SF（Service Flow rate）服务流率
Single-point Diamond Interchange 扁菱形立交
Sight Triangle 视距三角形
Signal Face 信号灯组
Signal Head 信号灯灯头
Signal Lens 信号灯透镜
Signal Timing 信号配时
Single-stream Door 单向车门
Side Street 旁路（是指与线控主路相交的道路）
Shock Wave 冲击波
Shoulder 路肩
Shoulder Bypass Lane 路肩分流车道
Skip-stop Service 大站快车
Skewness 非对称性
SMS（Space Mean Speed）空间平均速度
Sneakers 抢行者（是指先于对向直行车辆到达冲突点而通过交叉口的左转车辆）
Spacing 车头间距
Speeding 加速
Split 分时相位
Split-diamond Interchange 分离式菱形立交
Spot Speed 地点车速
Standard Vehicle 标准车
Standard Deviation 标准差
Standee 无座乘客
Start-up Lost Time 启动时损，绿损
Static Visual Acuity 静视力
Statistical Estimators 统计量
Stimuli 刺激物
Stop Sight Distance 停车视距
Stopped-time Delay 停车延误
Street Car 有轨车
SSD（Stopping Sight Distance）停车视距
Subject Approach 指定引道
Sub-phase 次相位
Suburban 郊区

Surface (Land/Highway/Roadway) Transportation 陆路运输或陆路交通
Sustainable Development 可持续发展
SV (Service Volume) 服务流量

T

TEA-21 (Transportation Equity Act for 21st Century) 21 世纪交通衡平法
The 30th Hourly Volume 第 30 位小时交通量
Threshold 阈值
Through Vehicles 直行车辆
Time Budge 绿灯时间分配
Time-in-queue Delay 排队延误
Time-space Domain 时空图
TMS (Time Mean Speed) 时间平均速度
Tolerance in Error (Given) 允许误差
Tradeoff 均衡
Traffic Engineering 交通工程
Traffic Modes 交通方式
Transit Reliability 公交可靠性
Transit Stop 公交停靠站
Transportation Engineering 运输工程
Traffic Calming 交通宁静
Traffic Crash 交通事故
Transverse Marking 横向标线
Travel speed 行程速度
Travel Time 行程时间
Trolleybus 无轨电车
Turnout 港湾
TWLTL (Two Way Left Turn Lane) 双向左转车道
Two-lane Highway 双车道公路
Two-way STOP 二路停车
TWSC 二路停车交叉口

U

Uninterrupted Flows 连续流
Uninterrupted Flow Facilities 连续流道路设施
Unsignalized Intersection 无信号交叉口

Urban 市区
Urbanization 城市化

V

Variance 方差
Video-frequency Detector 视频探测器
Visual Acuity 视力
Vehicle 标准车
Vertical Alignment 竖曲线
VMT (Vehicle Miles Traveled) 车公里
Volume/Capacity Ratio 负荷度

W

Walkway 人行道
Warning Signs 警告标志
Weaving 交织
Work Zone 施工区

X

Y

Yellow Ball 全黄

Z

Zebra-striped Crosswalk 斑马线人行横道
Zero-emission 零排放
Zone 小区

References

[1] A Policy on Geometric Design of Highways and Streets, American Association of State Highway and Transportation Officials, 1994.

[2] Roger P. Roess, Elena S. Prassas, and William R. Mcshace, Traffic Engineering, 3rd Edition, Upper Saddle River, NJ, 2004.

[3] Paul H. W RIGHT, and Norman J. Ashford, Transportation Engineering Planning and Design, 4th Edition.

[4] Nicholas J, Garber, and Lester A Hoel, Traffic and Highway Engineering, 3rd Edition, Brooks/Cole, 2002.

[5] Manual on Uniform Traffic Control Devices, Millennium Edition, U. S. Department of Transportation, Federal Highway Administration, December 2000.

[6] Highway Capacity Manual 2000, 4th Edition, Transportation Research Board, National Research council, Washington, DC, (revised) 2000.

[7] Highway Capacity Manual 2010, 5th Edition, Transportation Research Board, National Research council, Washington, DC, (revised) 2000.

[8] Traffic Engineering Handbook, Institute of Transportation Engineers, Prentice-Hall, Englewood Cliff, NJ, 1992.

[9] 任福田,刘小明,荣建,等.交通工程学[M].北京:人民交通出版社,2003.

[10] 任福田.新编交通工程学导论[M].北京:人民交通出版社,2011.

[11] 徐吉谦.交通工程总论[M].北京:人民交通出版社,2005.

[12] 王炜,过秀成,等.交通工程学[M].南京:东南大学出版社,2000.